For a Spell

GENDER AND AMERICAN CULTURE

Martha S. Jones and Mary Kelley, *editors*

Editorial Advisory Board
Cathleen Cahill
Rosalyn LaPier
Jen Manion
Tamika Nunley
Annelise Orleck
Janice A. Radway
Robert Reid-Pharr
Noliwe Rooks
Nick Syrett
Lisa Tetrault
Ji-Yeon Yuh

Series Editors Emerita
Thadious M. Davis
Linda K. Kerber
Annette Kolodny
Nell Irvin Painter

The Gender and American Culture series, guided by feminist perspectives, examines the social construction and influence of gender and sexuality within the full range of American cultures. Books in the series explore the intersection of gender (both female and male) with such markers of difference as race, class, and region. The series presents outstanding scholarship from all areas of American studies—including history, literature, religion, folklore, ethnography, and the visual arts—that investigates in a thoroughly contextualized and lively fashion the ways in which gender works with and against these markers. In so doing, the series seeks to reveal how these complex interactions have shaped American life.

A complete list of books published in Gender and American Culture is available at https://uncpress.org/series/gender-and-american-culture.

JASON EZELL

For a Spell
Sissie Collectivism and Radical Witchery in the Southeast

The University of North Carolina Press *Chapel Hill*

© 2025 Jason Ezell
All rights reserved
Set in Arno Pro by Westchester Publishing Services
Manufactured in the United States of America

Library of Congress Cataloging-in-Publication Data
Names: Ezell, Jason, author.
Title: For a spell : sissie collectivism and radical witchery in the Southeast / Jason Ezell.
Other titles: Gender & American culture.
Description: Chapel Hill : University of North Carolina Press, [2025] | Series: Gender and American culture | Includes bibliographical references and index.
Identifiers: LCCN 2025013870 | ISBN 9781469690438 (cloth) | ISBN 9781469690445 (paperback) | ISBN 9781469683089 (epub) | ISBN 9781469690452 (pdf)
Subjects: LCSH: Gay liberation movement—Southern States—History—20th century. | Gay men—Political activity—Southern States—History—20th century. | Communal living—Southern States—History—20th century. | Witchcraft in activism—Southern States—History—20th century. | BISAC: SOCIAL SCIENCE / Gender Studies | HISTORY / LGBTQ
Classification: LCC HQ76.8.U6 E94 2025 | DDC 306.76/62097509047—dc23/eng/20250512
LC record available at https://lccn.loc.gov/2025013870

Cover art: *Mulberry House Collective: Fayetteville, Arkansas, 1976,* by Trella Laughlin. Thanks to Laughlin's wife, Marie Howard, for granting permission to use the photo.

Frontispiece: *Mulberry House—Fayetteville, Arkansas* (1976), drawing by Dimid Hayes.

For product safety concerns under the European Union's General Product Safety Regulation (EU GPSR), please contact gpsr@mare-nostrum.co.uk or write to the University of North Carolina Press and Mare Nostrum Group B.V., Mauritskade 21D, 1091 GC Amsterdam, The Netherlands.

Invocation

calling xxx-xxxx

    Big Joy

    The Red Queen

    Faygele

    Melba'son

    Stacy Brotherlover

    Aurora

Contents

List of Illustrations ix

Main Sites and Collectivists xi

Introduction: Figuring, Housing, Witching 1

Part I
Mulberry House: The Ozarks, 1971–77

CHAPTER ONE
Mulberry Chemistries: Coming Together in an
Ozark Separatist Landscape 29

CHAPTER TWO
Drawing Down the Dialectical Moon: Faggot Witchcraft's
Leftist Invocations 52

CHAPTER THREE
Pied Pipers: Ozark Collectivism Pitched against
White Christian Supremacy 75

Part II
The Louisiana Sissies in Struggle: New Orleans, 1977–79

CHAPTER FOUR
A Bus Named Desire: Turning Melba'son in New Orleans 101

CHAPTER FIVE
Sissie Majik: From Sissystories of Terror to an Unqueer Street Pedagogy 122

CHAPTER SIX
Mapping Dreams: Gathering Sissie Solidarities into a Regional Network 150

Part III
Short Mountain: Appalachian Tennessee, 1979–81

CHAPTER SEVEN
After Milk: Performing Sissie Collectivism at New National Volumes 177

CHAPTER EIGHT
Way Stations to Revolution: Sustaining Liberation with Short Mountain 193

Conclusion: Unqueer Dreams Left 209

Acknowledgments 221
Out of the Stacks: Leaning into Librarianly Excess 223
Notes 227
Bibliography 245
Index 255

Illustrations

Flaming Faggot, drawing by Kenneth Pitchford, 1972   7
Fag Rag cover, 1971   9
Mulberry House letter to *RFD*, 1976   47
Poem by jai d. elliott, 1976   72
Cover of *The Torch*, 1977   87
"Sissy" photo, 1978   142
"Sissie Terror" photos, 1978   143
"Sissie Networking" map, 1978   171

Main Sites and Collectivists

To help trace this mercurial culture, the following table lists key collectives/sites, their locations, the focal years (within this book), and key associated collectivists (with adopted names). I have italicized the names of those interviewed for this project.

Collective/Event Site	Location	Years Covered	Key Collectivists
Mulberry House	Fayetteville, Arkansas	1976–77	Dennis Williams (Melba'son); *Michael Oglesby; Charlie Thornton; Dean (Dimid) Hayes*; Jack Kendrick (Carlotta Rose); Sam Edwards (Lawanda Rose); Robert Reich (Stacy Brotherlover); *Trella Laughlin*; Patricia Jackson
Louisiana Sissies in Struggle (LaSIS)	New Orleans, Louisiana	1978–79	Dennis Williams (Melba'son); *Dean (Dimid) Hayes*; Robert Reich (Stacy Brotherlover); *David Speakman (Aurora House Corona)*
Running Water Farm Gatherings	Bakersville, North Carolina	1978–81	*Mikel Wilson*; John Singer (Faygele Ben Miriam); *Franklin Abbott*; Ron Lambe
Early Short Mountain Sanctuary	Liberty, Tennessee	1979–81	*Clint (Milo) Pyne; Clarence (Clear) Englebert; Cathy Gross (Cathy Hope); Dean (Dimid) Hayes*

For a Spell

Introduction
Figuring, Housing, Witching

Late on Wednesday, August 13, 1980, at the second annual gathering of Radical Faeries in Estes Park, Colorado, a group of thirteen convened around a raging fire.[1] Most of these thirteen were "Southeast Fairies," and among them were the Louisiana Sissies in Struggle (LaSIS), a gay liberationist collective based in New Orleans. LaSIS member Dennis Melba'son recognized the coincidental thirteen as an improvised "coven" and their "Kali Fire" as a good place for him to "burn out . . . all the anger and pain" he was just then feeling. Earlier, he had participated in a group discussion about racism and classism at the queer gathering. As a leftist, he was frustrated that too few recognized how inaccessible the event was along those particular fault lines. In his journal he wrote, "I've fought these battles among het liberals for years and it hurt alot to havta fight them all over again among Fairies." Many of Melba'son's battles had begun in Arkansas and continued in New Orleans, where LaSIS had helped to link regional gay liberationist houses into what they then referred to as the "Southeast Network." The sissies at the national Radical Faeries gathering must have felt, however, that the winds had shifted. Melba'son recorded that "one of the things burned in the Kali Fire last night was the regionalism of LaSIS."[2] For good or ill, their scope had stretched, and national *faerie* networks had begun to eclipse regional *sissie* ones. Their Kali Fire ritual served as a kind of control burn—a way to alchemically transform outworn political modes to make way for new ones.

In this book I tell the story of those Southeast sissies, from the early 1970s to their diffusion in the early 1980s. Their early bonds were braced in answer to the terror sparked by the rise of the New Right. They were gay leftists in an unexpected place: the US Southeast. Their ways of living were unorthodox: They lived in collective houses. This was but one practice they adapted from lesbian feminists. They also conducted consciousness-raising, participated in alternative print cultures, and practiced feminist witchcraft. They referred to themselves by proudly reclaiming epithets, like *sissie, faerie,* and *faggot*. In this book I seek to understand their situated radicalism by looking closely at these aspects of their praxis. How they came to their queer way of living in the Southeast of the late 1970s, though, is a long and crooked story. They remade themselves as *sissies* in reaction to a gay liberationist faggot genealogy that they primarily encountered in *RFD* magazine and in visits to the West Coast. Before launching into their story proper, it's helpful to sketch the outlines of this earlier faggot subjectivity as it sprang from the splintering of the New York Gay Liberation Front (NY-GLF).

Out of New York: A Short, Forked Faggot Genealogy

According to its early chronicler Toby Marotta, the NY-GLF included outspoken revolutionary women, like Lois Hart, who inspired men whose radical experience had been won elsewhere than the Stonewall Riots: in other movements (like antiwar or civil rights work), in university classrooms and student activism, or in the counterculture.[3] These vocal NY-GLF revolutionaries were often ambivalent about, if not hostile to, the sites of urban gay male social and sexual life—cruisy bars, streets, and piers. Some of these revolutionaries joined the NY-GLF's Radical Study Group, reading classic Marxist texts and scouring history for the roots of Western homophobia. Their purpose was to build a radical gay political analysis that could match the powerful arguments in Black and feminist revolutionary movements. Through their studies, they fixed on socialist strains of early European gay liberation and the expressly religious roots of homophobia.[4] The latter lines of research led them to latch onto a politically charged etymology of *faggot* as a word that referred to homosexual men in the Middle Ages whom the Radical Study Group members claimed had been cast onto pyres by the Church, fueling the fires that burned liberated women, or witches. As a result, the gay liberationist *faggot* figure emerged in their imaginations as a centuries-old ally of radical women—whether they be the witches of yore or the contemporary revolutionary women who raged alongside them in the NY-GLF. As the city's GLF began to splinter, though, two important variations on this faggot figure emerged.

The first group—John Knoebel, Kenneth Pitchford, and Steven Dansky—called themselves the Flaming Faggots. They formed when, in the summer of 1970, at Chelsea's Elgin Theater, they bristled at how revolutionary Venceremos Brigadiers—who organized trips to Cuba in support of socialist revolution—critiqued the effeminacy of GLF men as a "quirk" and worse: a hindrance to serious revolution. Pitchford penned a poem-manifesto in response and broadly connected Venceremos sexism to the historical witch trials, claiming "androcide and gynocide [as] their one response to/any heretical blasphemy against/a god-given manliness."[5] In doing so, the Flaming Faggots clapped back at the hypermasculine, homophobic, militant revolutionary figuration evidenced at the time by the likes of Fidel Castro or Eldridge Cleaver. The poem also referred to any such militant posturing as "an expiring masculinity." The Flaming Faggots thereby, as Terence Kissack has observed, "reversed the value of 'machismo' and 'effeminacy.'" "'Flaming faggots' and liberated women," he asserted, "have taken [macho leftists'] place at the forefront of the revolution."[6]

Dansky—also a member of the GLF's Radical Study Group—went further. He defined male homosexuality as an early but woefully incomplete step in the dismantling of the patriarchy. Dansky advocated further action: "breaking down male roles," in the "process of 'de-manning.'" The issue, as he saw it, was that "the ways we [gay men] express homosexuality have been molded by male supremacy," and part of the solution was for the GLF "to demand the complete negation of the use of gay bars, tea rooms, trucks, baths, streets, and other traditional cruising institutions."[7] Some of their GLF peers surely read this "complete negation" as an erasure of the originating landscapes of US gay liberation, including the Stonewall Inn, as well as the nearby streets which hosted sex work and sustained protest. Central to the Flaming Faggots' revolutionary vision, then, was absolute alliance with radical feminists and an utter betrayal of masculinity, even gay men's.

Pitchford was also married to radical feminist Robin Morgan, who sharply criticized drag, comparing it to blackface, arguing through her analogy that gay queens mocked women's oppression through parodic performance.[8] The Flaming Faggots took up a similar position, eventually calling themselves *effeminists*, inspired by a San Francisco Bay Area group of the same name. The Effeminists' new 1973 manifesto blasted camp sensibility, transvestism, transsexualism, androgyny, BDSM, "sexual libertarianism," and ("beefcake") pornography. Gay femme social identities and leather/cruise culture drew the sharpest of their critiques, as examples of insulting parodies of extreme gender roles.[9] In order to distance themselves from femme presentation while still holding on to some form of effeminacy, Pitchford began to denounce "body-type" as a "typically straight-male fixation" and asserted that "effeminancy [sic] appears in men as the willingness to cooperate rather than compete, as the preferring of collectivity to individualism, personal solution, or privatism, and as the valuing of what is tender and gentle in men, what is delicate, sweet, lyrical, affectionate, considerate, aesthetic."[10]

It must be underscored that the Effeminists understood the unquestioned leaders of the revolution to be radical women. The Effeminists' manifesto further argued, then, that the main way effeminate men should contribute to women's liberation was to assume an expanded role in childcare, as a way to free radical women to dedicate their time to dismantling the patriarchy. As leftists, as radical feminists, they understood care labor to be unevenly assigned to women, and they increasingly saw shared mothering as one of their primary revolutionary contributions.[11]

At roughly the same time, the Gay Activists Alliance (GAA) improvised a second faggot form, emphasizing other performative aspects than the radical "de-manning" urged by the Flaming Faggots/Effeminists. Arthur Evans, a founding member of the Radical Study Group, also cofounded the GAA, writing most of the preamble to the organization's constitution. The GAA had split with the NY-GLF in late 1969, determined to focus exclusively on gay issues. The Flaming Faggots saw this as a betrayal not only of a wider women's liberation, but also of basic revolutionary methods. Pitchford asserted, "From the first, we understood that the Gay Activist Alliance had moved rightward in pressing for homosexual reforms within the system."[12] Others have interpreted Evans's vision for the GAA differently. For example, Lillian Faderman has described Evans as a revolutionary with an ongoing commitment to solidarity with all the oppressed.[13] Marotta also characterized Evans as a radical who feared that the NY-GLF could never consistently show up for their revolutionary allies, or contribute to sustained political actions, because their variable membership and unstructured decision-making process was too chaotic and fickle. Evans believed, per Marotta, that gay revolution, to be successful, would first have to proceed through multiple reformist phases.[14] For Evans, then, the GAA's singular focus on gay rights was one of these early phases of a longer revolution, a phase that would concentrate gay anger in order to produce more committed partners in future revolutionary solidarity.

Whereas the Effeminists decried sexually charged gay spaces, Evans attended his first NY-GLF meeting because he "thought it would be a good place to cruise," and his GAA preamble argued for "the right to treat and express our bodies as we will."[15] In part this was a defense of the gender nonconformity and sexual freedom so common to the urban spaces which the Flaming Faggots sought to negate. In fact, the gender-nonconforming activist Sylvia Rivera was a member of the early GAA, possibly in part due to such stated values. However, she would also ultimately have ample reason to critique the limits of GAA's gender inclusivity.[16]

While the Effeminists latched onto the faggot figure as (1) a heretical traitor to masculinity and (2) a radical support for women's liberation, what caught Evans's attention in the faggot narrative was the transformative magic implicit in its fiery iconography. As religious studies scholar Cynthia Eller has pointed out, feminist witches of the 1970s used the imagery of the executed witch, of the Burning Times, as part of a "martyrology" that called attention not only to these women's victimhood but also to the witches' *power*, which had so seriously posed a threat to church and state in the first place.[17] The GAA sought to dramatize the plight *and* power of the contemporary homosexual in similar ways, mobilizing fiery gay anger. From such lines of questioning, the early GAA leveraged its members' cumulative expertise in media, performance, and political tactics to make public zaps their most successful form of intervention.

For their first zap, the GAA would confront Mayor John Lindsay at the Metropolitan Museum of Art's 100th anniversary—April 13th, 1970—hounding him with questions in front of celebrants and journalists, demanding why he had done nothing to stop police harassment at gay bars. They specifically referenced the recent Snake Pit raid, which had resulted in the near death of an Argentinian immigrant who had fallen onto spiked fencing when trying to escape arrest. The city looked on as Lindsay uncomfortably smiled, offering nothing concrete to protect gay citizens. The GAA continued to pester Lindsay at event after event—his wife Mary even physically attacked GAA members at the Imperial Theater on October 28. The following spring, in May of 1971, Lindsay—under the persistent pressure of these zaps and of declining trust in his leadership—signed an antidiscrimination law into place.[18] The idea was that such public pressure not only would change oppressive laws but also would project contemporary homophobia into gay citizens' homes—on newspaper pages and their TV screens—and hopefully fire an outrage that would bring them together as a formidable political bloc.

Arthur Evans credited fellow Radical Study Group and GAA member Leo Martello for first suggesting a connection between gay politics and feminist witchcraft practice.[19] At Martello's prompting, Evans took the affective politics of the zap and expanded its repertoire to include actual ritual and spell-work. Although Evans's book *Witchcraft and the Gay Counterculture* wouldn't appear until 1978, he published his research about the place of homophobia in historical witch hunts in serial form in New York's *Out* magazine (December 1973) and Boston's *Fag Rag* (beginning in December 1974).

From the beginning, then, we can see how variable this faggot figure was. It was mercurial. Although it emerged from the splintering of the NY-GLF, it didn't remain in the city long. In fact, its culture was highly mobile. By 1972 Pitchford had moved to Sarasota, Florida, to the New School. He observed that there were then new faggot households established in Washington State and the Bay Area, and that there was a vocal interest in a national network of faggot collectives.[20] The year 1972 was also when Arthur Evans moved with his new partner and a third queer man to eastern Washington State, to a rural area near the Canadian border. In true faggot spirit, the three called themselves the Weird Sisters, and their rustic encampment New Sodom. Evans would begin publishing his work on witchcraft in 1973, and he often traveled from New Sodom to Seattle to do his research, sending drafts to his East Coast publishers.[21] As early as 1972, then, the faggot figure had established a presence on the US East, West, and Gulf Coasts.

The faggot figure (to be followed by the effeminist, sissie, and faerie figures) found its way into the Southeast in three main ways: through (1) circulation of gay liberationist print culture, (2) attendance at faggot-themed events, and (3) collaboration between collective households. In fact, as we will see in chapter 1, the Arkansas collective Mulberry House announced themselves as a "collective of five angry faggots" in a 1976 issue of *RFD*—a gay liberationist newspaper whose spring 1975 cover had dedicated itself to "country faggots everywhere." In chapter 2, I trace how Mulberry House would also refer to themselves as sissies rather than faggots after attending the 1976 Faggots and Class Struggle conference in rural Wolf Creek, Oregon. As sissies, they would, however, continue to riff on certain cultural inheritances of the faggot genealogy sparked from the ashes of the NY-GLF. I analyze the Southeastern sissies' faggot cultural inheritances through three main lenses: *figuring* (their bodily, iconographic, and relational dynamics), *housing* (their domestic and collectivist practices), and *witching* (their ritualistic and magickal performances). As the faggot figure took root in different regions over the course of the 1970s, its new manifestations continued to improvise liberationist ways to inhabit body, spirit, and home.

Figuring: The Radical Body's Composition and Orientation

For revolutionary gay liberationists, the bodily figure of the faggot mattered for several reasons. First, editors and artists consistently circulated faggot images in their print materials, producing a martyrological iconography meant to fire political anger. Second, gay leftists hoped that the faggot figure would come to index a specifically gay subjectivity that others—Black Panthers, Young Lords, radical women, and labor agitators—would easily recognize as being committed to revolution. And third, the *ways* in which the faggot figure was drawn—whether in print illustrations or descriptive manifestos—gestured toward these gay liberationists' primary alliances. These three aspects of faggot figural practice were intended to articulate a clear, bold picture of exactly where 1970s faggots stood. However, I argue that with such a widely diffused culture, there emerged regional variations on the faggot figure that we can

Kenneth Pitchford's drawing of a faggot for his article "Who Are the Flaming Faggots?," *motive* 32, no. 2 (1972): 18.

read closely for political distinctions. By attending to the specifics of the Southeast sissies' figuration, then, we can see how they riffed on faggot movements elsewhere.

The earliest iconography, however, was consistent in conveying its martyrology. The images usually featured flames, which represented the alchemical transformation of oppression into liberation and also registered the conversion of righteous anger into action. The effeminacy of the faggot was often signaled by his countercultural long hair. Beyond these commonalities, though, small differences could matter. For example, the faggot illustration accompanying Pitchford's 1972 "Who Are the Flaming Faggots?" visually minimizes the faggot's genitalia, perhaps seeking to displace masculine phallocentricity and thus "de-man" society. Further, the figure's nodding head may both register the martyr's defeat *or* the gentle, tender facets of male effeminacy as touted by Pitchford.

By contrast, the faggot on the cover of the second issue of *Fag Rag* stares steadily back at the reader, head lifted, as the flames consume and blend in with his hair. This rendering hews closer to an earlier register of brazen defiance.

In the following chapters I will at times read how such figures are drawn in order to tease out key variations on this early faggot iconography.

For leftists, it had long been important to highlight and celebrate the revolutionary body. For example, socialist realist art idealized the bodies of the robust peasant or factory worker. For workerists and labor activists especially, the latter became the very image of revolutionary subjectivity: the insurgent (white, male) industrial worker. However, as the twentieth century wore on, the face of the revolution changed. For example, widespread anti-colonial revolutions, Black civil rights/radical movements, women's liberation, and student protesters drastically refigured the look of the left, particularly along racial, ethnic, gender, age, and geographic lines. In the wake of Stonewall, leftist gay liberationists sought to sketch what the face of a specifically gay revolutionary would look like.

Many of these leftists were particularly eager to answer Huey Newton's 1970 call for gay liberationists to join in the wider revolution as agitated by the Black Panthers. In a startling reversal from some Panthers' previous homophobic and sexist rhetoric—as exemplified at the time by Eldridge Cleaver's provocative statements—in August 1970 Newton addressed his fellow Panthers and urged them to join in solidarity with revolutionaries in the women's and gay liberation movements.[22] Right after, in September, delegations of lesbian feminists and gay liberationists were invited to the Panther-led Revolutionary People's Constitutional Convention, in Philadelphia. For

Cover of *Fag Rag* 2, Fall 1971. Drawing unattributed.

many this was a concrete step toward liberationist solidarity in which queer revolutionaries had a place.[23] For many reasons, though, real and lasting solidarity did not materialize. Certain leftist gay liberationists still struggled to articulate a gay revolutionary subjectivity, in a faggot form, even years later.

This was the main purpose of an event which significantly influenced sissies: the 1976 Faggots & Class Struggle conference in rural Wolf Creek, Oregon. Attendees argued bitterly, along different leftist ideological lines, about the very need for a revolutionary figure. The Marxist-Leninist organizers proposed the conference for radical gay liberationist men to improvise and test the viability of the faggot figure as a vehicle for uniting them under a common leftist analysis and for galvanizing them to take their place in the long revolution. The New Communist Lavender & Red Union, from Los Angeles, however, argued that embracing *any* single revolutionary figure was doomed to be exclusionary and only temporarily useful—just as the white male factory worker had failed to address the breadth of previous revolutionary factions. The faggot organizers rebuffed this argument by saying that refusing to articulate a revolutionary figure at all promoted a faceless movement that, in practice, would only default to a de facto straight white male leadership. They insisted that a historically situated—and therefore temporary—solidarity demanded several revolutionary figures representing major different experiences of oppression. This was exactly what was needed to advance revolution in practical, everyday steps. The faggot was just one possible such figure. In the end, most conference attendees agreed with the need for a gay revolutionary figure. By the event's close, though, not all were equally invested in the capaciousness of the faggot to embody all their ranging experiences. Chapter 2 will offer more detail on these differences, but race, gender, and class were key points of contention at the 1976 Oregon event.

As we have seen, race, gender, sexuality, and class had unevenly inflected the gay liberationist faggot story since its inception. I argue that this is so thoroughly true that we can only describe faggot subjectivity by how it orients itself along *all* of those lines. For example, the Flaming Faggots affirmed themselves as radical feminists *only* by facing away from gay femmes and cruisy streets and bars—a move that would have also oriented them *away* from street queens of color like Marsha P. Johnson and Sylvia Rivera. Later, they more aggressively made such queens their foils as they redefined their effeminacy as being overtly opposed to drag, crossdressing, and other femme embodiments. For such reasons I argue that it is important to attend not only to how these figures were visualized, but also to how they were *oriented*.[24] Tracing these gay liberationist figures must also account for how their orientations shifted, because the earliest faggot alliances did not simply remain the same as they migrated into different places, with different dynamics and needs.

Fag Rag is a crucial early example. One of the first places that the faggot figure traveled was Boston. One year after the Flaming Faggots formed, the Boston newspaper *Fag Rag* appeared, in June 1971. In their second issue, the editors felt compelled to explain the publication's name, given the shock the first issue provoked. In their note, they cite a Flaming Faggots leaflet given them at a Christopher Street parade. However, Black faggot-identified authors were regular *Fag Rag* voices, and the editorial collective came to overtly orient themselves to Black radicalism. Kevin Mumford has pointed out that it was a publication in which Black gay liberationists themselves embraced the faggot as a figure that invited them to proclaim their race and sexuality at once. Mumford emphasizes that this was, in part, due to how "in the radical gay press the strategy of queering black power signaled a level of serious engagement with black liberation ideas and served to prove the revolutionary potential of black gay men."[25] One way Boston's early *Fag Rag* queered Black power was by embracing the legacy of George Jackson, an incarcerated young Black revolutionary who in 1970 published his widely read prison letters—one year before he was killed when attempting to escape from northern California's San Quentin Prison.[26] *Fag Rag* was, therefore, in dialogue with a wider West Coast faggot orientation that both orbited the Black Panthers' headquarters in Oakland, California, and linked a loosely networked set of gay liberationist and lesbian feminist collectives up and down the coast. This network's influence was strongly felt at the 1976 Faggots & Class Struggle conference. In facing the West Coast, Boston's early *Fag Rag* often oriented itself primarily toward a Black radicalism that featured militarism more than gentleness.

In Seattle, the faggot figure took on an especially militant orientation. Daniel Burton-Rose has detailed the story of the Seattle-area George Jackson Brigade, formed in 1975. The core group of five was racially and sexually diverse, including an African American and three avowedly queer members (a lesbian couple and bisexual co-founder Ed Mead). They leveraged leftist violence—often bombs—against oppressive institutions (government and industry sites), and published communiqués afterward to explain their reasons for doing so.[27] Around the same time, Seattle's Morning Due collective formed in 1974, under the auspices of the city's Gay Community Social Services.[28] They began as a men's group that grew increasingly feminist, like the Flaming Faggots. As they refined their politics, they also formed a Marxist study circle, but their political position was really strained when, in 1975, they received requests to publish communiqués from the George Jackson Brigade in their newsletter. Morning Due buckled under fierce debates over whether nonviolent or armed struggle was the more necessary revolutionary strategy. The group eventually did publish two of the Brigade's statements—concerning the bombing of a Safeway (September 1975) and the bombing of a power substation (December 1975). Over the Labor Day weekend of 1976, Morning Due members—including those in support of publishing the Brigade communiqués—attended Oregon's faggot conference. In the orbit of the George Jackson Brigade, this Pacific Northwest faggot figure took on an especially militant form.

At the conference, various faggot variations mixed, and sometimes clashed. Alongside overtly political discussions, the faggot conference featured group rituals styled after the gay witchcraft that Evans had further articulated since leaving New York. In this West Coast context, the militant politics of *Fag Rag*—taking its notes from Black radicalism—and the fieriness of Evans's faggot witchcraft mixed to once more vary the template of earlier faggot forms. However, the Pacific Northwest organizers planned the faggot conference and only later invited Bay Area liberationists of color (the Gay Latinos Alliance, Gay American Indians, and the Black Gay Caucus)—all of whom declined the invitation. Their reasons were not only that they hadn't been involved in planning, and that the conference excluded women, but that they felt the titular witchy faggot figure drew primarily upon white European colonial experiences and, as such, could hardly represent them. Many conference attendees who agreed with this critique, and who also embraced their own outward effeminacy, called themselves sissies rather than faggots, in solidarity with the critique.[29] We can see from this 1976 Oregon event how the faggot figure migrated to the Pacific Northwest and then was rebuffed for its tacit white masculinity, ultimately failing to translate queered Black Power from Boston's *Fag Rag* or from Seattle's George Jackson Brigade. As a result, a new body, the *sissies*, descended from a faggot precedent. The Arkansas Mulberry House faggots were among those who agreed with the critique and began calling themselves *sissies* after the conference. By facing elsewhere, as the 1970s marched on, the faggot body that had sprung out of New York morphed as it moved.

In the context of revolution, clearly the composition of the faggot figure mattered. Did it convey the fire necessary to spark revolutionary analysis and action? Were its contours and features capacious enough to include the range of radical gay bodies fired under its umbrella? But this figure's orientation mattered, too. Tracing the social positions of the figure helped not only to identify primary allies but also to describe the forms of (often uneven) collaboration offered under that alliance. For example, did their alliance take the shape of publishing communiqués, or did it involve collaborative conference planning? In the 1970s, how such questions of embodiment were answered could divide houses, produce alternate revolutionary figures, and generate new alliances—as was the case with the Arkansas Sissies of Mulberry House.

Housing: From Radical Interiors to Regional Undergrounds

The Flaming Faggots saw living collectively as fundamental to who they were as revolutionaries. As we have seen, they negated gay bars and street culture. Their coming out was less focused on living hyper-visible lives in public spaces, in wide-open exteriors, and they turned more often to overhauling their interiors. Like many lesbian feminists of the time, they made consciousness-raising a priority, and that work was conducted in collective households where everyday domestic life was utterly transformed in accordance with revolutionary values. By their own count, the Flaming Faggots collective started fifty such consciousness-raising groups in New York in the early 1970s.[30] And faggot households had, according to Pitchford, popped up on all three US coasts by 1972. Clearly, faggots gave much thought to what happened within the walls of their collective houses, but how these houses connected with each other—across diverse geopolitical terrains—was also quite intentional.

Stephen Vider has described how 1970s gay liberationist men's communal homes were sites for reimagining and then practicing "domestic liberation": "The gay commune offered a glimpse of an alternative future, where the home would be unbound to monogamy, to capitalism, to patriarchy and to the state, molded only to the needs, desires and ideals of its makers."[31] As they learned from many of the lesbian feminists of the time, these gay liberationists, to some extent or another, withdrew from the oppressive institutions around them to design more accommodating ones for themselves. For example, proscribed family forms, home economics, gendered labor division, care practices, and sexual politics were interrogated and then reconfigured. Such intense inward-facing work, however, often prompted questions about who was included within these tightly redrawn circles and who was not. When considering the period's collectivism, it's crucial to think through what forces routed some groups into one house and not another.

For example, Martin Duberman has speculated as to why so many early gay liberationist organizations were largely white, despite their anti-racism. He admits that subtler, sometimes subconscious, forms of racism were a major factor, but he proposes that another influence was the difference in how white and Black liberationists regarded the nuclear family. He notes that Black families were more likely to accept, or accommodate, their gay members than were white ones, suggesting that white liberationists, as a result, took up harsher critiques of the traditional family, and forged other forms of collective living.[32] But Sylvia Rivera and Marsha P. Johnson, as street queens of color, also presented a collectivist solution when they formed STAR (Street Transvestite Action Revolutionaries) House.[33] As femmes, STAR House residents wouldn't have found a place in effeminists' anti-drag houses, either. Clearly, race, gender, and class separated collectives.

Of course, lesbian feminism has often been sweepingly critiqued for its separatist excesses. Sometimes, though, separatists conceived of what they were doing as a necessary tactic in a longer strategy. Julie Enszer has suggested that we do better to understand lesbian "separatism" less as a static and permanent isolation and more as a stage in a longer political process of alliance.[34] I find that this observation applies beyond lesbian feminism, to multiple New Left groups. For example, this was an aspect of Arthur Evans's conceiving of the single-issue GAA as a first step toward a wider revolution to which gay liberationists would be better prepared to contribute. The strategy was *not* to permanently separate gay issues from the wider revolutionary movement. Similarly, Huey Newton had not only organized the September 1970 Revolutionary People's Constitutional Convention to unite diverse leftist groups. He had also proposed that white anti-racists form their own White Panther Party to work in tandem with the Black Panthers. In these cases, a strategic and temporary separatism was necessary for groups who experienced unique forms of oppression to carve out the space to prioritize their issues and solutions before bringing them, in the spirit of a robust solidarity, to the united revolution.

Some scholars have characterized this uniquely 1970s way of doing radicalism as a disappointing identitarian departure from earlier 1960s New Left organizing. For example, Todd Gitlin has contrasted the successes of the earlier (early to mid-1960s) New Left to the oversteps of its later (1968–73) forms.[35] Max Elbaum has questioned views like Gitlin's, though, which see "the early 1960s movements [to] stand out as humane, sensible, and worthy of emulation in contrast to the heartless, violence-prone and irrational tendencies dominant after 1968."[36] Scholars like Elbaum, Jeremy Varon, and Van Gosse nuance this perspective by looking closer at the challenges of the later period, such as the relative youth of the activists, the New Communist embrace of a more strident Marxist-Leninism, the (incorrect) assumption that anti-imperial insurrections would increase, and an underestimation of the conservative backlash against radicalism.[37] The later New Left—to which gay liberation generally belongs—was simply up against a new set of circumstances. As activists broke with the "old left," they also lost traditions of "organizational discipline, ideological coherence, and programmatic sense of purpose."[38] They had to remake such tools.

Further, as they formed into political groups according to shared (racial, ethnic, sexual, gendered) experiences of oppression, they were challenged as to how to deal with intersectional experience.[39] Many groups responded to this challenge by conceiving solidarity as a practice that required some measured separatist processes, such as the practice of subgroups forming breakaway caucuses within movements. As a result, though, organizations, social groups, and communal houses often formed along identitarian lines and, although they shared visions of wider alliance, often struggled to know *when* and *how* to rejoin others in unity. For this reason, it is absolutely critical to attend to the specific vectors, tenors, and temporalities of primarily white gay collectivists' orientations and alliances. Did these houses face, recognize, engage, and vocally and/or materially support other movements? Did they regularly ask whether the time, conditions, and mutual interest for inclusion had come? And if so, how?

Collective houses rarely wanted a pure withdrawal from society; rather, they often served important political functions. For example, Emily Hobson ascribes the term *collective defense* to how lesbian communal households of the 1970s developed a strategy of harboring women—some of whom sought shelter from domestic and sexualized violence and others of whom eluded imprisonment for their radical politics. This practice brought intense government scrutiny to queer homes in cities across the United States.[40] Although Hobson's history is anchored in the Bay Area, she references lesbian radical Susan Saxe. The FBI's pursuit of Saxe led to the arrest of the Lexington Six, a Kentucky collective who had harbored Saxe. Houses in the deeper US South also practiced collective defense, as evidenced by the arrest of Vicki Gabriner in 1973, for passport fraud, in an Atlanta Little Five Points lesbian household. Gabriner had briefly worked with the Weathermen, gone to Cuba as part of the Venceremos Brigades, and later cofounded the Atlanta Lesbian Feminist Alliance (ALFA).[41] Radicals often eluded capture by moving from one collective house to another, forming both a network of sympathetic houses and well-trod paths through an underground that these networks made possible. To the degree that faggot, effeminist, sissie, and faerie households insinuated themselves as part of such radical underground networks, they committed their homes to the practice of collective defense, a strategy that Hobson maintains was itself adapted from the Black Panthers.

For radicals to make their way through the underground, they often depended on rural or small-town households. It wasn't only that these were sometimes necessary as way stations between urban destinations, across entire regions; they also offered a much lower profile than did the cities' collectives, which were under heavy surveillance. Also, many of these households formed in areas where countercultural, back-to-the-land enclaves took root in the 1960s and 1970s. Lesbian feminists and gay liberationists were embedded in these rural socialities. For example, the serial *RFD*, since its inception in 1974, had wed a gay liberationist political tenor to rural, countercultural, back-to-the-land sites and culture, thereby linking urban and rural collective households. Just as faggot, effeminist, and sissie households were inspired by lesbian feminist collective defense, Scott Herring has shown how *RFD* likewise modeled its rustic print aesthetics and its queered back-to-the-land versions of domestic liberation on lesbian precursors documented in serials like *Country Women*.[42]

If such rural sites were less sustainedly visible to urban perspectives, it doesn't follow that they were short-lived. Vider notes that, whereas many such collective households quickly folded, some of the rural ones—especially those that would become associated with the Radical Faeries—have persisted.[43] Similarly, while Martin Duberman has proclaimed that "the Effeminists succeeded in enlisting almost no one other than themselves," Dansky himself has retorted that even if they didn't become a fully organized movement, effeminists "influenced thinking across this country, and had a global reach to Australia, England, and France."[44] I propose that the habit of historicizing gay liberation as an urban phenomenon (with a fixed address and formal organizational records) misses how mobile, transient, intimate, and dispersed its adherents were. They moved a lot—often from one liberationist household to another, often to places without formal gay neighborhoods. I contend that the role of the faggots' rural–urban networks was not simply a matter of chance, but part of faggot design. After all, when Arthur Evans published his book in 1978, he insisted that rural collectives, well away from urban centers of surveillance, would be best situated to instigate the revolution, but that they should also form networks with those urban houses so closely watched as radical refuges.[45]

As these collectivist networks linked rural and urban landscapes, they took on regional scales and often confronted other regional forces. The persistence of Jim Crow segregation and violence was pervasive in the sissies' Southeastern geographies. So were government anti-poverty programs, like the Appalachian Regional Commission and the Ozark Regional Commission, both of which were begun in the mid-1960s. Booming college towns were also a factor as they not only connected regional young adults but made inroads for student movements into new rural and small-town contexts. As I trace the networking of these collective households, I resist the urge to isolate either rural or urban narratives, instead opening up to a regional geographic scale, to transnational imaginaries, and to countercultural transience as features of faggot and sissie collectivist design. I describe successive iterations of domestic liberation, leftist separatism, collective defense, underground networking, and regional political cultures. With this description, I hope to attend to how the entanglements of race, gender, and sexuality that are implicit within the sissie figure were themselves mirrored by the racist, sexist, and homophobic dynamics of the white supremacist geographies through which the Southeastern houses threaded themselves. As a fledgling gay liberationist underground, this particular Southeastern network struggled, unevenly, to define itself in the hollows of a New Right cultural geography that clung to its Jim Crow contexts.

Witching: New Socialist Covens, Rituals, and Magic

It was Arthur Evans who most fully described faggot witchcraft as a magical practice wed to radical politics. However, Evans's articulation of this form of witchcraft was only possible due to his synthesis of both East and West Coast faggot cultures. When he published *Witchcraft and the Gay Counterculture* in 1978, New York was still very much on his mind. He opened the book with "Once upon a time" but proceeded to describe a particular GAA zap of Mayor John Lindsay.[46] Those zaps were themselves a kind of magic. They used street theater tactics to provoke cowed public figures into either material support for reform or outsized homophobic outbursts, while the GAA positioned the media to project the results before the wide eyes of witnesses everywhere. When the public saw unfiltered homophobia in the daily paper or the nightly news, pockets of red anger flared, and these flashes would politicize a growing bloc of New York's homosexuals. This was a magic that worked kind of like routing sunlight through a lens to produce fire. It magnified public anger to unite resistance.

There were other examples of gay witchy politics in early 1970s New York City. Just a few days after the GAA's Imperial Theater zap, on Halloween 1970 Leo Martello staged a "Witch-In" in Central Park's Sheep Meadow, performing pagan rituals for the passing public and the media. He had done this in Central Park before, but this time, as a practicing witch, he demanded protection of his religious right to work spells openly, in public green spaces. Martello clearly used the sensationalism of witchery to manipulate media attention toward an injustice.[47] As we have seen, Evans credited Martello for first recommending a connection between gay politics and feminist witchcraft. I argue that, at Martello's suggestion, Evans took the affective politics of the zap and expanded its repertoire to include actual ritual and spell-work. Condemned by religions and legal institutions alike, gay liberationist revolutionaries like Evans increasingly thought of themselves not only as defiant traitors but also as unabashed heretics. To deepen his profane practice, Evans went west—to Washington State's New Sodom and then to San Francisco's Haight Ashbury.

British historian of witchcraft Ronald Hutton has characterized late twentieth-century California as an epicenter of modern paganism.[48] In the 1960s and 1970s, California witchcraft was often openly feminist, and fairly welcoming to homosexuals. In 1971, lesbian Zsuzsanna Budapest founded the women-only Susan B. Anthony Coven #1 in Los Angeles. In the Bay Area, in Alameda County, Victor and Cora Anderson had begun initiating their own coven members around 1960. The couple would, over time, come to mythologize the universe's creation more as a product of feminine ecstasy (rather than fertility) and to articulate a theology with a complex gender system—both of which proved especially attractive to sexual and gender nonconformists who were interested in witchcraft. Starhawk (Miriam Simos), a bisexual woman who had spent most of her teenage years in Southern California, moved to San Francisco around 1975, and to defend against the legal challenges faced by the growing number of witches in her new city, she helped to found the Covenant of the Goddess as an official body to represent the interests of area witches.[49]

That there was a need for such a group is testament to the rising profile of witchcraft in the mid-1970s Bay Area. Starhawk had studied with the Andersons and would publish *The Spiral Dance* in 1979, ultimately helping to found the Reclaiming Collective for feminist spirituality in 1980. *The Spiral Dance* described witchcraft as a very political practice, and Starhawk placed antihomophobia alongside her feminist, peace, and environmentalist activism. Although *The Spiral Dance* and the Reclaiming Collective didn't officially emerge until the end of the decade, Starhawk refined her beliefs in the mid-1970s through her study with the Andersons, through her collective spiritual practice, and through her advocacy work with the Covenant of the Goddess. As a visible leader in witchcraft circles and as a theorist of the political and spiritual dimensions of the reclaiming process, Starhawk was an important figure to many spiritually minded gay liberationists and lesbian feminists—on the West Coast and beyond. Evans and Starhawk both came to San Francisco in the mid-1970s, when feminist witchcraft was already in the air.

In her discussion of the Bay Area "politics of faggotry," Hobson doesn't mention spirituality. Describing the San Francisco activism of Reverend Ray Broshears and Bishop Michael-Francis Itkin, however, Christina Hanhardt does reference a "[not] uncommon mold for gay activists in the 1970s"—sex radicals who were "also spiritually oriented and often members of small, offbeat religious groups—some of which they themselves founded—that combined a wide variety of traditions, including paganism."[50] Evans, who relocated to San Francisco in 1974, easily fit this mold. From his Haight-Ashbury apartment in 1975 he began hosting a spiritual "fairy circle," and in early 1976 he gave a series of public lectures on his witchcraft research. As with Starhawk, Evans's work was active in the witchcraft and liberationist circles of the Bay Area well before his book appeared, published by Fag Rag Books in 1978.

It's important to understand the ways Evans's faggot witchcraft melded East and West Coast faggot cultures. Obviously, the street theater and media manipulation of GAA zaps still captured his imagination. Further, as we have already shown, Evans—like the Flaming Faggots—recommended collectivism, but he imagined it as a network of urban and rural collective houses. Evans's gay liberationism, like that of many others, was also deeply anti-institutional. He proposed that revolutionary faggots should unplug as much as possible from all institutions and network in collectives to take care of each other without the aid of the state, industries, prisons, hospitals, schools, and the military. This echoed the strategy of radical lesbian feminists whose separatism was primarily aimed at creating alternative institutions. It shouldn't be surprising, then, that the first chapter of *Witchcraft and the Gay Counterculture* highlights as a foundational case study the relationship between the gender-nonconforming Joan of Arc and her close friend Gilles de Rais (who was not only accused of being a pagan but a sexual predator of boys). Evans noted how both they and their networks were "tortured by methods rather like the CIA today."[51] Like the Flaming Faggots, Evans defined faggot witchcraft by a primary alliance of vilified queer men and women.

Although the Flaming Faggots had taken sharp exception to the hypermasculinity of socialist revolutionaries like those in the Venceremos Brigade, Evans didn't distance himself altogether from classic leftism. He pitched faggot witchcraft as a practice toward a "new socialism." The book's analysis of Western history is consistently socialist feminist. His historical narrative traces the violences of an autocratic Christian church that colluded with emergent colonial and capitalist forces, which were anchored in urban industrial areas. Central to these forces' power was control over the reproductive processes necessary to swell the ranks of their military and labor pools. It fell to the Church, he explained, to regulate sexuality as a valve for childbirth, to sanctify the traditional family and its gendered division of labor, to professionalize medicine, and to make humility a virtue. This role required the Church to vilify those women, and men, who not only worshiped other gods but defied proscribed sexual duties, gendered scripts, familial obligations, work ethics, medical obeisance, and pervasive body shaming. As Evans showed in multiple case studies, this meant that independent women and homosexuals were often the ones targeted by the witch hunts conducted by the conflated Church and State, which was determined to stamp out those who were especially defiant.[52]

The primary element that was new about Evans's "new socialism" was its willingness to correct for the "failures of industrial socialism and ... [make] room for the special contributions of Gay people, women, and ancient Third World cultures."[53] He described faggot witchcraft through New Left frames, underscoring the importance of it maintaining a global anti-colonial stance. This position closely aligned with the Bay Area "politics of faggotry" observed by Hobson. He rejected the single-minded workerism of industrial-based traditional socialism, turning to New Left politics around more expansive analysis of class, race, gender, sexuality, and ability in order to imagine a host of potential revolutionary subjectivities.[54] However, it is important to remember that, on his path to San Francisco, Evans had also published his witchcraft research in Boston's *Fag Rag* and had lived in Washington State. He would have also been familiar, then, with a faggot militancy inspired by the George Jackson Brigade.

He characterized the 1970s United States as a capitalist military state and took some time to comment on how mental hospitals were organized on military models, how federal agencies used domestic surveillance and infiltration (including entrapment of homosexuals), and how the Bay Area economy had come to heavily depend on the US Department of Defense.[55] He summed up the problems of the 1970s by saying, "The whole industrial system is like one great night of the living dead ... It has deadened us to the environment, deprived us of art, sterilized our human nature, robbed us of the skills of survival, degraded our labor and leisure, and decimated our sexual lives. And so it has made us like the living dead—dead to nature, dead to each other, dead to ourselves." Still, he imagined it possible that vital, connective sex and magic could still thrive "among the zombies."[56] He conveyed magic as a social practice—"group song, dance, sex, and ecstacy [sic]"—that was necessary for revolution: for successful collectivization, alliance, and networking; for identification with nature as a "corrective for 'civilization'"; and for raising "great inner power."[57] Magic was the practice of materializing the basic social units of revolution—from developing the social psychologies of revolutionary classes, to forming local collectives, to forging the alliances which themselves accrued to comprise the wider network—and building a radical underground. As a result, Evans's model for the collective, as actively practicing this radical magic, came to resemble a witches' coven.

And Evans didn't shy away from baneful work. He thought that strategic violence against those in control was sometimes necessary, and he encouraged new socialists to "fan out like viruses in the body politic, when the time is right, carrying our secret weapons, and striking without warning against ruling institutions, and the politicians, industrialists, warlords, and academics that run them. Many will undoubtedly disagree, but without a revolutionary underground, I fear we will again perish like burning faggots."[58] Riding a visionary and ecstatic wave, he closed his book by calling on goddesses: "Come, blessed Lady of the Flowers, Queen of Heaven, creator and destroyer, Kali—we are dancing the great dance of your coming."[59] In the end, his book is best understood as a gay witch's prayer for revolution. And the means of that revolution was a new socialism, which Evans insisted was "not just political, but also magical and sexual."[60]

Evans's witchcraft inflected the daily life and politics of many faggot houses, but its rituals were often improvised to fit the needs of the specific place. Its spells were adapted to shape local variations on the faggot figure. This would certainly be the case in the Southeast. And as these new figures met—on the faggot page and off the main roads—their chemistries would spark and their coven-houses would link to form regional undergrounds set against the storm clouds of surging New Right violence.

The Deeper-South Setting

In his analysis of 1970s gay liberationist communes, Vider mentions Mulberry House as a collective that fissured over class differences, and also names Short Mountain as a rural collective that survives into the present. Treating them as discrete instances, he presents the former as but one of many examples that prove how short-lived most of these experiments were, and the latter as a durable, rural exception.[61] In this book, however, I show how members of Mulberry House hived off to form New Orleans's LaSIS collective, which in turn, helped form Tennessee's Short Mountain Sanctuary. Further, all three collectives—through *RFD* and gatherings at North Carolina's Running Water Farm—synergized even more Southern gay liberationists into a wider group that called itself the Southeast Network. By seeing how these households linked, we are able to uncover a much wider, influential network, an underground galvanized in response to the rise of the New Right. We are also able to see their strategies for sustaining liberation. Scott Lauria Morgensen has proposed that Short Mountain Sanctuary may have had roots in "histories of radical southern and rural gay collectivism." I trace one of those roots in order to narrate the story of those collectivists through a period and place that they didn't always trust they would survive.[62]

The sissie collectivist story in this book picks up important implications of Ian Lekus's account of early lesbian and gay liberationist experiences on the Cuban Venceremos Brigade. His work points not only to (1) how the Southern civil rights movement faced a Jim Crow establishment whose racism, sexism, and homophobia were entangled with an anti-communism inspired by their proximity to Cuba, but also to (2) how "the [US gay] communes sprouting up all across the land came closest to replicating the personal and political intimacy of the Brigades, but they differed in their small household size and in their highly decentralized nature."[63] Lekus, perhaps offhandedly, refers to a "deeper-south" ideological geography, which I describe as the backdrop of the Southeast sissies' political cultures. While the events described in this book completely take place within US territory, their liberationist politics were shaped by cross-border visions, sometimes especially attuned to a wider Caribbean world.[64]

As a history of the specifically queer south, this book benefits from the work of scholars like John Howard and E. Patrick Johnson, whose scholarship has not only been foundational for the field but also has offered more nuanced analysis about race and visibility to broader LGBTQ+ studies, showing how Southern queer networks often formed tacitly, within traditional social institutions.[65] It is less common, though, for expressly radical LGBTQ+ culture to be placed in the South. In that this book treats explicitly political (liberationist, leftist) and countercultural gay networks committed to building alternative institutions, it bears a closer resemblance to James T. Sears's documentation of the "Stonewall South."[66] But where Sears's narrative method is kaleidoscopic, my own is to trace an important linear throughline within such dispersed regional circulations. More recently, Jaimie Harker's *The Lesbian South* also presents a departure from Howard's focus on tacit networks and traditional institutions to describe an openly radical Southern lesbian feminism, which she culls from the print culture of the time.[67] Text, politics, and geography informed each other, as Harker shows; and as I argue, this book's faggots, sissies, and faeries adapted strategies from lesbian culture for gay liberationist purposes. By looking at documentation of the collectives' practices, I also hope to show how their printed values and dreams were put into action.

Both Sears and Harker pitch their histories at a regional scale. This is unusual because most histories of the LGBTQ+ movement have been local ones, using, for example, archival records of local activist organizations to tell the queer story of a single city. As is by now widely recognized, such common practice feeds a metronormativity in LGBTQ+ studies.[68] I argue that it also denies how often historical queer activists circulated from place to place, connecting rural, urban, event, and media cultures across wider swaths of geography. Instead of treating each place discretely, I connect them to describe how 1970s gay liberationist networks often assumed a regional character—inflected by counterculture transience and transnational yearnings. La Shonda Mims has recently taken a similar approach, linking communities in Atlanta and Charlotte to suggest a late twentieth-century lesbian South.[69] It is my hope that this book complements the work of Harker and Mims by demonstrating how Southeastern gay liberationists were inspired by the lesbian South—just one way in which Southern lesbians' political cultures radiated beyond their immediate circles. This book, then, adds to the existing literature by tracing an openly radical and countercultural gay liberationist network across the South; by demonstrating what might be gained by doing LGBTQ+ movement history at the regional scale; by describing an effeminate, nonbinary gay liberationist political culture most inspired by lesbian feminism; and by fleshing out how these sissies improvised a figural, collectivist, and witchy design to survive the terror-filled rise of the New Right in the late 1970s.

The resulting portrait not only places lesbian and gay radicalism in the South; it also proposes that we reconsider how we have framed the late-1970s New Right in US LGBTQ+ history. It is a central premise of this book that, because popular narratives have satirized Anita Bryant as an unwitting midwife for the national gay rights movement, we often forget the real violence and terror that followed the June 1977 success of Save Our Children and persisted past the November 1978 assassination of Harvey Milk. It is understandable that scholars have been interested in the organizational, legal, and media practices that formed the gay response to Save Our Children at a comparable national, gay-rights scale.[70] However, it has also been helpful that critical studies of the New Right have allowed us to understand Save Our Children's homophobia as interwoven with racist, sexist, Christo-centric, and anticommunist agendas, and also to consider local and regional contexts for Bryant's influence, rather than a monolithic national one.[71] I have found it particularly interesting, though, that most such histories frame gay liberationist responses to Save Our Children as a naive or passé liability when compared to that of savvier gay-rights activists.[72] I take seriously the sissies' Southeast Network as an example of a sustained gay liberationist response to late-1970s New Right child protectionism.

This book proceeds chronologically, in three parts. Part I describes the Mulberry House collective in Fayetteville, Arkansas. Part II describes how the Louisiana Sissies in Struggle (LaSIS) hived off from Mulberry House and formed a linked collective in New Orleans. Part III traces how LaSIS helped to form Short Mountain Sanctuary, in Appalachian Tennessee. The book, then, traces the proliferation of sissies' houses in the Southeast, from one to the next, fomenting a significant enough regional network of gay liberationist collectives to function as an underground during New Right violence. The narrative form of this progression, from house to house, sometimes shapeshifts. By turn, the book reads like a small-group romance, a hermetic biography, or an arcing movement chronicle. This is, in part, because I try to depict the collectives' politics in their most personal *and* social forms. Also, although the story is propelled by violence, I try to keep my main focus on how collectivists responded to that violence with gay liberationist tones.

Part I, on Mulberry House, has three chapters. Chapter 1 describes how each main collectivist came to Arkansas, how the Ozarks facilitated their gay liberation, and how Mulberry House originally oriented themselves to the area's socialist lesbian feminists as well as to the *RFD* print network. Chapter 2 recounts the complex politico-spiritual dynamics of the 1976 Faggots & Class Struggle conference that led Mulberry House to call themselves *sissies*. Chapter 3 offers an account of how Mulberry House critiqued the Oregon conference, articulated a domestic liberation around regional food justice, and ultimately split over a crisis of collective defense in the wake of Save Our Children.

Part II, on LaSIS, also consists of three chapters. Chapter 4 is an account of how one lone Mulberry House collectivist reoriented himself to New Orleans as a place where he could learn to care across race and class lines, and how he adapted feminist witchcraft practices to produce a radical self-conversion in line with his leftist ideals. Chapter 5 is an account of the formation of LaSIS through their shared radical conversions and information activism. I describe this formation by applying Marlon Ross's hermeneutic for sissy liminality to describe how LaSIS answered the Briggs Initiative and ongoing local segregationism with a nonbinary street presence that was both heretical and pedagogical. Chapter 6 describes how LaSIS further articulated their collectivist practice through a regional networking that emphasized the importance of both solidarity and dreamwork.

Part III, on sissies' collaborations with Short Mountain, consists of two chapters. Chapter 7 details LaSIS's response to the assassination of Harvey Milk and the rush toward a national gay rights movement. This period included their sissie media performance for an ABC docuseries and their qualified participation in several events: Running Water Farm gatherings, the National March on Washington, and the first Spiritual Conference for Radical Faeries. Chapter 8 covers LaSIS's partnership with Short Mountain and their use of their shared editorship of *RFD* and the Short Mountain Re-Inhabitation Project to translate sissie collectivism into a sanctuary practice within the emergent Radical Faerie culture. The chapter closes where this Introduction started: with an account of LaSIS ritually relinquishing their regional collectivism. I argue, though, that they did this with hopes that their radical spiritual and collectivist practice would survive through the faerie figure, which seized latter-day gay liberationist attention as the Reagan era dawned.

From a certain angle, the subject of this book is a light one. The period of time within which the sissies captured an already seriously thinned gay liberation movement was brief—roughly two to three years. There were relatively few who really embraced the figure as part of their doggedly radical politics. However, I argue that the sissies were part of a longer radical gay liberation galvanized by faggot subjectivity, which then mutated into the Radical Faerie culture, which—like Short Mountain Sanctuary and *RFD*—exists to this day. I also contend that these sissies not only improvised a uniquely Southeastern variation on faggot radicalism that grappled, with uneven success, with the white Christian supremacist context of late-1970s child protectionism. They also suggested spiritual and collectivist strategies for sustaining a revolution that was presumed to be exhausted. To overlook the sissies for their small numbers and their short time on stage is to misread how they themselves conceived gay liberationist visibility. Their loud figures and teeming houses were designed to be seasonal, thoroughly historical. What lasted was their collectivist praxis, which we see replicated even a half-century later, at Short Mountain and in *RFD*. If as historians we shift our view of gay liberation as a culture of coming out to a practice of coming together, we can see how critical their sissie stories are to our learning how liberation endures. While offering nothing like a pat answer, their experiences are useful at a time when (white supremacist, sexist, homophobic) New Right child protectionism has proven itself completely capable of staging its own violent return.

This book, then, invites us to give our attention to the fleeting in order to discern a longer circulation, often into those places off our usual maps: in crude periodicals, at hushed house meetings, and on once-abandoned mountain farms. It also urges us to follow how, for these faggots, effeminists, sissies, and faeries, turning each house into the next involved a bit of magic. They dreamed that their daily pathworking might lead to something like a future.

Part I
Mulberry House
The Ozarks, 1971–77

CHAPTER ONE

Mulberry Chemistries
Coming Together in an Ozark Separatist Landscape

We can think of that which brings a collective together as a kind of chemistry. It is not altogether different from what unites a couple, except that the political mingles overtly with the personal as the collective bonds form along multiple axes: interpersonal and ideological. This chapter falls into two parts. In the first, I introduce each of the early, primary collectivists of Mulberry House. Stylistically, I weave mini-biographies (based on oral histories and personal letters) into descriptions of the early-1970s cultural climate of northwest Arkansas, tracing what brought each collectivist to the region. I take this approach as a way to narrate the composition of Mulberry House, to wed the personal and the political, to cast their ideological formation as a meeting of interpersonal chemistries and larger social forces. In the second part, I analyze Mulberry House's 1976 *RFD* manifesto in order to read the group's early figural development as a faggot collective with a primary orientation to (1) Ozark lesbian socialist feminism and (2) the countercultural, networking enabled by *RFD*. By this two-pronged approach, I offer both a domestic view of those who resided *in* the house alongside a nuanced description of how they first looked *out*, addressing the wider liberationist world.

Finding Each Other in Fayetteville

In 1974, when Dennis Williams rented the "little wooden shack that was sliding down the hillside" at 438 West Lawson Street ("a lush Southern environment," with "honeysuckle everywhere"), he had barely survived his last love.[1] Still, there must have seemed something graced about his finding the bowered house. He'd left his previous home—with its beautiful mulberry tree—in a rush when the owner sold it to be razed for development. Williams quickly took the Lawson Street house, rented to him by a local named Honey Dawn, and called it "Mulberry House II." He envisioned the place full of others, like him, dedicated to liberationist causes. In a year that vision would materialize, and the future collective would name themselves after the house. There was clearly a generous magic to the place, but upon first moving in, at the age of forty-one, Williams had taken a long and winding road to find it.

Williams's childhood had been conventional, middle-class. Born a Capricorn in Dallas in 1933, he saw his father—a businessman who traveled frequently—very little. He felt his mother smothered him. Although homosexuality seemed hardly to appear on her radar, she stressed that he should *never* enter intimate relations with "Catholics, Negroes, or Jews."[2] In school he was notably effeminate—identifying with the girl characters in his reading and adoring his female teachers. Later, armed with a degree in English and drama from the University of Texas at Austin, he moved to New York City, making a living there as a theatrical costume designer and then as an editor of academic books. He did well. However, despite the fact that he moved in the city's 1960s arts and intellectual circles during the period leading up to the Stonewall Riots, he referred to that time as his "straight years" and, of gay culture, exhibited only a vague familiarity with the cruising circles around the piers.[3]

Stifled by city and career, he took night classes at CUNY to get a master's degree in history, a subject that, at the time, he considered his true passion. Not long before Stonewall erupted, with his diploma fresh in hand, he headed upstate to teach at a Stony Point countercultural "free school" run by a radical couple: Leo and Mary Koch. After locals shut the school down over a zoning technicality, Williams moved into the Kochs' attic. By this point he had no biological family to speak of; his mother had passed away in the late 1960s, and his father, soon after, dismissed him as a "deranged communist."[4] Regaining a sense of family then became a personal mission for Williams. After some soul-searching, though, he told the Kochs he was pulling up stakes in the States and heading to India.

In early 1970 he hitchhiked with other hippies to San Francisco. From there he took a boat to India. Western hippies—or "heads," as he called them—were everywhere, traveling in groups, smoking pot, sporting Indian clothing, and seeking various religious experiences. Williams considered himself one of them, but he chose to travel alone, to keep to his American countercultural garb, and to visit the local cafes on his own. As a result, he got to know more Indians. In 1970 Indira Gandhi was emerging as a prime minister dedicated to eliminating national poverty, and Williams with great interest watched her "steer the very tricky middle course of democratic socialism."[5] He took careful note of Sikh, Hindu, and Buddhist interactions and developed sympathies with the exiled Tibetans. Politically, he put his faith in a libidinal, youth-led revolution as he saw younger Indians reject the older generation's strict gender divisions and sexual repression, both of which he felt contributed to the country's remarkably high suicide rate.

He enjoyed tense, brief sexual interactions with various local men, but struggled to define his sexuality, finding himself emotionally also drawn to women and to the idea of family. In India he struggled both to hone his political analysis and to keep an outsider's modesty, regularly sending his reflections back home, by letter, to old New York friends. He spent the bulk of August on a grueling group pilgrimage, through rain and cold, to Amaranth, "to pay homage to a gigantic phallus formed out of living ice," where, he observed, all who made it to the end were "touched by the Shiva madness."[6] He was devastated, however, arriving at a post office in September, to find that not one friend had responded to his letters. (He didn't know then that his letters had been unwittingly addressed to a friend's former workplace.) Intensely alone, he kept writing letters that increasingly felt like the diaries of long-lost selves. He thought he might try to stay on, to finish the year in India. He did not. Instead, by the spring of 1971 he had rejoined the Kochs, who had relocated to Boles, Arkansas, to form an anarchist farming collective.

By the 1960s, most small Ozark farms had been effectively choked out by the rise of larger-scale agricultural and extraction industries, forcing many locals in the impoverished mountain South to leave their land and the region. This phenomenon brought the counterculture to the Ozarks in various ways. Foremost, the mountain South figured prominently in Johnson's War on Poverty. The Ozarks were somewhat overshadowed by the national sympathies, policies, and programs extended to Appalachia through the formation of the Appalachian Regional Commission (ARC), but Arkansas quickly learned from the example.

Moved by the poverty and isolation of Appalachia, John F. Kennedy responded in 1963 to pleas from that region's governors by forming a multistate commission, which his successor Lyndon B. Johnson would legally formalize as ARC, a federal agency, in 1965. This act situated the wide area's economically depressed counties not only as a new Appalachian geography of abjection, but also as principal recipients of federal support in Johnson's War on Poverty. Local leaders in Arkansas noted how, where the acute needs of a single, sparsely populated rural site could never hope to grab national attention, the articulation of a whole networked region of such sites could very well attract federal aid. Those entrepreneurial leaders, from several counties spanning the Ouachita and Ozark National Forests in western Arkansas, put together their own Ozark Regional Commission (ORC), and in late 1964 they secured federal support from the newly formed Volunteers in Service to America (VISTA), a domestic program modeled on the Peace Corps. From then on, the Ozarks would host many VISTA volunteers—locals and newcomers, many of whom, through the late 1960s, were also both hippies and activists.[7]

Writer Marvin Schwartz shares the story of one Ozark volunteer, Bob Gorman, who was assigned to the Ozarks in 1968, in Newton County. Gorman, who came from a poor white Boston background, recalled that, by his time there, the early Ozark VISTA focus on teaching and regional culture had shifted to community organizing. Gorman had been trained for that work in urban Black neighborhoods and noted the irony of his appointment to the mostly white Newton County. He slowly integrated into the local community, however, by coordinating area youth to cut and sell wood, which he would deliver to remote households in a truck, the bed of which was outfitted with a shelf for library books and a hidden cache of bootleg alcohol. Gorman's audacity and leftist leanings earned him an odd reputation with locals, who, he said, regarded him fondly but as a sort of "village idiot." Such bemused relations between locals and the counterculture became part of the wider social landscape. Gorman remembered that, in nearby Fayetteville, almost all VISTA projects were delivered with some context of "alternative lifestyles," which "Arkansas kids ... would [take] into their own homes."[8] These relations settled into a unique culture of affable overlap between hippie and "hillbilly," a mix that historian Jared M. Phillips named "hipbillies."[9]

This connection produced frictions, though, as the local political and business leaders who had formed ORC in order to draw federal money for their development plans inadvertently helped produce entrenched countercultural enclaves with different visions for the Ozarks than their own. Schwartz says local leaders' concerns were answered when Nixon came into office and quickly shifted the VISTA culture again—this time toward more clearly circumscribed practical projects implemented almost exclusively under local governmental direction. In effect, fewer hippies were invited in from then on. Historian Blake Perkins argues that what is now widely perceived as an Ozark culture of anti-federalism is, at times, actually better understood in the context of tension around local leadership's hijacking federal aid from the populace.[10] The 1970s reshaping of Ozark VISTA projects often reflected that dynamic. As a result, in many parts of the Ozarks, rural locals and recently arrived hippies bonded not only over rural folkways but over a populist distrust of the political and economic elite at both the national and local levels. By the time Williams and the Kochs arrived, the counterculture was already dug in as an Ozarks fixture, and hippies flocked to the state on their own, without VISTA invitations.

Heady from his experiences in India, Williams described their collective at Koch Farm humorously, in spiritual and political terms: "Religiously we run the gamut from militant atheist to backsliding Buddhist, but spiritually our rallying cry is Freedom. If Prince Kropotkin were alive I think he would call us a functioning anarchy, even though I'm sure he would disapprove of our voting on whether to watch *Bonanza* or turn the TV off."[11] He quickly assumed the role of what Leo Koch called the "Minister of Information," writing letters to old friends and fellow hippies interested in the latest rural, countercultural collective to break ground in the hipbilly Ozarks. He secured what would at first be the collective's only source of income by reviving his freelance editorial career, mostly with the regional University of Oklahoma, and he took responsibility for writing the farm's newsletter. After discovering the radical Atlanta newspaper *The Great Speckled Bird*, in mid-1971, he was able to connect Koch Farm to wider movement networks so that, by January 1972, he could count nine Europeans and twelve US inmates among his readers.

He entered a relationship with a far younger Gloria, who encouraged him to discuss his same-sex sexuality in correspondence with some of his incarcerated readers, and with her blessing he began openly calling himself a *homosexual* as he and Gloria planned a family of their own. When the Kochs began to assert a parental authority over the new couple, Williams and Gloria decided to move out, with Gloria expecting a child. Gloria miscarried, though, and left Williams, alone and deeply depressed, living in the attic of a countercultural household called Putnam House, in Fayetteville. While editing a collection of Inuit folklore, he isolated himself at first. In letters to friends he declared the old Dennis dead and announced that a new figure called "The Mole" had taken his place.[12] Slowly, though, he started to defiantly embrace his new gay identity, and to acidly dismiss the straight world, including his old friends. Testing new waters, he found some accepting community at the gay-friendly hippie bar George's, where, in January 1973, for his fortieth birthday, a fellow queen named Toad gave Williams a striptease and a new nickname—Ms. Buddha—that united his spiritual and femme sides.[13] Williams welcomed both and assumed yet another identity.

Through his Koch Farm correspondence, Williams had grown to see the prison system as a central tool of US imperial social control, particularly through the oppressive registers of race, class, and sexuality. As a result, he offered Koch Farm as a re-entry option for radicalized inmates, some of them gay, to reunite with a more politically sympathetic society upon their release. Some of this perspective was sparked when he had discussed with curious

Indians the racism he had witnessed as a child in Texas. However, it's important not to think of the Ozark hipbilly meld of the early 1970s as easily or exclusively made between newly arrived white hippies and backward white locals.

On the one hand, Perkins does observe that many rural whites in the Ozarks resented VISTA programs as being, at their root, measures meant only to aid poor Black populations. Gorman remembers how VISTA programs elsewhere in Arkansas were more combustible, dealing as they did with the racialized poverty produced in Black communities by the entrenchment of Southern Jim Crow practices. He recalls one time when two buses of Black children on a nearby Russellville Upward Bound program came to Newton County, and the locals, according to his observation, silently fumed at the intrusion.[14] Whether the rural locals actually felt like a color line had been crossed or Gorman projected that feeling, VISTA programs did link rural white and urban Black poverty, and therefore did sometimes bring the two groups into physical proximity. Rural whites surely responded variously. For those who embraced the emergent hipbilly culture, we can only speculate a range of reasons they were not so troubled by the linking of their lot with poor Blacks. But other rural Ozark whites, as Perkins shows, shifted their allegiances from VISTA workers to local white elites at this time because of racial resentments.

We *can* show, though, that Ozark VISTA activism wasn't exclusively the work of whites from elsewhere. Both Schwartz and Perkins cite the sustained VISTA organizing conducted by Black Fayetteville native Bobby Morgan. The son of a town tavern owner in the Black community of East Fayetteville, Morgan showed early achievement when, in the mid-1960s, he won a $480,000 grant to fund a county mobile clinic program, but implementation was stalled when monies were routed elsewhere under the watch of local white elites. Frustrated, Morgan relocated to Little Rock, where he organized around voting issues, ultimately exposing Ozark racist voter fraud and committing himself to wider voter education. His late-1960s VISTA-related activism earned him a Ford Foundation leadership fellowship, which led to his wider exposure to Southern radicalism, with groups like the Weathermen and the Black Panthers. Upon his return to Fayetteville in the early 1970s, he set up a breakfast program for Black children out of his own home, which the local health department promptly ordered him to relocate. Also subject to police harassment and wiretapping over the course of his early activist career, Morgan serves as an important reminder that the VISTA-related politics and counterculture of the time did not only originate with whites brought into the Ozarks from elsewhere but was also spurred by Black locals who persistently took on the region's elite power structure.[15]

In the mid- to late 1960s, then, the War on Poverty came to the Ozarks through VISTA programs that not only connected locals with populist leanings to wider countercultural activist networks but also surely made the racial dimensions of poverty impossible to ignore. It was tangible in the wide awareness of racial conflict related to other Arkansas VISTA projects, in the crossracial contact resulting from rural–urban programming, in the defensive maneuvers of the regional white establishment, and in the work of local Black activists like Bobby Morgan. I take some time with this point in order to qualify the whiteness of the 1970s Ozark hipbilly counterculture. Even if it was mostly composed of white people, it is difficult to imagine that—given the 1960s roots of this counterculture in the VISTA programs—theirs was a network wholly unaware of the role of race in constituting their new place in those hills. This is a factor I find important to remember when making the argument that gay liberationists like Williams found their place in the Ozarks via countercultural routes. If Williams's letters to US prisoners were often occasion for him to reflect on the whiteness of Koch Farm, this was certainly due not only to his own discussions of US racism while in India but also to the racial dynamics that inflected the counterculture's place in the Ozarks in the first place.

Williams cultivated a "guru" status in Fayetteville. At the local university he screened avant-garde films by gay directors (Warhol and Pasolini) and taught courses on fabric arts and the *I Ching*. By the spring of 1974, he openly espoused a "gay militancy." He shared in a letter, "Sometimes my younger friends do not understand . . . but when I try & explain to them what it was like to be queer during the fifties, they begin to get a glimmering."[16] There is no indication that Williams understood this militancy in conventionally gay liberationist terms—he makes no reference to Stonewall or the burgeoning gay press of the time. His context had, to date, primarily been within countercultural circles. However, his leftist, broadly anarchist focus on freedom would have made him amenable to the goals of liberation. His experiences of repression, at home and in India—especially given his complex gender and sexual identity—produced a politics invested in sexual freedom. His correspondence reveals a particularly fiery anger focused on the repressive roles of family and prison. As an effeminate man, Williams might have glimpsed a place for himself in hippie circles. That vision was hard to maintain, though, once he had settled into his first Arkansas home, at Koch Farm.

His experience was not unique. In the very first issue of *RFD* (Fall 1974) Allan Troxler bitterly described how quickly straight, masculine men in rural hippie collectives won the approval of locals by visibly taking on butch farmwork and reestablishing the dynamics of the traditional family, thus themselves shedding the label "commie hippie faggot," betraying countercultural sexual and gender politics, and leaving women and queers doubly isolated in their new backwoods homes. Nascent gay liberationists like Troxler and Williams found themselves painfully trapped in exactly the sorts of traditional families that they had imagined themselves transforming. Troxler recalled his time in the country, "I had hoped to find other faggots.... But I hadn't reckoned on the function of repression in counter-culture."[17] As a middle-aged, effeminate, queer hippie, "Ms. Buddha" took up residence in Honey Dawn's Fayetteville rental house and took some heart in the more accommodating gay-hippie overlap he found in the Ozark college town and the generally accepting bar life at George's.

That same spring he would meet a young gay couple, driven by the promise of gay liberation, recently arrived from points further south. Charlie Thornton and Michael Oglesby came to Arkansas as a pair. They had met in Monroe, Louisiana, in 1972 at the Pit Grill, which, as Thornton remembers it, was a place where "truck drivers and professional wrestlers and queer people would go in and have a bite to eat."[18] It was late (or early, rather): four in the morning. As Oglesby took a seat in a nearby booth, Thornton noticed his eyes, his "long hair coming down to his shoulders"—"this beautiful man." He immediately thought, "*This* is the man"—a prescient statement, given that their relationship would last over half a century. Thornton would have read Oglesby's long hair as a kind of countercultural badge. This mark of the social outsider was definitely a part of their connection. Oglesby remembers the Pit Grill as situated in this tiny stretch of Monroe's downtown, near the Catholic church and the bus station, a place where gay street kids like himself hung out, cruising to be picked up by older men. That night at the Pit Grill, Thornton had gotten off his shift at the gas station, and after eating, introduced himself before asking Oglesby back to his apartment. Oglesby went, intrigued, not knowing anyone who had their own place. He was thrilled to find that "Charlie had books by Allen Ginsberg. He had some information on the Gay Liberation Front. Poetry, Ezra Pound.... I felt like I had finally found a kindred spirit, and I was just amazed at all the information he had."

The powerful chemistry that so enduringly connected Thornton and Oglesby belonged to the compressed social space of a few blocks. It belonged to the hours before dawn. It was decidedly blue-collar, and it was Southern. More specific was their mutual recognition—unique within Monroe's small-town gay circle—over countercultural style and offbeat reading habits. The spirit they shared was bent on gay liberation and, as such, their love was thoroughly political. As a couple, they each determined to discover, as Thornton put it, "how to be open as a gay man without being killed."

The couple had an overt investment in gay liberation well before they arrived in Fayetteville. Oglesby still remembers the GLF literature back in Thornton's Monroe apartment. Despite their Deep South upbringings in the 1950s and 1960s, neither remembers having had a particularly hard time with being gay when it came to their birth families. Oglesby attributes this to his growing up in Monroe in a single-parent household, alone with his mom and four older sisters—after his dad and brother left home. His mother, wanting "to create a more liberal environment" for her son, remarkably, gave the young teenager a copy of John Rechy's *City of Night*. Oglesby's later teen years as a gay street kid in Monroe might have been inspired by the Texan author's seamy tales of gay hustler life in cities like New Orleans.

Five years older, Thornton knew, as a child in rural Winn Parish, *that* he was different, but it was at the age of sixteen, when his family moved to the cotton town of Winnsboro and he fell in love with another boy—"an artist, classical pianist, valedictorian"—that he knew *how* he was different. Heading to Monroe for college, Thornton made an equally unabashed gay friend there, Terry Flaherty, and the two styled their lives after what "inklings" they could glean from their reading: "I hid out in the library and started reading things [e.g., the Beat Poets, Krafft-Ebing's *Psychopathis Sexualis*]. I was trying to figure out how to live as a gay man." He also vividly remembers Tom Burke's 1969 *Village Voice* article "The New Homosexuality," which pronounced the midcentury dandy dead and raised a defiant, countercultural liberationist in his place. They had no formal collective living experience; however, Oglesby says, "Charlie ended up not only getting *me*, but the gay street gang came with me, so we kind of headquartered ourselves in his apartment." Part information center and part crash pad, Thornton's apartment became part of a little gay circuit connected to the Pit Grill area.

Oglesby and Thornton met in the birthplace of Huey Newton, and they were acutely aware of the Jim Crow context of their gay identities. Both grew up relatively poor, a fact that sometimes prompted better-heeled white Southerners to draw analogies between their poor white kin and Black families. They both remember the Ku Klux Klan and White Citizens' Councils as aggressive, naturalized social forces. As a student journalist, Thornton covered the efforts of a campus Black nationalist group, insisting that their story deserved a fair telling. As a couple, while visiting New Orleans in 1972, they happened on a protest in support of Baton Rouge–born Black radical H. Rap

Brown (by then, Imam Jamil Al-Amin) who was in New Orleans for resentencing, and the two chose to join the rally.[19] Such experiences set the potential for a regional anti-racism as part of their budding gay liberationist perspective. In fact, back in Monroe, after a cross was burned on a car belonging to dear friends—an interracial lesbian couple—they decided it was time to leave Thornton's apartment and move to New Orleans.

They went, with hippie relatives of Thornton's, in the summer of 1973, just weeks after the UpStairs Lounge arson. The fire at the French Quarter gay bar had killed thirty-two people, and Florida-born Reverend Troy Perry of the Los Angeles Metropolitan Community Church referred to the event as "the Stonewall of New Orleans," even though the event produced no comparable formal gay liberation in its wake.[20] The fire diminished the young couple's faith in their new city as a "sanctuary" for gay people in the South. Still they went, determined to find opportunities to practice gay liberation. They say that they found none. Instead they encountered a vibrant bar culture and, according to Thornton, "beautiful street queens who would not be suppressed." Living at the corner of Dumaine and Royal, they worked constantly, earned little, and weren't really bar people, although they considered just entering a gay bar "a privilege." They held hands on the street, and as openly gay longhairs, they were stopped by police every single day they lived there. Thornton feared that if they were "taken to central lockup, no one knew what would happen." The prevailing logic was that "we would have no recourse, even if we were victimized . . . because we were criminals also and we deserved it."

One night after Thornton left the corner market, gunmen entered five minutes later and shot everyone inside. Shortly after, the couple decided to move to the Ozarks, where they heard the counterculture was taking root. They had hopes of finding a place for themselves in the back-to-the-land movement, due to hippies' "free sexuality and acceptance—*limited* acceptance," as Thornton calibrated their dreams. Before they left, though, Thornton spotted a recently published book on display in a store window: *Out of the Closets: Voices of Gay Liberation*. The cover art was a closet door with a little keyhole cut out. The book was a big expense, so he discussed this purchase with Oglesby. They decided they had to have it. Said Oglesby, "We just consumed that book all the way up to Fayetteville." Whoever was passenger would sometimes read aloud, or otherwise summarize passages. He adds that it was "just what we were looking for: liberation philosophies or liberation stories, including gay people going to Cuba to cut sugar cane, and we were pretty much leaning in that direction, being socialist-communist radicals." It is not surprising that Allen Young's accounts of gay experience in revolutionary

Cuba resonated most with the young couple. After all, rural Louisiana was a sugar cane producer, too. Also, their working-class backgrounds in the Jim Crow South inflected their gay liberation with an interest in socialist *and* antiracist views. Stories of Cuban revolution would have mirrored both those concerns.

They arrived in Fayetteville in late March 1974. With gay liberationist readings so fresh on their minds, Thornton started collecting some of the related serials that had cropped up elsewhere—*RFD* and *Gay Sunshine*, for example. They networked with other gay men, mostly steering clear of bar culture, save the hippie, gay-friendly George's. Their first step was to create gay discussion groups. They moved to an apartment near downtown, and in a room with no furniture they hosted potlucks, with a blanket spread on the floor. Around a dozen men came. Several found the couple's ideas too wild—visions of gay life unimaginable within the frames of their prior experience. A few were intrigued and hung in to see where it would all go.

It wasn't long before Oglesby met Dennis Williams at a house party, and he remembers that Williams enjoyed a certain "guru" status in town.[21] The short, animated, effeminate man in his early forties often wore, according to Thornton and Oglesby, colorful Indian clothing, cut like caftans. He had an altar in his rental house, featuring the gender and sexual complexity of Hindu iconography. It's fair to say he raised a few eyebrows in Fayetteville. Here was someone with a similarly wild vision for gay life. He asked the couple to move in. They did, but left shortly after to see the West Coast before fully settling in the Ozarks. Thornton, though, the avid literature collector, introduced Williams to the fledgling *RFD* before they left, and Williams soon counted himself among the Iowa magazine's readership of "country faggots everywhere." Oglesby and Thornton would keep up with Williams by letter, likely unaware that they would be back before long, moving back in with Ms. Buddha, along with other newly arrived, nascent gay liberationists.

Like Oglesby and Thornton, Jack Kendrick came to Fayetteville as part of a relatively new relationship. His queer 1950s childhood in the "redneck" small town of Hahira, Georgia, was full of violence and fear. As was true for his fellow sissie Southerners, his memories of his hometown featured racism alongside homophobia. He can trace his attraction to young boys as far back as the age of three, and his early taste for dressing in his mother's clothes "marked" him. Going to school was "hell": "being taunted daily, and being physically abused, beating on me, practically every day, for being queer. . . . It was a miracle I even got out of there without offing myself. It was pretty awful." His family moved to Dublin, Georgia, his senior year of high school—a new start. Determined to avoid the Vietnam War draft, he enrolled in junior college and transferred to the University of Georgia in Athens. His parents agreed to foot the bill as long as he majored in accounting, which he did—despite the fact he was miserable, being far more interested in art. In his last term, he read about Stonewall and realized the odds of his being drafted were statistically low, so he dropped out and shocked his parents by moving to New York City. While there, he got a job doing photography and graphics for NBC News, in Rockefeller Center, and he attended the GAA Firehouse dances when he could. It was at one of these dances in 1973 that he met Sam Edwards, a Kentucky native then living in Fayetteville, Arkansas. The two connected immediately, and Kendrick kept up with Edwards by letter. Over the next months Kendrick's relationship with a much older man in New York tapered off, so in 1974 he went to Fayetteville to spend the summer with Edwards.

Edwards had come to Fayetteville in 1966 as a graduate student at the University of Arkansas.[22] After trying psychedelics, he left school in 1970 to run a small antiques store on Dixon Street. He ran his Proustian business, "Remembrance of Things Past," on the second floor of a town building, above a flower shop and next to a pool hall. It was a short-lived venture, and he sold it to some fellow hippies for a dollar. In 1972 he moved to the scenic Markham Hill, into a rustic rental cabin, which was where he welcomed Kendrick that summer of 1974. It was while living on Markham Hill with Edwards that Kendrick met Williams at the first Mulberry House. Because the Cleveland Street Mulberry House was a town hub for the Ozark counterculture, all manner of hipbilly people dropped by or crashed there on their daily visits to Fayetteville to shop at the thrift stores or at the new co-op. It was clear Dennis was the "anchor," but so many familiar faces came and went that it was hard for any newcomer to say who "lived" there. The same would be the case for the future Mulberry House on Lawson Street. Outspoken and audacious feminists were some of the most regular of those to frequent both Mulberry Houses, especially after Williams embraced gay militancy.

Two women's communities in particular would very much shape Mulberry House as it formed. The first was Sassafras. Even while at Koch Farm, Williams had been in touch by letter with an acquaintance from his days teaching at the Kochs' school in New York. Diana Rivers remembered having to shoo Williams and some fellow skinny-dippers off the property at Gate Hill Coop—the Stony Point artists community where she then lived. Rivers divorced in 1970 and left Gate Hill. After searching the country for an apt space for rural community, she eventually chose land outside Newton County's Jasper, in

Boxley Valley, calling her new Arkansas hippie home "Sassafras."[23] After his breakup with Gloria, Williams was too depressed to meet Diana, but after his rousing fortieth birthday at George's, he attended Sassafras's one-year anniversary in March 1973—themed the "Welcome Back the Ticks Celebration!"— and it bolstered his new optimism and sociality.[24] Rivers and Williams grew close, and when Williams had to move into the second Mulberry House in late 1974, Rivers financed the sudden move.[25] Over the following years Rivers came to identify as lesbian, and Sassafras evolved as a women-only community where its founder wrote women-centric speculative fiction.

The second community was Yellowhammer. Kendrick recalls about Mulberry House, "There were these dykes who came and went a lot." He particularly remembers Trella Laughlin and her partner Patricia Jackson. The couple were Southern by birth—the former from Jackson, Mississippi, and the latter born in Tennessee but raised in Louisville, Kentucky. Zajicek and Lord tell us that the two women came to Arkansas by way of Austin, where they played together in an all-girl band, lived in collectives, promoted alternative energy use, and participated in war protests. They first joined the hipbilly "Doobie Plantation" in Pope County, but when the women became increasingly vocal in their protest of the regional use of the Agent Orange derivative 2,4,5-T, the men abruptly left the community, concerned that this politicization might draw local violence. In 1974, with a modest inheritance, Laughlin and Jackson bought eighty acres in Madison County, naming it "Yellowhammer," for all the woodpeckers on the land, and raised interest in the space as a lesbian community through the forum *Lesbian Connection*.[26] Making the land livable and expanding their collective took time, however. Kendrick remembers the couple as powerful "Amazon dykes," and that they were actively networking for Yellowhammer in 1974.

Jared Phillips's hipbilly characterization of the 1970s Ozarks, while helpful, hardly does justice to the region's counterculture which influenced Mulberry House the most. In the 1970s, northwest Arkansas witnessed the burgeoning of a remarkable grassroots women's movement. According to its chroniclers, Zajicek and Lord, many of the region's dispersed consciousness-raising groups dated back to the late 1960s, but when the Women's Center was established on the University of Arkansas campus in 1972, it quickly networked the once discrete groups and led to visible organizing around women's health, employment, arts, and publishing. Many women's housing collectives also formed at this time, and the tensions between "town and gown" became pronounced when a radical lesbian group called the Razordykes pushed the university and more moderate feminist groups to question the institutional role of the center.

This was a synergy and friction not unlike that described by La Shonda Mims regarding the Charlotte Women's Center, Piedmont Community College, and the Drastic Dykes, except that, in the case of Fayetteville, a rich women's land movement in the surrounding Ozarks extended the network into hill country.[27]

Several rural women's communities had also cropped up in the early 1970s, a number of them lesbian—like the one historian Brock Thompson mentions: Huckleberry Farm, outside Eureka Springs.[28] Thompson describes lesbian feminist activist Suzanne Pharr moving there from New Orleans. Pharr left the Crescent City after she was fired from her high school teaching job at Metairie's Country Day School for being openly lesbian, and she described what she found in the Ozarks as "a women's movement raging there, because it was outside of Fayetteville. It was in the time when women's culture was rising, rising up. We had the great lesbian migration of people going back and forth across the country."[29] Nearby Eureka Springs served as another town anchor for Ozark lesbian feminists when, in the early 1970s, Barbara Scott also moved from New Orleans, bought a grand old hotel in town, and placed an ad in *Ms.* magazine: "Feminist hotel, the New Orleans, in the Ozarks, Eureka Springs."[30] The women then poured in, to the hill towns and to the country. Lesbian feminists were a significant presence in the hipbilly Ozarks, and they certainly exerted a powerful political influence on Mulberry House.

Such sites as Huckleberry Farm, Rivers's Sassafras, and Laughlin and Jackson's Yellowhammer must be understood through the lens of lesbian separatism, of course, but also as part of a wider Ozark back-to-the-land phenomenon. In his history of the hipbillies, Phillips discusses the common appearance of the Ozarks in national back-to-the-land serials like *Mother Earth News* and *Communities*. Many of these appearances took the form of ads for rural land as Arkansas locals sought to sell abandoned rural farms and countercultural back-to-the-landers looked for cheap property in areas with strong folk traditions. However, Phillips only gives passing mention to the lesbian presence on the hipbilly landscape. Zajicek and Lord center it, as does Thompson, the latter referencing a 1972 *Ms.* magazine ad offering 1,000 acres of land in rural Johnson County. Such an ad underscored the eagerness of locals to sell rural property specifically to women. Some of the Ozark lesbians living on the land also likely came to Arkansas through ads in serials like *Country Women* and *Lesbian Connections*, geared specifically for rural women, many of whom were lesbian separatists.

When Kendrick and Edwards met Williams in 1974, his hippie revolving door at Mulberry House was notably turned by many of these Ozark lesbian feminists, embedded as they were within the wider regional hipbilly culture.

Kendrick must have been favorably impressed. He and Edwards returned to New York City for a year, sharing an apartment. Jack was hired back by NBC. They saved a little money and returned to Fayetteville in 1975, initially moving into the second Mulberry House. Kendrick remembers how full the busy house seemed. Easily joining the gender confusion of Williams's hippie way station and its retinue of Amazons, Kendrick adopted the name "Carlotta Rose"—the first name for the character in George Cukor's *Dinner at Eight* (1933), an indomitable aging actress, and the surname for his habit of wearing rose essential oil. Edwards lent the couple a family air by himself taking the name "Lawanda Rose." Perhaps because the house was so crowded, or maybe because Kendrick admits he himself was newly bitten by the back-to-the-land bug, the two Roses soon moved to a dilapidated farmhouse outside Pettigrew, Arkansas, agreeing, in return for rent, to refurbish the place for the owner, a professor at the university. They promptly named their new home "Mulberry Farm," linking its spirit to the Fayetteville house, and they invited a local feminist, Evalina, and her boyfriend John to join them. The farm was short-lived, though. The Roses had wanderlust, and the landlord professor noted no real renovations. Like Oglesby and Thornton, Kendrick and Edwards went west, in Kendrick's black 1959 Ford named "Nighthawk," in the early winter of 1975, and like the Louisiana couple they would soon return to the Ozarks to join Mulberry House. Unlike Oglesby and Thornton, though, the two Roses drifted apart not long after, leaving only Kendrick as a committed collectivist.

The last of the founding Mulberry House collectivists was new to the South. East of Fayetteville, in Harrison, Arkansas, Dean Hayes read a 1975 letter that Williams published in *RFD*. Hayes had just begun to discover his own gay identity that very year. He was born the middle of seven children, in 1952, near Clarissa, Minnesota, and his family moved all over the rural southern part of that state when Hayes was a child. His father was a grocer whose career grew along with the emergent midcentury supermarket industry. His father wasn't particularly spiritual. His mother set the religious tone for the Hayes family: liberal Lutheran. Hayes asserts, though, that he personally felt "much more at home, in a spiritual sense, outdoors in nature." He also shares, "I lost myself in books. I've always been a reader and that was a way to survive." After high school, in the early 1970s, he went to college in St. Paul and then vocational school in Farmington, studying landscape architecture and then design, but he dropped out due to the unstructured nature of the first program and not feeling challenged by the second. He accumulated practical experience working in greenhouses, but felt a nagging need "to get out of the family realm." He called a cousin who was working in Harrison, Arkansas, as a

VISTA volunteer, and asked if he could join her. When she gave him the okay, he fled south and soon found work in a nursery.

A young local lesbian couple, on a hunch, gave him a copy of *RFD*. Recalling his first encounter with the serial's content, Hayes says, "It really personified what I internally felt: my nature orientation. I was living rural." Also, his sexual interests were piqued by photos of "bearded hippy-esque" men who identified as gay. Reflecting the queer postal intimacies of *RFD*, he painted his mailbox a vivid lavender and scrawled the homophone "male" on the side. Williams's letter snagged his attention, and Hayes hitchhiked over to Fayetteville in late 1975. He and Williams quickly became close. He remembers Williams as "very captivating, very charismatic, very intelligent, very well spoken. Passionate speaker. Had an incredible cackle of a laugh. Not like anything I had ever met before." Williams spoke about his plans for a gay collective, which inspired Hayes. They corresponded through the rest of 1975, and Hayes made plans to move into Mulberry House in the 1976 new year. He explained the move to his parents, but now carefully distinguishes the closets he was then navigating: "It wasn't really just about coming out . . . it was really the exhilaration of meeting these people and beginning to do this political work." He says, as evidence of that, that his mother and grocer father were less concerned about his sexuality than they were that his radicalization might mean he would refuse to repay his lingering student loans. Hayes had managed, in a relatively short time, to leave his upper Midwest, Lutheran family realm far, far behind.

Mulberry House was formed, then, that winter of 1975–76. Its main founding members were Williams, Oglesby, Thornton, Kendrick, and Hayes. Their clustered stories reveal some commonalities. To the one, they followed countercultural paths to the Ozarks. In many ways the region exerted a certain hipbilly magnetism, drawing together VISTA activists, politicized locals, and back-to-the-land homesteaders. Within this countercultural mix was a significant network of lesbian feminist collectives—both college-town houses in Fayetteville and rural communities like Huckleberry Farm, Sassafras, and Yellowhammer, all importantly linked and synergized by the university's women's center. Circulation between town and country, mountain and delta (New Orleans), was common, as was hippie road travel to gay urban hubs like those on the West Coast, and New York City. Mulberry House's gay liberationists were drawn to the potential of a countercultural landscape with a notable, existing queer presence.

Most had pursued higher education, but only a couple remained in school to obtain a degree. All of them were heavy readers alert to the alternatives suggested by the gay liberationist press, especially guided by Thornton's canon.

They differed in other qualities. Some were from decidedly working-class backgrounds while others were from more middle-class origins. About half of them (Williams and Kendrick especially) lived marked lives as obviously femme men. Oglesby and Thornton were inspired by a queer translation of the Venceremos Brigades experience into a deeper-south countercultural milieu while Williams and Kendrick inevitably saw things through the lens of their New York experience, whether that was the sexual cultures of the cruisy piers and GAA firehouse dances or their creative professional lives in academic publishing, experimental education, or broadcast journalism. Hayes served as a kind of bridge here, not only because of his Midwestern home, but also because his landscape architecture studies and his greenhouse experience gave him both a blue-collar *and* middle-class air and also outfitted him with essential skills for back-to-the-land living. Only Williams had traveled internationally and cultivated a non-Christian spiritual perspective, based on his time in India. He complemented it with an express faith in the libidinous potential of youthful cultural revolution, possibly because, as someone twenty years senior to any of his fellow collectivists, and as a former teacher, he still romanticized the student movements of the past decade. Williams was also fiercely critical of the prison system.

This profile of Mulberry House describes some personal motivations and geographic contexts that were quite different from those of the Flaming Faggots or the GAA. Their immersion in faggot print culture and their staunchly feminist political lens, though, suggest a strong family resemblance.

Pressing Themselves: The Orientations of Early Mulberry House's Faggot Figure

One of the first things the new collective did as a group, in late 1975, was to visit the *RFD* editors in Iowa. For the fledgling Mulberry House, *RFD* wasn't just a destination, it was a map. Sears has thematized the successive editorial focuses of the magazine, showing that its Iowan tenure emphasized networking and skill-sharing between queer homesteaders.[31] Part of this networking goal was to mitigate the isolation that many queer men felt in back-to-the-land communities, as both Troxler and Williams experienced. Rural readers would publish their addresses, and countercultural travelers would build itineraries around stays with the queer homes on their paths. When the two Mulberry House couples—Oglesby and Thornton, and the two Roses—traveled from the Ozarks to the West Coast, this was how they went.[32]

Another way Iowan *RFD* fought rural queer isolation was to amplify the ways in which the text operated as a surrogate for the bodies of its reader-writers.

In the very first issue the editors wrote, "*You* write, sing, dance and are R.F.D."[33] This sequence of verbs animates the publication, turning its written words into an audible voice, then a palpable movement, and finally a full somatic presence. Readers were to take the pages in their hands as they would the bodies of their fellow queers, and to see their reading as a fully intimate act. During *RFD*'s Iowan days, the editors adopted many textual practices to convey this feeling. It's not surprising, then, that when Mulberry House published their introduction to the *RFD* community, the text was visibly haunted by a shadowy faggot figure.

We have already described the individuals who came together to form Mulberry House, but here we see how they attempted to legibly present themselves, as a collective body, to the wider world beyond the Ozarks. The primary purpose of the article they wrote for *RFD* was to place themselves on the *RFD* map, to offer their house as a well-lit way station for transient countercultural gay liberationists. However, it also functioned as a first manifesto, echoing earlier liberationist writings. Kathi Weeks has characterized the manifesto as a genre that galvanizes a collectivity—a "we"—as it takes up textual methods of fomenting urgent action.[34] There is little of the latter here, but the text is eager to orient the collective in several key ways.

They opened by introducing themselves as "five angry faggots still burning with the rage of our oppression."[35] Calling themselves *faggots*, we might anticipate this reference to the fire and anger of the Flaming Faggots' and early GAA's witchcraft genealogy, and the fact that Mulberry House was *still* burning reflected their efforts to sustain that liberationist position. The figure they drew, though, hardly resembles a martyrology—visually featuring the flame, stake, and bound witch as a means to transmute victimhood into fiery revolution. That imagery had been central to early *Fag Rag*'s figuration, along with the androgyny of countercultural long hair. Instead, the visual figure behind their text had a nearly gender-neutral, almost alien appearance. While the white space on the page—at the chest and crotch—*might* suggest breasts and a uterus, this faint femme air appears only by a process of negation, a "de-manning" reminiscent of the effeminists. Such a reading seems supported by the fact that Mulberry House defined themselves against the patriarchal forces of "oppression, exploitation, competition, aggression" but stopped short of listing opposite values, as the effeminists did. They named themselves feminists, and their opening line might be read as a reference to the Radicalesbians publication "The Woman-Identified Woman": "A lesbian is the rage of all women condensed to the point of explosion."[36]

Mulberry House is home for a collective of five angry faggots still burning with the rage of our oppression in 1976 when Bicentennial joy reigns unabashed. We are white and come from working- and middle-class backgrounds. We live and work together collectively not only for economic reasons, but in order to overcome our heterosexual conditioning as men. Our politics entails separating ourselves from straight male energy and living as outfront faggots.

We are exploring our feminist nature and struggling to rid ourselves of being oppressors and being oppressed, which limits us. Our freedom is our spirituality. The patriarchal culture is based on oppression, exploitation, competition, aggression, and our lifestyle reflects our determination to struggle against these destructive forces. We are aware of the power and privilege that comes with money and want to be supportive of other poor and nonwhite faggots.

We love the earth. We see the next step as securing land for a faggot space--a fairy farm--free from the oppressions of straight society. In order to survive, faggots must have land. Not as an escape, but as a retreat to a more free space where we may learn to teach each other, heal each other, love each other. We want to save the earth. The land is being raped by speculators, poisoned by chemicals, and carved up by nuclear family breeders. We as faggots on the land see ourselves as caretakers, not possessors. We cannot go on eating poisoned foods and supporting the systems that are destroying us. We are what we eat. We can't be strong and powerful faggots eating the Man's food. We are removing our bodies and spirits from dependence on prepackaged processed foods. We want to grow our own food, returning what is given us, nurturing as we are nurtured.

The land we envision would not be individually owned but held in common. We realize that people with money intimidate those without, and are determined that everyone who lives on the land will have equal power. Decisions will be made by consensus.

We are all political faggots committed to the world-wide struggle against oppression. We realize that we benefit from our brothers' struggles in the cities, but we feel that many city faggots are not aware of the benefits that everyone can receive from an energy exchange with faggots on faggot land. We seek a dialogue on ways to support each other. We see many possibilities of a city-country energy exchange. We are learning ourselves and seek to exchange survival skills such as growing and preserving food, building structures, making clothes, raising consciousness, reclaiming our faggot history and magick.

To secure land we need money from those who have it. But you don't need to have money to come here. We also need time and energy and support to create the reality of our vision. It's necessary for poor faggots to have time and space which have always been denied them, the freedom to develop without intimidation. We know that words come easy. We expect our actions to speak for us.

Time is short. Land in the Ozarks is still relatively cheap ($200-500 an acre), but it's being gobbled up fast and prices are rising. Growing season is long (March-November). Population is sparse and wilderness isolation is still possible. People here are fighting to keep the air and water clean. These hills are the oldest on the planet and are very beautiful to us.

We said we wanted a dialogue. So write.
Charlie, Dean, Dennis, Jack, Michael
Mulberry House, 438 W. Lawson, Fayetteville, Ark. 72701

* * * * * * * * * * * * * *

First of all RFD is not a political pamphlet and, I believe, was not intended to be one. It is a gay orientated (oriented) back-to-the-land magazine for those who are there, hope to be, or just want to keep a finger on what's happening. It should be involved with helping people contact other people and with providing information about areas of the country, both good and bad, about methods and aids for those who are starting, and about those of us who are serving as examples for those coming. It should be a place for us to express and share our thoughts and feelings.

Country living is an alternative life style. We do not escape from being gay or from the problems connected with trying to find our place in a straight oriented society. If anything we augment some of the social problems. There is an anonymous quality to the city that the country doesn't have. In the country people know who you are, where you live, and usually know more of what you're up to than you do. But they have a respect for the individual and for his production! On one hand they know what you're doing, and on the other they give you enough room to sink or swim on your own. But, while they may doubt whether the "new folks" will ever get their crop in and if, when they do they'll ever figure out how to harvest it, they give a grudging respect to production.

Moreover, in the big cities you can pick your society. You can live in a gay ghetto, go to gay bars, and restaurants, and pretty much keep your contact with straights down to a minimum. Yes you do have to work and live in the world of the straight majority, but it's one thing to live an honest open life as a gay being and another to flaunt your sexual orientation. The straight world, for the most part, doesn't wear its preferred position on its sleeve.

In the country, the gay person, couple, or commune must mix with and get along with the

Mulberry House's introduction letter in *RFD*, Fall 1976, 8. Illustration by John Steczynski.

Their orientation to lesbian feminism was not abstract. Mulberry House collectivists credit their politics to Ozark lesbian collectivists, most of whom were socialist feminists and separatists. Of these women, the most immediately influential were Yellowhammer's Laughlin and Jackson, who called themselves "Amazon Dykes." Yellowhammer was not immediately habitable. To generate interest in their nascent community, Laughlin and Jackson moved to the Bay Area to network in the lesbian communities there. When they returned to Fayetteville, they came back with their political vision as fiery as ever. Other Ozark feminists called the couple "Berkeley dykes"—and sometimes cast them as more radical than other women's collectives in the Arkansas college town. In 1976, already aware of the teeming gay radical energy on Lawson Street, local women suggested that Laughlin and Jackson contact the newly formed Mulberry House. The couple did so, and ended up staying. Being separatists, they first kept some distance, living in their van, which they parked in the driveway. Slowly, however, a closeness developed and the women moved into the house.

This was roughly the time when the "five angry faggots" of Mulberry House wrote their first collective piece for *RFD*, saying themselves that their "politics entails separating ourselves." Clearly, their shared separatism requires some qualification. As already noted, Enszer has nuanced our understanding of lesbian separatism, suggesting that we shift from seeing it primarily as a hard spatial boundary or a permanent divorce and think of it instead as an important temporary repositioning within a longer, careful political process. I argue that Mulberry House shared this lesbian feminist theoretical position. They clarified that their separatism was not an "escape" but a "retreat... where we may learn to teach each other, heal each other, love each other." They also defined their separation as being specifically away from "straight male energy," an orientation that might, by a logic of one-to-one inversion, involve turning to face lesbians. This was so much the case that these five angry faggots and the Amazon Dyke couple shared a home in 1976. Further, Oglesby says, "Even though [Laughlin and Jackson] were separatist, we had much in common and we all kind of fell in love with each other." Laughlin recalls meeting the Mulberry House collectivists with the same warmth.

Early New Left concepts of revolution required a process of struggle and unity, differentiation and solidarity. Those experiencing similar forms of oppression often required time apart to collectively analyze that oppression, to raise their consciousness, and to build their movement strategies around that analysis before they were ready to join other movements (which were often also based on identities forged by this process) in a wider revolution. Knowing *when* to come back together was often a matter of intense debate. As a result, various forms of separatism were central to the revolutionary process, not a feature of lesbian feminism alone. I have elsewhere described this orientation of "radical adjacency"—a "'good fences make good neighbors' form of connection . . . a togetherness characterized by respect but not by erotics or wonder."[37] In that they shared a house and love with Laughlin and Jackson, Mulberry House demonstrated a faggot separatism characterized by a notable, possibly unexpected intimacy with Ozark lesbian feminists.

They adopted other orientations from this primary one. For example, Carl Wittman, a cofounder of *RFD*, in his manifesto "Refugees from Amerika" (1970) urged a broader gay solidarity with women's liberationists as "our closest allies" and considered the priority of the day to be "among ourselves—self educating, fending off attacks, and building free territory." But he also felt that gay coalition with Black liberation had to be "tenuous" at the time due to the latter's masculinist rhetoric, which he referred to as "uptightness and supermasculinity."[38] Demonstrating his own radical adjacency, Wittman didn't easily imagine the queered Black liberation that would later amplify Black faggot voices in publications like *Fag Rag*. Six years later Mulberry House acknowledged their position as white faggots and shared their desire to leverage "power and privilege" to "be supportive of other poor and nonwhite faggots." The Southerners among them had grown up in Jim Crow contexts where the Klan and White Citizens Councils violently policed white, straight masculinity and femininity as a way of preserving white dynastic supremacy. Mulberry House shared this perspective with Ozark socialist feminists, a significant number of whom, according to Zajicek and Lord, came to their activism out of prior civil rights experience. As Jaime Harker notes, "For Southern lesbian feminists, race was not something that was later 'added' to feminism; it was always an essential part of their understanding of their region and their identities. Many southern lesbian feminist writers came to feminism through civil rights activism and continued anti-racist work as a key part of their feminism."[39]

As was the case with Wittman, however, a certain unevenness exists in the orientation of early Mulberry House's faggot figure. In 1976 they had an active, intimate solidarity with area lesbian feminists but still desired such a relationship with other Black faggots or Black liberationists. For example, Black radical Bobby Morgan practiced a very similar liberationist activism in Fayetteville, Arkansas, just before the formation of Mulberry House, but there is no record of their sharing work or home with Morgan. They faced Black faggots, then, far more theoretically than they did Ozark lesbian feminists.

Spatially, the urban gay street or apartment didn't figure for them. Instead they most associated themselves with their dream of a "fairy farm." This was fitting for their debut in the Iowan *RFD*, with its focus on a queered back-to-the-land culture. After all, the *RFD* map brought them not only to the Iowan editors' home, in 1975, but also to similar queer farms in rural New Mexico and to Oregon's Magdalen Farm. They'd not only had their brief taste of faggot farm life when the two Roses lived at their sister Mulberry Farm, but they also shared Laughlin and Jackson's dream of Yellowhammer, helping them to transition there. It's also important to recognize that Mulberry House's letter appeared in *RFD* alongside notes from similar queer homesteaders—most notably Faygele Ben Miriam, formerly of the Elwha Land Project outside of Seattle, and Allen Young, the gay Venceremos founder who at the time lived at Massachusetts's gay Butterworth Farm. Therefore, Mulberry House's understanding of the countercultural faerie farm was never isolationist but critically linked. There were several ways that this kind of networking had already proven concretely useful to them. First, the earlier Mulberry House (and Putnam House before it) had served as a crash pad for rural hippies who made regular trips to town. Regional countercultural mobility united rural and urban houses into a more concerted cultural presence, as we have seen from how the University Women's Center had synergized Ozark feminist collectives. Second, this not only enabled safer queer countercultural travel but mitigated rural queer loneliness, which was one of early *RFD*'s aims.

Third, building on this idea of safety, linked rural and urban houses were important to collective defense. Mulberry House was aware of this from early on. In his 1975 letters to Hayes, still in Harrison, Williams envisioned rural spaces of freedom connected to cities, which he understood as centers of increasing despotic power. Disappointed by the fact that a rural gay couple he knew planned to move to Little Rock, Williams argued that they needed some experience to "jolt those country boys into the realization that the land is the only place faggots can be free."[40] He enjoined Hayes to imagine "how important it's gonna be in terms of Darwinian 'survival of the fittest' for country gays to know what's happening *immediately* in the city—which is where the oppression is going to come from in the new fascism happening all around us."[41] This suggests Williams's awareness of the surveillance of urban lesbian households, which Hobson describes as one of the main drivers for collective defense. Once Laughlin and Jackson were installed at Yellowhammer, Mulberry House offered traveling women—several of them women of color moving through Jim Crow rural geographies—regular transport to women's communities, with the small, effeminate Williams as a frequent ferryman.[42] And these networks did go beyond Arkansas. For example, Ozark Women on the Land (OWL), in the Eureka Springs area, networked with the Atlanta Lesbian Feminist Alliance (ALFA) for financial support in 1976.[43]

Fourth, a more ineffable benefit was rural-urban skill-sharing that might enable faggots to withdraw their bodies from the capitalist conditioning achieved through dependence on the market for all basics: shelter, clothing, and—most importantly—food. Mulberry House did not situate their faerie farm in a bucolic past or a fantasy future. Rather, they understood it as a site of relief, of small-scale "freedom," within a larger capitalist system of environmental degradation, expanding agribusiness, biopolitically distributed hunger/health, and heterosexist property relations. This perspective was drawn directly from their Ozark experience. Laughlin and Jackson had made a reputation for themselves as environmental activists protesting the use of an Agent Orange derivative on area fields, and as Jared Phillips has shown, this was part of a wider Ozark feminist position that saw such crop-dusting as poisoning the reproductive capacities of both the land *and* women.[44] The countercultural Ozarks had also become a hub for organic food distribution, and the Mulberry House faggots collectively took a single position at the affiliated Ozark Food Co-op in Fayetteville, a role that—as I will show in chapter 3—would politicize them further. Following the lead of earlier ads in *Country Women* and *Lesbian Connections*, the five angry faggots went further than asking for interlocutors and visitors; they urged *RFD* readers to consider reclaiming the (still cheap) rural land in the Ozarks as a way of expanding on the hipbilly and lesbian feminist network in the Ozarks.

This illustrates why Mulberry House named their primary political orientation as an intimately shared separatism *with* the socialist, Ozark lesbian feminists around them. They did, though, always add that *RFD* was their spiritual compass. In their 1976 *RFD* debut, they asserted the importance of "reclaiming their faggot history and magick," a phrasing that reflects parallel concerns with Arthur Evans. Perhaps they had read his thoughts in *Fag Rag*, or heard rumor of his fledgling fairie circles on their road trips to the Bay Area. However, neither their faggot iconography nor their lesbian feminist orientation suggests as much, so the reference is a thin one. Claiming that "freedom" was their spirituality, they echoed the anarchist Koch Farm and their countercultural circulation through the *RFD* map. Their debut was composed in the days leading up to the Labor Day 1976 Faggots & Class Struggle conference at Oregon's Magdalen Farm, an event they would all attend. That experience would redefine the faggot figure they had drawn in their first six months as a collective body.

CHAPTER TWO

Drawing Down the Dialectical Moon
Faggot Witchcraft's Leftist Invocations

Thornton remembers hearing about the conference, not from its host, Chenille, at Magdalen Farm, but from the collective who started the Bay Area socialist faggot serial *Magnus*. Still, Mulberry House was familiar with the routes to the conference through their previous travels within the *RFD* map, and they promptly registered, making plans to attend the Oregon event. They drove a retired postal truck cross-country, and their doing so extended *RFD*'s tradition of queering the postal service. If *RFD*, by its title, evoked the expanded reach into rural areas by the Rural Free Delivery of the US mail service at the turn of the twentieth century, then the "journal for country faggots everywhere" brought a new kind of intimate correspondent to the nation's heartlands. In Harrison, Arkansas, Dimid (formerly Dean) Hayes had plastered the homophone "male" on his mailbox, and painted it lavender. Now, by traveling in a postal truck, Mulberry House further conflated the faggot with the circulating letter, and countercultural travel with gay print culture. The group of them—Williams and Hayes, Thornton and Oglesby, and Kendrick (Carlotta Rose)—took the trip, stopping as they traveled west, to soak in the views. Although it was a route several of them had made before, it was a long one, and they arrived at the Wolf Creek site late at night.

Their reception was not as warm as they had hoped for. The organizers had, in part, chosen the rural Wolf Creek site as a strategy of collective defense. The remote location alone was not enough to secure the event, though. As they put it, "Certainly, the recent rash of Grand Juries and FBI-CIA exposures seem pretty unfriendly. So we figured we had to come up with some kind of security system."[1] This was especially true, they felt, given the conference's focus on revolution, with at least one session on armed struggle. Their security system consisted of requiring advance registration, researching registered attendees through gay liberationist networks, and keeping a gate to take tickets and confirm registration. When Mulberry House arrived, the gatekeepers claimed that the unfamiliar Southern faggots had not registered.

Road-weary, the Arkansas collective pleaded that they *had* registered and could not help it if their paperwork had gotten lost. The tense conference security must have looked askance at these unfamiliar faggots. Entry was stalled by a tense standoff until a Seattle attendee, an associate of the journal *Morning Due*, interceded on their behalf, and they were—finally—admitted. Although conference planners insisted that such safeguards were necessary due to West Coast run-ins with surveillance, informants, and raids, their report conceded that security was a controversial aspect of the conference, with bitter disagreement over whether it was needed and how it was enacted. Despite this, it is likely that organizers held Mulberry House particularly responsible for affronting security. They noted in their report, "We are angry that some used emotional manipulation (I had to drive a long way) to gain sympathy without validating the group need for pre-registration."[2]

The Faggots & Class Struggle conference was divisive in other ways. West Coast faggot collectives often sought, mid-decade, to situate themselves within an internecine "new communism." The conference organizers were Pacific Northwest Marxist-Leninists who pitched the event as a laboratory for discovering a uniquely gay liberationist analysis that they might offer to the wider revolution. Informing the event's political philosophy were two broad tenets: (1) that Black radicalism was the vanguard of the people's revolution, and that gay liberation still needed to formulate its own unique leftist analysis, offering an organized strategy to the cause; and (2) that it was key to this forthcoming strategy to discover a compelling revolutionary figure that might represent and galvanize gay liberationists in a period when the New Left no longer saw the white masculine industrial worker as the face of their proletariat force. The conference was meant to forge the faggot as that revolutionary figure. Bay Area liberationists of color had declined their belated invitation to the event in part because they saw this figure as being too Eurocentric, and white, to represent them. Los Angeles's new communist Lavender & Red Union (L&RU)—a "group of dyke and faggot communists"—did attend the Oregon Faggots & Class struggle conference, but they ultimately used their attendance to launch a critique of the event's premise: They held that a romanticized embrace of *any* revolutionary figure whatsoever was a strategic error that would foreclose wider solidarity.[3]

The Marxist-Leninist conference organizers retorted that the L&RU dogmatically assumed that the conference idealized a separatist faggotry when, in fact, the conference had clearly described that work as a *temporary* retreat meant to explore whether the politics of faggotry could offer common gay liberationist strategies to the historical phase of revolution immediately before them all. For them, the proposal to skip over the work of articulating historically specific (and therefore impermanent) revolutionary figures was antithetical to the work of solidarity.[4] Dispensing with the particularity of the faggot, the sissie, the Black Panther, or the Amazon dyke was to repeat the old "left error": to sideline racial, gender, and sexual analysis in pursuit of an abstract class perspective that would ultimately only be white, male, and straight by default. Most of the Oregon conference attendees themselves approved the improvisation of revolutionary figures, finding it helpful to (1) unite uniquely oppressed groups, (2) galvanize historically specific analysis and praxis, and (3) underscore the endless work of difference necessarily embedded in processes of solidarity.

Although the Bay Area liberationists of color declined their invitation, others from San Francisco did accept, and in quite large numbers—ultimately constituting about half of the attendees. Emily Hobson notes that socialist feminist organizations, like the Berkeley-Oakland and San Francisco Women's Unions, then held the most traction with gay and lesbian radicals in the Bay Area. As a result, the men began actively participating—following an effeminist strategic line—in childcare, vocally owning the responsibility of men to perform care labor.[5] Unlike the Los Angeles L&RU, these Bay Area socialist feminists tended to agree with the utility of a revolutionary figure; they just disagreed with the masculinist overtones of the faggot as it was performed at the Oregon conference. As a result, many, along with a small number of anarchists, threw their weight behind the sissie figure instead.

The conference organizers, in the end, agreed with the critiques of the Bay Area gay liberationists of color, the socialist feminists, the anarchists, and the sissies, but thought their error was in their isolationist processes rather than in the faggot figure itself. If they had but invited others to the planning table, the faggot figure might have been articulated more capaciously: less whitely, and less masculinely. They remained hopeful about their original project, seeing the nascent sissie figure less as a negation of the faggot than as a complementary figure that provided a helpful corrective in the process of solidarity. Mid-1970s West Coast faggot politics, then, remained inspired by a queered Black radicalism, embraced a militant femme embodiment, practiced socialist *ef*feminist care labor, and improvised a revolutionary complementarity around the faggot and sissie figures. These were the ideological ingredients of their revolutionary bent. Such were the topics of their houses' consciousness-raising. These commonalities also allowed West Coast faggot households the common ground that made their networking all the easier.

As fractious as the conference was, it both re-energized faggot political culture and suggested *sissies* as a figural variation. Mulberry House faggots were active, if unexpected, participants, bringing their own Ozark socialist feminist collectivism, learned from lesbian communities back home. To more fully understand the dynamics of the conference, though, it is helpful to, first, more finely describe the West Coast faggot politics that informed the event. I will then demonstrate faggot witchcraft's variable leftist functions by contrasting the very different poetic accounts of a single ritual documented in *Morning Due* and *RFD*. In the process, I fan the range of new leftist ideological positions around race, ethnicity, gender, and class, which defined a complex West coast faggotry in 1976. I offer this as necessary background for the ways Mulberry House would, later that fall, operate *as* sissies (not faggots) back in the Ozarks.

Bringing Up the Rear: The Belated Feelings of West Coast Faggot Politics

The Seattle attendee who interceded on behalf of Mulberry House at the security check was Faygele Ben Miriam (originally John F. Singer). Then nearly thirty-two, Ben Miriam had grown up in a not particularly religious Jewish family in Mount Vernon, New York. When he came out in the 1960s, his activist mother Miriam required only a short time to accommodate herself to the idea, and he took her first name ("Ben Miriam" is Yiddish for "son of Miriam") when he legally changed his name to Faygele (a Yiddish homophobic slur meaning "little bird"). In the 1960s, Ben Miriam went to school at the City University of New York, joined the Students for a Democratic Society (SDS), worked as a VISTA volunteer in urban St. Louis, did military duty in Germany (as a medic, because he was a conscientious objector), and returned home to work briefly with the Gay Activists Alliance (GAA) before leaving New York in the spring of 1970. After a short stopover in San Francisco, he settled in the Seattle area.[6]

Sharing his family's activist spirit, Ben Miriam hit the Seattle ground running.[7] He joined the local GLF, and in 1971, with fellow member Paul Barstow, applied for a marriage license; he sued when they were denied, ultimately losing in 1974. He won another case that year, though. In 1972 he sued the Equal Employment Opportunity Commission (EEOC) for firing him from his typist job—for wearing women's clothing and openly declaring his homosexuality. The courts were unsympathetic with the EEOC's having so casually fired someone, and they ruled in Ben Miriam's favor. In another activist mode, he helped to produce the first known queer country-western album, *Lavender Country* (1973). A voluble figure in the Pacific Northwest's radical, gay liberationist networks, Faygele's support ensured that Mulberry House was admitted to the conference. As we will see, he would remain a friend of the Southeastern sissies for years to come.

The Lavender Country song "Back in the Closet Again" nicely conveys the West Coast gay liberationist spirit of the times.

> The Revolution started outright
> Black Panthers were leading the fight
> The Lords were in the left flank
> The women drove a Sherman tank
> And the workers were a hunk of dynamite
> A battalion of Gay men brought up the rear
> Packing two grenades in each brassiere
> Every purse was filled with mace
> Carbine rifles trimmed with lace
> Them campy Gay guerillas knew no fear.[8]

The spatial ordering of this liberationist phalanx follows faggots' shared understanding of the chronology of the New Left revolution. As we have seen, the Black Panthers were regarded as the vanguard of a succession of revolutionary forces. Seattle's Lavender Country clearly embraced a militant vision of this solidarity. Note, though, that "gay men brought up the rear."

There was a sense that, of the liberationist movements, gay liberation did not just arrive last, with Stonewall not happening until 1969, but that gay liberationists had by the early 1970s yet to offer their own unique leftist analysis and militant figure for the wider revolution. By 1973, according to Lavender Country, the revolutionary promise of 1970 had already been defused—by police and intelligence officers planting internal suspicions among revolutionary forces—and gay liberation was forced "back in the closet again." However, three years later the Labor Day Faggots & Class Struggle conference was put together with the express purpose of finally building that gay liberationist analysis under a faggot banner.

Faygele Ben Miriam was good friends with Lavender Country vocalist Patrick Haggerty, and both were also on good terms with the lesbian members of the George Jackson Brigade: Rita "Bo" Brown and Therese Coupez.[9] Given the Brigade's commitment to the strategic destruction of property as a way of neutralizing nodes of systemic oppression, we can see why Haggerty might have featured gay men with bras, purses, and lace who carried grenades, mace, and rifles in his Lavender Country song. Ben Miriam was also a member of the Morning Due collective in 1975 when they published the Brigade's communiqués about recent bombings. The ongoing sense of revolutionary belatedness thus added urgent militancy to Pacific Northwest faggot culture, and that militancy was most often depicted with the figure of an armed, violent femme. Such figural details offer a richer frame for the politics of Ben Miriam, the cross-dressing typist, who did not *just* fight audacious gay legal battles—which is how he is often memorialized—but also published George Jackson Brigade communiqués and produced country albums with images of grenade-slinging femmes. It is possible, then, to position Ben Miriam as a Seattle counterpart to the Bay Area's Tede Matthews, who added a gun to his drag when marching at anti-rape rallies. Both unapologetically femme liberationists also attended the 1976 Faggots & Class Struggle conference.

We may now find it difficult to identify with their armed stance. It's important to recall that the 1970s were an era characterized by open state violence and systemic control. Burton-Rose references how Brigade founder Ed Mead had followed the coverage of officers waiting for news crews to arrive in LA's Compton neighborhood before they shredded the Symbionese Liberation Army's safe house with more than 5,000 rounds of ammunition, killing six of the members inside.[10] This news sent a message: It confirmed that the US state was literally at war with its radicals. In a post-Nixon Vietnam era characterized by government deception, conscription, political imprisonment, and police violence, few held to hopes that mere talk could lead to any real social change. Brute force was the only language. Many radicals practiced increased militancy, following the model of similar groups abroad. The nation's aggressive tactics were broadcast to increasingly vivid degrees in the years following the Vietnam War and Watergate. Acutely aware of how democratic processes had been co-opted and of how radicals were cast as fanatics, and then violently neutralized, some New Leftists grew militant and weighed the possible roles of violence in their own political repertoires.

In fact, Jeremy Varon has cautioned that historians have, in the name of a kind of intellectual propriety, shirked their responsibility to look at this period's violence more closely, to fully understand its dynamics. He suggests approaching its record differently than sorting the rightly reasonable from the wildly irrational, urging us to think of the period not as a climate of "'normal' politics" but instead as "the rarefied world of the underground—a world of extraordinary danger, determination, fear, arrogance, trust, triumph, togetherness, suspicion, exhilarations, and despair," a world that requires our taking seriously the "seemingly religious longings" within radical political cultures.[11]

It's important to emphasize just how different this West Coast armed, femme faggot figure was from (1) the Flaming Faggots' stance, which disavowed effeminate appearance, or (2) the GAA's use of zaps, which more heavily used public theatrical confrontations and strategic media coverage to broadcast homophobia and spark gay anger. West Coast faggots, to the degree that they looked to area Black Panthers as the revolutionary vanguard, likely also followed the Panthers in adopting a militant aesthetic, which as historian Donna Jean Murch has suggested, matched the hypervisibility of soldiers on Bay Area streets once the military-industrial complex dominated the area's postwar economy.[12] In fact, as we have seen, Arthur Evans would make a similar observation once his book appeared in 1978: The streets of San Francisco already looked like a militarized zone.

It's also important to distinguish the 1976 conference from other leftist genealogies within the faggot print culture—especially in *RFD*, whose editorial move from Iowa to Wolf Creek, Oregon, overlapped with the conference. At one point there were rumors that Harry Hay would take a central role at the Faggots & Class Struggle conference. If so, his status not only as a veteran gay activist but as a former communist might have lent the conference a certain leftist cachet.[13] This arrangement never came to pass, however. It is quite likely that Hay, still living in New Mexico with Burnside, his partner, was already moving in a different direction than the Marxist-Leninist organizers of the Wolf Creek conference. Hay's biographer Stuart Timmons comments that in 1976, responding to the acrid bickering he read between gay and straight leftists in the radical press of the Pacific Northwest, Hay began a "position paper" called "Gay Liberation: Chapter Two." In it, he expanded on his "biosocial" theory of gay identity published the previous year in *RFD*, elaborating on the importance of "subject-SUBJECT consciousness," but also clearly distancing himself—and the whole movement—from Marx and Engels.

He submitted a draft to the Oregon editors of *RFD*, who, as Hay put it in a letter to a friend, "rejected it as gobbledygook," even though Carl Wittman was sympathetic enough with the ideas to offer Hay help with revision.[14] The article never appeared, in that form at least, and Hay didn't attend the Faggots & Class Struggle conference. It seems that Hay was recoiling from his Marxist past—understandably, given his expulsion from the Communist Party—just as young West Coast gay radicals were improvising a new leftism in the name of a militant faggot figure. In fact, Timmons further tells us that in 1976 Hay and Burnside considered joining the gay collective at Wolf Creek, but ultimately returned home to New Mexico. Hay would forge different alliances, for the time being, and West Coast faggotry would go through its growing pains without him. The conference itself mostly exposed raw nerves and ideological differences among area leftists, and the visiting Ozark gay liberationists of Mulberry House immediately found themselves at the center of those divisions. But they also encountered a faggot witchcraft that was flexible enough to accommodate the different political facets of faggotry. Its rituals exercised the "religious longings" of their politics.

The Revolutionary Rituals of the Mad Subject

The conference's main ritual was slated for 11 p.m. on Sunday, September 5.[15] The moon wouldn't have been full until Wednesday, but the witching hour preceding Labor Day 1976 would have been a bright one, lit by a waxing moon. The *Morning Due* report offers a short description of the "moon ritual" at the heart of the conference. The magic began with about fifty "fairies from all corners of the land gather[ing] in the tipi" while a "fire sparkled in the center." A musician named Blackberi played guitar and struck up "a children's tune": "I can feel Her magic . . . everywhere," offering a soft echo of *RFD*'s dedication to "country faggots everywhere." The faeries called upon "the spirit of the land," and the four elements, before—one by one—they put water on the fire and headed out into damp, moonlit grass. They joined hands to make a circle, which they rotated and also contracted: "The line snaked in and out, a breathing bursting circle." The fifty faeries ultimately collapsed into a heap, chanting together, until the group fell silent. Shortly after, individual voices began to express their thanks: "some thanked the Mother of Us All— the Deliciously Dialectical, Mother History. The force and power of the inevitable great changes, the changes growing within each of us." They "ended with the witches' spiral. A spiral turning back on itself to kiss each one as you passed him, sharing our passion, our tenderness, our saliva with each every. Delicious. Fifty times fifty kisses." The following day, attendees recreated this circle in a group goodbye hug, referring to it then as "the fairy circle" and "the faggot-witches' spiral."[16]

This ritual was central, rather than tangential, to the political aims of the conference. The *Morning Due* record offers us some details for making out what aspects specifically expressed their faggot spirit. The ritual reverently linked the figure of the nearly full Harvest Moon with the "Deliciously Dialectical, Mother History." With this description, the celebrants suggested that just as the moon drew the tides, so did materialist history shape the changing lives of her actors.[17] The ritual served a stronger political purpose than mere satire, however. To understand the political strategies embedded in this faggot leftist spirituality, we must first contextualize its emergence on the heels of gay liberationist antipsychiatry and of leftist debates about revolutionary subjectivity.

In the 1970s, community-based spirituality emerged as a viable alternative to institutionalized versions of mental health. This was because one of gay liberation's prime targets had been the US psychiatric profession, which treated homosexuality as a sickness. The first edition of *The Diagnostic and Statistical Manual of Mental Disorders* (*DSM*), published in 1952, classed homosexuality as a mental disorder. Some of these diagnoses built on Freud's focus on infantile sexuality, family relations, and personality development at a time, during the Cold War, when the nuclear family became a crucial metaphor for national security. While psychiatrists developed a range of treatments, some of which involved forced hospitalization and shock therapy, McCarthy-era governments conducted purges of homosexual civil servants and teachers, dismissing them from their jobs, claiming that they were inherent security risks and perverts. Lesbians and gay men were regarded as mentally unstable, aberrant, and therefore socially and politically unreliable. Their activity was policed, leading to loss of jobs and alienation from their families, forcing them into extreme levels of ostracization and financial precarity—conditions that psychiatrists of the time more exacerbated than helped.

During the Vietnam War, as arbiters of who was fit to serve on the front lines, psychiatrists were sometimes seen by anti-war activists as a crucial arm of US imperialism. However, some of these same practicing psychiatrists were themselves homosexual. In 1972 two notably outspoken veterans of homophile activism, Barbara Gittings and Frank Kameny, organized a panel on homosexuality at the annual American Psychiatric Association (APA) conference in Dallas, sharing the stage with a disguised gay psychiatrist, Dr. John E. Fryer. Possibly as a result of staging their critique of the psychiatric profession within its own governing bodies and in the voices of its own practitioners, and of exposing a dearth of scientific evidence for their homophobic stances, in December 1973 activists succeeded in getting the APA to change its classification of homosexuality as a mental disorder.

Abram J. Lewis has shown how, where more reformist-minded lesbian and gay activists may have felt affirmed because the proper authorities reversed their view of homosexuality as a sickness, many liberationists maintained a more thoroughgoing critique of psychiatry as an insidious institution within US imperialism.[18] Lewis adds that many of these liberationists turned to other models of health—from ones that were official, scientific, skeptical, and "reasonable," to more religious or spiritual models. Even though this practice coincided with the rise of "New Age" and "self-help" movements, gay liberationists took care to distinguish their practices from that context, as when a Jewish *RFD* reader expressed his faggot spirituality through his anger at "the

New Age Growth Movement ... because it only recognizes problems as personal and internal. They blame the individual for not being spiritual, skilled or mature enough. By emphasizing individual solutions they don't recognize societal caused problems," specifically ones of class and race.[19] Further, many began to see madness as the direct mental result of imperial oppression and violence, and some considered madness a necessary psychological orientation for revolution. For example, in 1975 a young *RFD* reader in rural Missouri openly embraced his own schizophrenic perspective as crucial to his emergent gay liberationist views.[20] The emphasis on open ritual and heightened emotion at the 1976 Wolf Creek conference stemmed from such veins of recent gay liberationist antipsychiatry.

As the *RFD* critique of New Age spirituality indicates, faggot antipsychiatry did not regard sanity as a personal matter, but instead as an issue of social psychology that required political solutions. These gay liberationists would have argued that an equitable society produced mental health, whereas an imperialist one—like that of the United States at the time—created, and operationalized, mental disorders as a form of institutional oppression. Therefore, many liberationists saw reclaiming one's madness as integral to revolutionary politics, as a way of pitching chaos against the oppressive order.[21] As the above young Missouri *RFD* writer speculated, maybe wide social "madness" could drive revolutionary change. We might also here recall that Evans himself had envisioned "a madness that tears the [repressive] new order itself apart."[22]

Such antipsychiatric positions reflected broader leftist concerns with what, if any, revolutionary perspectives were most fit to foment change. Of course, many earlier leftists had placed all their faith in the revolutionary social subjectivity of the radicalized industrial factory worker. New leftists generally agreed that this focus was too single-minded because it remained blind to the complex, adaptive nature of capitalist economies. Factory workers were never really the only exploited class. And this seemed increasingly true in a world that appeared to be inching away from the industrial economic model toward industries rooted in technology, service, and communications. However, these newer leftists often disagreed in terms of how to revise their theories regarding revolutionary subjectivity.

As we have already seen, at the Faggots & Class Struggle conference, the Los Angeles L&RU argued against proposing any revolutionary figure whatsoever, contending that such strategies always narrowly defined solidarity. Most other conference attendees—the Marxist-Leninist organizers, the Maoists, the socialist feminists, working-class faggots, and the anarchists—disagreed. The working class, in particular, pointed out that the L&RU

leadership was, at the time, only composed of gay men, giving lie to their argument that not naming revolutionary subjectivities would lead to a more inclusive liberation; to the contrary, the working-class faggots suggested, the L&RU's *refusal* to define a revolutionary class allowed their leadership to center their own agenda without considering the specific experiences of the variously oppressed. The Marxist-Leninists, based in Eugene, Oregon, countered that solidarity was a process that required recognition of different historical, classed experiences and that it was not only naive but insulting to imagine that, in the name of unity, revolutionaries could skip over that process of struggling with those subjective differences. Recognizing this, the organizers had, from the beginning, planned the rural faggot conference as a "transitory historic tactic"—"with a limited scope and purpose" of sharing attendees' different experiences in order to explore possible points of unity.[23] By this logic, faggotry was a temporary and strategic subjectivity that could galvanize gay revolutionary transformation. Most attendees agreed with this broad logic but were not fully sold on the idea that the faggot—considered from racial, ethnic, and gendered perspectives—was a figure they could all embrace.

The moon ritual, then, allowed conference goers to use performance to explore the positive potential of the faggot social psychology in a collective context. In line with the conference organizers' intent, it acknowledged the historically materialist, rather than transcendent, quality of that subjectivity. As a group activity asking participants to hold hands and kiss, it defied the isolating and physically passive format of the counseling session conducted on the couch. Because it stressed the use of imaginative, somatic, erotic, and emotional faculties, it diverged from purely reflective, intellectual analysis. And it is possible that, with its lunar focus over a Labor Day weekend, it suggested cultural links with lunacy in a leftist antipsychiatry context that encouraged ritualists to try on the revolutionary potential of the madness the APA had saddled them with as recently as three years before. The ritual performed a kind of politically charged bonding around these shared values.

If gay liberationist antipsychiatry and newer leftist debates about subjectivity lend context to the moon ritual as dialectical, how should we consider the personification of the moon as "*Mother* History"? Both the L&RU and the Marxist-Leninist organizers considered themselves "autonomous communist" organizations, and this leftist line had its own history, which eventually included a feminist take on reproductive labor. Italian communists of the 1960s, like Mario Tronti, hungrily looking to a new Italian edition of Marx's *Grundrisse* for applicable revolutionary lessons, developed theories of labor as creative and active, and conversely, of capitalist exploitation as *reactive*.

This view fueled a workerist movement (*operaismo*) that valorized the factory worker as utterly capable of escaping compulsory labor altogether and sparking revolution. Following this perspective, factory workers, especially those in northern Italian automobile plants, discovered their power through the widespread staging of strikes, slowdowns, and sabotage. These workers came to see themselves as the true leaders of economic operations.

In the wake of May 1968, however, European industrial workers forged alliances with classes not always associated with waged labor—students, housewives, and artists, for example. The industrial worker was clearly no longer the sole revolutionary class. Instead of dispensing with the importance of labor subjectivity altogether, the Italians improvised a new autonomist communism (*autonomia operaia*), which turned to analyzing and celebrating the unique historical potentialities of each social subjectivity, and they expanded how they conceived the revolutionary site of the factory floor to include the wider "social factory"—performing activism in everyday public streets and in populist media. Whereas some communists responded to workerism's narrow glorification of the factory worker by refusing to invest in any revolutionary subjectivity whatsoever, these autonomists tended to expand their cadre of subjectivities to imagine what students, housewives, and artists might uniquely contribute to revolution.[24]

One important branch of autonomist communism was the International Wages for Housework movement, sparked in Padua in 1972. It included Italian feminists Mariarosa Dalla Costa and Silvia Federici, as well as New Yorker Selma James.[25] Their central critique was that, by focusing on *waged* labor, the old left obscured how women's unwaged reproductive labor not only gave birth to and raised future workforces but also cared for—that is, fed, clothed, nursed, and sexually and emotionally satisfied—those workers, sending them off daily to the factory fit, sated, and healthy. They argued that the entire capitalist system depended on housewives' *un*waged labor. These autonomist feminists proposed that wives and mothers demand salaries from the state for doing the work of making the waged economy possible in the first place. Their strategy depended on women feeling empowered *through* embracing a radicalized mother/housewife subjectivity.[26]

It is possible that gay West Coast new leftists like the L&RU and the Marxist-Leninist conference organizers thought of their "autonomous communism" through the lens of recent Italian leftist feminism, particularly the Wages for Housework movement. Dalla Costa and James toured North America in the spring of 1973, and shortly after, Federici, living in New York at the time, founded a New York City chapter. Other Wages for Housework groups popped up in cities across the country, including in Los Angeles in 1975 and in San Francisco in 1976.[27] The Bay Area chapter would have certainly jibed with the socialist feminism teeming in San Francisco at just this time. If this were the case, the Wolf Creek moon ritualists—so many of whom were likely Bay Area socialist feminists—would have understood motherhood as a labor subjectivity with revolutionary potential. As faggots and sissies and effeminists, they would have embraced their own feminization along with their own capacity to share in reproductive labor. Many ecofeminist spiritual movements of the time, including witchcraft, of course, also valorized the figure of the mother. For its part, faggot witchcraft invoked a left-leaning mother.

If the Wolf Creek conference aimed to reclaim the political role of the faggot, to rebirth a leftist gay liberationist revolutionary figure, witchcraft was the spiritual method for their doing so. Spiritual modalities were common within Bay Area gay liberation. Joey Plaster has described the queer street ministries of the Tenderloin, and Christina Hanhardt has noted some San Francisco liberationists' membership in pagan groups.[28] Because Hanhardt emphasizes the centrality of "New Age" and "self-help" in such groups, we can easily distinguish West Coast faggots from the mainline that Hanhardt describes, but her reference to paganism *does* make liberationist overlaps with Bay Area witchcraft conceivable. Activist gay and lesbian witches emerged from this spiritual mix.

We already know that Arthur Evans was the most central figure in articulating faggot politics through the vehicle of witchcraft. Evans claimed in his book's acknowledgments, however, that *Witchcraft and the Gay Counterculture* resulted less from single authorship than from collective work. The lion's share of his gratitude went to fellow liberationists laboring in nascent political and print cultures. These included the members of his Fairy Circle and the sponsors for his lectures. While he didn't mention any of the major West Coast witchcraft practitioners of the time—Budapest, the Andersons, or Starhawk— he did top his list with a nod of thanks to fellow GAA cofounder Leo Martello for suggesting that he graft feminist witchcraft to gay politics. Evans also thanked Faygele Ben Miriam for the loan of a typewriter, a nod that confirms Evans's place within the wider West Coast faggot network of the time.[29]

He also listed several who provided important "social energy." One was Assunta Feria, whom Hanhardt mentions as being a member of the left-leaning Bay Area Gay Liberation (BAGL).[30] BAGL formed a very vocal presence at the Faggots & Class Struggle panel presentations, and Evans himself was an early member. In fact, he took a good bit of space in his book to laud BAGL for its actions in protest of commercial bathhouses, owned by gay liberals, who promoted hypermasculinist Castro clone culture with policies excluding effeminate men, people of color, and older queers. According to Evans, BAGL's vocal critique led to bathhouse owners banning anyone wearing a BAGL T-shirt because of the activists' overly critical and "communist" stance.[31] Another person Evans thanked was Tede Matthews, the highly visible femme instigator of faggot political culture in the Bay Area. Having pitched himself against the rising clone culture, Evans would have cheered the femme protest figure Matthews cut. In fact, almost as if embodying "the Lady of the Flowers, the Queen of Heaven" invoked at the conclusion of his book, Evans began calling himself "the Red Queen" in the late 1970s and distributed pamphlets protesting the Castro's "butch conformity."[32] In this, he seemed to have come through the looking glass as a full-fledged new socialist ("red") femme.

In other words, Evans used magic to assume the revolutionary subjectivity he invoked. Far from being a personal idiosyncrasy, this practice was at the heart of the gay liberationist witchcraft that suffused the West Coast politics of faggotry in the latter half of the 1970s. It was often *the* purpose of the invocations that appeared in print culture and in rituals at political events. Such invocations aimed to animate revolutionary social psychologies and generate new leftist figures. It took the reflective, critical, and interpersonal work of consciousness-raising and fleshed it out—with group performance, ecstatic interactivity, collective fantasy, shared affect, and revolutionary character development. The *Morning Due* report on the 1976 Faggots & Class Struggle conference began with such an invocation, featuring a chorus, "our song: / sissies / fairies / & / witches and all / discovering together our revolutionary spirit."[33] By 1976 gay liberation was widely seen to have failed and Evans regarded industrial society as a mass of the living dead. Faggot witchcraft was meant to revivify gay liberation, to animate its new socialism. One of its main methods was the invocation, what many Wiccans of the time referred to as "drawing down the moon," a way of inviting the lunar goddess to possess ritualists' bodies. The Wolf Creek moon ritual invoked the "Deliciously Dialectical, Mother History" for the express purpose of jump-starting revolutionary subjectivity into an electrified network of faggots, sissies, and faeries.

Roses, Too: RFD's 1976 Faggot Spirituality and the Raising of the Violent Femme

However, the very same ritual could raise different radical spirits. *RFD* and *Morning Due* ascribed distinct political tenors to it. In the winter 1976 issue of

RFD, the Oregon editors published a "Collective Statement" in which they claimed, "Most of us call ourselves faggots," and they described that figure just as Evans would.[34] Among the issue's listed *RFD* editors was a "jai d. elliott," whose poem "bread & roses revisited (for the sissies)" documented the moon ritual. There are enough similarities with the *Morning Due* account to confirm that the poem refers to the same event. There are the fifty attendees, called "faggots" here rather than "fairies." There is reference to the moon, the crowded tipi, the fire, and the spiral dance outside. In elliott's poem, though, we learn that there was actually a workshop to carefully design the communist aspect of the ritual "of faggots & the mother / and together we merged / ceremony with solidarity / demystified."[35] Noting that elliott footed the poem with a mailing address for a "Mao House" in Eugene, we might infer that he was also friendly with the Marxist-Leninist organizers of the conference. What is most striking, though, is how the poem's refrain, its fiery focus, and its parenthetical closing invoke a revolutionary figure quite different from that of *Morning Due*.

Lacking the tripartite invocations of Evans (Isis, Diana, and Kali) or *Morning Due* ("sissies, fairies, and witches"), the central refrain of elliott's poem is the phrase "bread & roses," repeated at six different instances, set off with quotation marks and a right-hand justification. The phrase therefore forms the spine of the revolutionary figure that the poem-spell ultimately summons, and it roots that figure's work in both industrial *and* reproductive labor.

Before diving into the context of the poem's title, we should first address its dedication: "for the sissies." As we have already seen, many conference-goers, especially socialist feminists from the Bay Area, called themselves sissies instead of faggots, as a way to show their alliance with those Bay Area gay liberationists of color who critiqued the faggot as too white and European to represent their revolution. There was another reason, though. The conference schedule devoted the days to intellectual lectures, while cultural events (such as shared meals, creative performances, and spiritual ritual) and body-work (such as massage, group sex) were slated for the end of the day. The labor for the cultural events, bodywork, and childcare duties fell to effeminate attendees, while lectures were delivered with masculine gravity. These serious leftist lecturers tended to belabor their talks, and the discussions stretched out, pushing the schedule further and further back, so that the (feminized) cultural, body, and childcare labor was deferred, and then rushed—basically rendered a mere afterthought. In a caucus, the marginalized, effeminate conference participants, calling themselves *sissies*, referred to the organizers and lecturers as STIFs ("straight-identified faggots") for their sexist masculinity.

The sissies emerged, then, as a revolutionary alternative to the faggots, who in conference practice were drawn from a narrowly white, western, *and* masculinist model. The *RFD* poem "bread & roses revisited" not only documented the conference moon ritual; it also attempted to heal this STIF–sissie rift.

The feminist origins of the phrase "bread and roses" were a little more than a half-century old. Chicago suffragist and factory inspector Helen Todd gave a 1911 account of her participation in an automobile campaign for women's suffrage, sharing that an acquaintance in her nineties requested that the campaign slogan "Bread for all, and Roses too" be embroidered on her pillow. Todd's account clarifies the phrase: "Woman is the mothering element in the world and her vote will go toward helping forward the time when life's Bread, which is home, shelter and security, and the Roses of life, music, education, nature and books, shall be the heritage of every child that is born in the country, in the government of which she has a voice."[36] The "Deliciously Dialectical, Mother History," the leftist goddess of the *Morning Due* moon ritual, here became the historically specific US mother-suffragists who saw their reproductive labor taking two necessary forms: the bread (emblematic of survival: nourishment and protection) and roses (metaphor for pleasure, growth, beauty, and culture). These suffragists staked their argument for women's vote on the importance of both forms of reproductive labor. As "faggots claiming the female aspect / as well as the male," the revolutionary sissies, to whom elliott's poem was dedicated, also took seriously their political obligation to mothering in both these forms—to provide, for example, childcare, and to maximize culture and pleasure in the world.

As with the Wages for Housework campaign, *RFD* faggots framed the perspective of reproductive labor as linked to industrial socialism. As such, the "bread & roses" refrain kept its workerist associations while expanding them to include reproductive concerns. Herself a factory inspector and labor activist, as well as a suffragist and mother, Todd nicely exemplified this perspective. The "bread and roses" slogan was later reproduced in a 1911 James Oppenheim poem that was then linked to the 1912 textile mills strike in Lawrence, Massachusetts—an action led by the Industrial Workers of the World (IWW) and composed of many marching women and immigrant textile workers. The Lawrence women marched as factory workers *and* as working mothers, expressing in one protest body an industrial-reproductive labor point of view. Oppenheim's poem placed new emphasis on political *affect* with the line "Hearts starve as well as bodies," allowing room for Evans's apocalyptic view that a politics that did not address "roses, too" would end in a society of the living dead, in which mere heartless bodies survived to walk the earth and labor endlessly.[37] Oppenheim similarly asserted the need to fight for "small art and love and beauty." Gay liberationist sissies committed to sexual liberation as well as to cultural labor would have been inspired by the political orientation that accrued around the phrase "bread & roses" in the early twentieth century.

It had a salience much closer to home for West Coast faggots, though. The phrase had traveled the twentieth century from suffragist slogan to embroidered pillow, from speech to protest poem to midcentury labor anthem. It was powerfully revived as countercultural folk music in 1974 when Mimi Fariña, Joan Baez's sister, recorded it as a song and in the same year founded a Bay Area nonprofit of the same name. Having performed the year before for prisoners at Sing Sing prison, with her sister and B.B. King, Fariña dedicated the Bread and Roses cooperative to defying institutional isolation by coordinating performances in prisons and medical facilities. In this manifestation, "bread & roses" took liberationist aim at the institutions used to divide and contain domestic subjects under US imperialism. It's helpful to note, too, that Fariña's Bay Area organization was founded in the same year that Tede Matthews began practicing open faggotry and Arthur Evans moved to San Francisco from Washington. In 1974 the West Coast folk scene sought ways to make good on the countercultural promise that experiments in art and everyday life would fuel liberation. Bay Area faggotry took up this refrain of "roses, too."

However, readers of elliott's poem could in no way mistake these roses for those of the flower children. The poem ends with a stanza set apart by parentheses—a vision bracketed for the very near future: "dreaming comrades in dresses/& with guns/commandeering a military base/dreaming faggots in revolution." The figure elliott's poem invokes is an armed faggot in women's clothing taking possession of a (Bay Area) military base. If we remember the West Coast context of the 1970s, this may not seem such an unexpected pose to strike. There were many handy examples of violent femmes at the time. As Hobson has reminded us, through figures like Patty Hearst and Susan Saxe the 1970s were a decade in which stories of armed radical women circulated in the media. But West Coast faggot culture produced its own cross-dressed violent femmes. In 1973, Lavender Country's song "Back in the Closet Again" appeared in Seattle, with its images of gay men with grenades in their bras. Hanhardt recounts how in San Francisco in 1973 the Lavender Panthers were formed to police street violence against sexual- and gender-nonconforming people, carrying "sawed-off pool cues and shotguns" and appearing in press releases with some members unabashedly "feminine-presenting" (labeled, as Hanhardt notes, "drag queens" by the *San Francisco Examiner*).[38] Hobson's cited photo of Tede Matthews at the 1975 San Francisco Gay Freedom Day features Matthews carrying a rifle while dressed in drag.[39] Also in 1975, Ben Miriam, the cross-dressed typist, helped to publish George Jackson Brigade communiqués in Seattle's *Morning Due*. The 1970s West Coast radically revised femininity in the figure of the militant femme. For socialist feminists of the period, it wasn't so difficult to imagine feminine revolutionaries demanding bread and roses while armed.

If Stephen Vider looks at the gay collective through the lens of "domestic liberation" and Emily Hobson sees it in terms of lesbian "collective defense," it is also important to remember that, for some faggots, like Evans, the collective was a single node in an underground—prepared to defend against violence, but also in some cases to strategically attack, dismantle, and reclaim sites of institutional power. In attendance at the Oregon faggot conference, Tede Matthews may have been a real-life model for the social subjectivity proposed at the end of elliott's poem. Evans bemoaned the stranglehold that the military industrial complex had on the Bay Area economy, and while critiquing the hypermasculinity of the emergent clone culture, he cautioned faggots to be prepared to "[fan] out like viruses" and "[carry] our secret weapons, and [strike] without warning" at those infrastructures within the imperial control system. This counteroffensive faggot move would have been a job fit for the likes of Evans's Red Queen. After all, in elliott's poem the focus was on commandeering the military bases that dominated the 1970s Bay Area economy.

The fact that the Morning Due collective had recently decided to publish the communiqués of the Seattle-based George Jackson Brigade's armed robberies and pipe bombings is key here. In the same winter 1976 issue—likely under Ben Miriam's guidance—*RFD* published Brigade founder Ed Mead's prison letters, in which he requested support for the organization of gay prisoners at the Walla Walla state penitentiary.[40] And, to bring the transnational intersections of femme radical violence full circle, when fellow Brigade member Rita Brown would detonate a pipe bomb in a Bellevue Mercedes dealership in October 1977, their group's communiqué expressed alliance with the anti-fascist German Red Army Faction (RAF).[41] Recently, three more German RAF members had died from (likely staged) suicides while in custody—a pattern begun when RAF cofounder Ulrike Meinhof was found hanged in her German cell the year before. Seattle's significantly queer George Jackson Brigade voiced its sympathies with their militant leftist German comrades. Their stance, as they saw it, was an international alliance.

This describes the climate out of which faggot witchcraft emerged. If the *Morning Due* account of the ritual underscored the moon's power to bond the moonstruck dancers together, then jai elliott's "bread and roses revisited" focused on the fire, stoking a martyrology of feelings: pain and injustice associated with the ongoing witch hunts conducted by the state. Out of these flames, the *RFD* poem dreamed up armed femme figures to answer such injustices: "comrades in dresses / & with guns." A single ritual had invoked a figure that politically was both lunar *and* fiery.

Faggot Spirituality as White Magic?

That the very same ritual prompted different accounts from *Morning Due* (moon) and *RFD* (fire) is testimony to the political range within the politics of faggotry and to the diverse registers of its witchcraft practice. The *Morning Due* account presented the ritual as a collective and broadly erotic exercise to ground faggot subjectivity in the historical materialist moment. *RFD* recounted it as a fire ritual with the power to alchemically transmute the burning witch and faggot into an armed, violent femme fighting for bread, and roses, too. Both versions were compatible with Arthur Evans's new socialist magic, and both were haunted by the specters of mothers, by the value of reproductive labor. In that both look back to the Labor Day 1976 Wolf Creek conference, each also had an opportunity to address the whiteness of their West Coast faggot spiritualities.

The *Morning Due* account committed gay liberationists to struggle with their own racism. The poem opening the conference report flatly states, "sissies / faeries / & / witches and all / 'from all color—of women / we anglos must fight our racism."[42] In fact, because this poem is simply titled "Sissies," and because there is no use of the word "faggot" anywhere in the poem, we might infer that the unnamed author was responding to Bay Area gay liberationists of color who objected to the Eurocentrism of the faggot figure. They had argued that the figure of the faggot was too rooted in European witchcraft, in white experiences of colonialism, to resonate with them. However, the inclusion of "faeries" and "witches" in the *Morning Due* poem evidences a continued investment in the broader European folkloric context of faggot witchcraft, even as the addition of the phrase "and all / from all color" signals an effort to create ample room for liberationists of color to add to the list with their own subjectivities. The poem indicates that the responsibility for making such room around the ritual circle should not be foisted on those in the Gay Latinos Alliance, Gay American Indians, and the Black Gay Caucus but should instead fall to white sissies, faeries, and witches, who would turn to consciousness-raising techniques to combat their own racism. The whiteness of *Morning Due* sissies' spirituality, then, was acknowledged and simply slated for ongoing work.

The whiteness of the *RFD* invocation was more complicated. The poetic account doesn't raise the issue of race at all. It also, like the Wolf Creek editors' statement, held tight to its faggot perspective—being "*for* the sissies" but spoken from a faggot point of view. Conspicuously, elliott omitted any reference to witchcraft or Europe. Perhaps this indicates an effort to couch the conference ritual, not as witchcraft at all, but instead as a form of updated mother-goddess worship. By using the refrain "bread and roses," the origin story for elliott's invocation took historical root on *this* side of the Atlantic and in the early twentieth century—at once giving it a less medieval European frame *and* a firmer industrial socialist bent than Evans himself would have chosen. The poem offers a thoroughly American, radical labor myth. Perhaps this shift was also intended to draw upon the widely recognized immigrant leadership in the Lowell textile mill strikes as a way to imply a more diverse, American ethnic composition for faggotry. However, this purpose is not supported elsewhere in the poem, and the move suggests that the author thought that unpinning the faggot figure from its European context and then planting it in the industrial United States could answer for the assumed white Eurocentrism of faggotry.

However, if elliott's poem linguistically skirted race in sticking to its militant faggot perspective, the *RFD* editorial collective chose to print the poem with a photograph from the conference itself—a photo that foregrounds a Black attendee apparently singing "bread and roses revisited" in unison with his white faggot peers. This "David," who appeared in photos elsewhere in the winter 1976 issue, was one of the five conference-goers of color among the event's 140 attendees. It is therefore difficult to imagine that David's appearance alongside the poem is coincidental. Rather, this editorial decision seemed bent on visually centering David's racialized body at the heart of West Coast faggotry while naturalizing that presence as unworthy of comment or reflection. In other words, the photo implied that faggot subjectivity was, naturally, at least as Black as it was white.

It could be that *RFD* editors took the objection of the Bay Area liberationists of color too narrowly, as an issue of simple representation, and assumed that, to correct it, they only needed to circulate images of Black conference participants. However, such a strategy only excised crucial narratives about how the few Black attendees, like David or Blackberi, found themselves at Wolf Creek in the first place and how other potential attendees of color came to be, significantly, absent. Just as the Eugene Marxist Leninists and the conference

bread & roses revisited
                      (for the sissies)

oh flaming comrades
you came down from the mountain
twilight chanting "bread & roses
                  bread & roses"
arm in arm/heart in heart
you came fresh from your caucus
hungry to no more food
and into the evenings culture
we followed you
eyes and repression
your shadows the same as ours

earlier
you had shared a workshop
designing the midnight ritual
of faggots & the mother
and together we merged
ceremony with solidarity
de-mystified
for all of our brothers
not just us

and
you joined in with the anarchists
caucusing for unity & to be heard
twilight chanting "bread & roses
                bread & roses"
and we voiced our concerns & support
creating a statement
together
for the rest of the conference
to wake up to

midnight
clouded over moon near full
fifty and more faggot comrades
huddled within tipi like shaman
we sang & chanted songs to Her
we held each other
             eye to eye
arm in arm/heart in heart
lips to lips
we performed a fire ritual:
faggots rising from the flames
faggots resisting the oppression
faggots joining the struggle
faggots claiming the female aspect
as well as the male
faggots working to be whole again
we gathered then outside
to dance our joy our love
in spirals and chants
we became seed for "bread & roses
              bread & roses"
last day
conference workshops delineated
one last time
interupted for sissy statement
"stiff" men gasp for denial
goats eat garbage
dresses blow in the wind

more workshops announced
interupted for anarchist statement
marxists shuffle silently
another barnyard perhaps
i feel warm with my comrades:
anarchist & sissy faggots

the moment becomes chaos
i head for the workshop:
terrorism & armed struggle

after workshop
and lunch and terrorist talk
criticism & self-criticism
and many comrades on departure
addresses exchanged
there is work to be done
smiles & tears & love
faggots creating "bread & roses
              bread & roses"
words spoken into microphone
from heart & soul
and finally i leave as i came
and it is all a memory:
faggots chanting "bread & roses
              bread & roses"

(and any night now
i wake up darkly
dreaming comrades in dresses
& with guns
commandeering a military base
dreaming faggots in revolution
& with love
tying scarves securely
twilight chanting "bread & roses
              bread & roses")

-jai d.-elliott

Mao House
2193½ Alder Street
Eugene, OR. 97405

Poem "bread & roses revisited (for the sissies)," by jai d. elliott, *RFD*, Winter 1976, 17. Photo by Candor Smoothstone.

working-class caucus critiqued the L&RU for its arrogance in skipping over the struggle with difference, in visually foregrounding and proliferating David's Black body, the *RFD* faggot editors cast David's belonging in faggotry as natural and easy, without acknowledging the complex work necessary for him to arrive at the Wolf Creek site and participate in the moon ritual at all.

It can certainly be argued that Evans commits a similar racialized "left error" in his celebrating the "Indian, wise-woman" and "Black sorcerer" as natural allies alongside the faggot and witch in his *Witchcraft and the Gay Counterculture*.[43] However, even though it is unclear whether he counted any Indigenous or Black participation in the collective production of his book, he did couch his new socialism and magic as an allied resistance pitched against settler and white supremacist colonialism. By contrast, the *RFD* account denies the faggot culture's whiteness by simply sidestepping any racial conversation or analysis, by visually asserting a black-and-white composition for faggot spirituality, and by denying a platform for the stories of the few attendees of color. As we will see, the whiteness of *RFD*'s West Coast faggotry would be challenged the following year by the serial's wider readership. For some gay liberationists—possibly those most inspired by Huey Newton's call for gay revolutionary analysis, or those whose introduction to activism was civil rights work, or those who held New Left alliances as an utmost priority—faggotry lost its appeal as a movement subjectivity the more it confirmed its whiteness by the very act of refusing to acknowledge and address its racial dynamics.

Mulberry House returned to the Ozarks calling themselves *sissies* rather than *faggots*. Their political, ideological reasons for this choice would be tried, refined, and strained through their collective life in Fayetteville, as chapter 3 shows. Their strong connections to people like Faygele Ben Miriam and Tede Matthews, and their engagement with serials like *RFD*, placed them within an expanding gay liberationist network with a rural vision and a complex swirl of subjectivities—faggots, faeries, or sissies, by turn. As dedicated sissies intent on establishing a "fairy farm," they were right at home in this fuzzy network.

However, the 1976 Oregon Faggots & Class Struggle conference dramatically underscored that if the liberationist collective worked like a coven, if its revolutionary politics were spiked with "religious longings," then its spiritual politics could register in quite different forms—from the proliferative and erotic faerie spiral of the *Morning Due* account, to the fiery, armed, and violent femme of the *RFD* faggots. The differences in these figures stemmed from important ideological distinctions, even as they occupied a similar space within the gay liberationist political cultures that were renewed in the second half of the decade. I suggest that, while both accounts shared a long-term goal, they prioritized different tactics—*Morning Due* emphasizing witchcraft ritual's function for strengthening the bond between liberationists understood as mad outsiders, and *RFD* highlighting witchery's capacity to valorize a femme militant figure to put imperialists on warning. These figures were uniquely West Coast invocations, though, with different responses to the whiteness of their faggot spirituality. It remained for Mulberry House to transform their Wolf Creek experience for an Ozark moon.

CHAPTER THREE

Pied Pipers
Ozark Collectivism Pitched against White Christian Supremacy

How did the Ozark collective respond to their Oregon experience once back home in Fayetteville? Although they now called themselves sissies, the look was not new to them. Oglesby remembers that, with Laughlin and Jackson under the same roof, they had already begun to "wear skirts and worship the goddess," mirroring how many Ozark lesbian feminists had taken on butch looks and masculine work.[1] (Zajiek and Lord shared how regional women, for example, started a trucking collective.[2]) After the conference they also doubled down on their socialist feminist domestic liberation. This meant that, at least initially, they focused more on bread than roses, working to denaturalize patriarchal notions of the domestic (home, family, labor, love, meals) in order to carve out a liberationist way of living. They also reached for their dream of a faerie farm by concentrating on food justice activism through their work at the Ozark Food Co-op. By their own admission, though, they devoted less time to the spiritual practice that would bond and shape them in the image of radical sissies. In many ways they simply returned to the work that they had named for themselves in *RFD* a year earlier.

In the coming year their house would divide. Certainly part of the story, as Stephen Vider notes in his reference to Mulberry House, was the exacerbated class tensions between working-class and middle-class collectivists.[3] In fact, members recall that that *was* the dominant theme. Those divisions were stoked on a couple of fronts. First, the socialist feminist Amazon dykes Laughlin and Jackson urged Thornton and Oglesby to, as the latter put it, "get in touch with our class anger." Second, Oglesby had taken a leadership role in the working-class caucus at the Faggots & Class Struggle conference, so at the time he was most driven by the intellectual work of distinguishing a working-class perspective within the wider politics of faggotry. Such processing, within the confines of a small house, was painful, just as it was within the Ozark lesbian households all around them. Ultimately the single Mulberry House would split into two separate, but linked, class-affiliated addresses. It is fair to say, then, that class differences divided the house.

Even today, almost fifty years later, Mulberry House collectivists feel regret around how they let those differences divide them, how they hurt each other in the name of their politics. The lingering pain is palpable. It is a main point of this book that the interpersonal *must* be given space in histories of collectivism, that such intimacies are at the heart of queer political stories. At the same time, I here suggest that the spike of regional terror caused by the rise of the white Christian supremacist Save Our Children campaign pushed otherwise manageable classed emotions, consciousness-raising, and ideological differences into a fever pitch. Mulberry House's internal relations took place, not in a vacuum, but in a crucible fired by regional violence. This is the climate Jeremy Varon refers to as "the world of the underground," a world pushed past "normal politics" into a "world of extraordinary danger."[4]

In this chapter, I open with a reading of Oglesby's *RFD* critique of the Oregon conference in order to clarify Mulberry House's socialist feminist bent and to link it to the collective's early commitment to food justice as aligned with their longer vision for an Ozark faerie farm. In doing so, I show how they sought to realize their domestic liberation on a regional scale. I then describe the regional white Christian supremacist facets of the Save Our Children campaign, and Mulberry House's gay liberationist responses to it. I close the chapter with an account of Williams developing a quite different collectivist vision when in complete despair over how ill-equipped their collective defense was for the terror they faced in 1977.

Table to Farm: Growing Domestic Liberation while Feeling the Co-Op Blues

Back in Oregon, Oglesby had been the one to share the working-class caucus's point of view with other conference attendees, and his later *RFD* critique was carefully couched to reflect the Ozark socialist feminist shape of his political thought.[5] In line with the broader working-class analysis, he objected to the theoretical bent of the "conference," which sidelined working-class faggots' networking, communication, and organizing. He additionally pointed out that both the gay liberationist press and the Oregon fixed conference fee were examples of the means by which the middle class continued to dominate faggot relations, creating access issues for the working class among them.

His socialist views took on a complexly feminist cast in a few of his other points, which demonstrated his collectivist stance on domesticated space and labor. For example, he critiqued how some faggots lived alone as couples in large homes, referring to it as a "ridiculously hetero" model by which privileged classes accumulated property and took up space in the name of privacy, leaving the working classes pinched into smaller, less desirable spaces. He wrote, "Privileged faggots have to MOVE OVER and share their resources." Oglesby would often express this in terms of his working-class childhood: He never had his own room growing up. His large family was only as emotionally close as they were physically. As a result, the privileged presumption of discrete, personal domestic space—a house for every couple—offended him. As a socialist feminist, he also questioned middle-class domestic arrangements as expressions of love, when in reality they had everything to do with maintaining a patriarchal division of labor. Even in same-sex relations, the feminized partner was required to manage the excessive domestic space while the masculinized partner left the home to work an outside job to pay for the property. As a gay liberationist, Oglesby's strategy was not to stretch capitalist logic by demanding a wage for domestic work, like the autonomist feminists did, but to replace the model of the domestic—predicated on a patriarchal nuclear family—by collectivizing the home and withdrawing from waged labor as much as possible. He urged couples to move over and share their homes, and the housework, with more of their comrades.

He further criticized how conference organizers feminized working-class faggots by assigning them to all reproductive labor. The working-class caucus was positioned near the Wolf Creek entrance and tasked with welcoming latecomers and keeping unruly children away from the most central conversations. In essence, they were compelled to absorb and accommodate any interruption, doing the endless work of gracious hosts and attendant mothers. Oglesby reminded *RFD* readers that he had come all that way to network with other working-class faggots. Such communication was rendered impossible by organizers' presumptive division of labor.

Oglesby deepened his point by an inspired analogy drawn from another form of reproductive labor. He referred to the organizers' revolutionary lectures as "a 'buffet' of ideology with mind-food galore." Just as a buffet offers the consumer diverse choice and limitless self-service while falling short of the more participatory *production* of, say, a potluck, the conference lineup, with its ideological lectures, only created the illusion of collective thought. Oglesby objected, "Well, I don't like to be waited on. It doesn't feel good to me." Instead, he argued, the conference political content should have been prepared collectively to avoid the false consensus produced by the format. He argued that "that kind of unity is fascist." By using an analogy from food cultures, Oglesby again underscored the priority of reproductive labor over waged work, and over masculinized intellectualism, and embraced a proudly feminized role for himself. In so doing, he gestured toward models of intellect that were collectivist, care-oriented, and feminine. He urged other faggots to couch important analysis and theories in "nurturing" modes, and in his written critique he consistently used the verb *feel* rather than *think* to convey his own thoughtful practice. This is why he closed his article with an appreciation of the cultural labor of his fellow sissies, who delivered similarly trenchant ideas but in performative and collaborative modes that didn't divorce the personal from the political.

This food analogy not only placed Oglesby firmly in the camp of his fellow conference sissies, as someone chiefly concerned with the reproductive labor associated with "bread," but it also reminded readers of Mulberry House's stated commitment to a faerie farm and food justice. Fayetteville's Ozark Food Co-op was largely run by regional hippies who allowed the Mulberry House collective to fill a single role, in shifts, in exchange for one paycheck. This freed Oglesby and Thornton, for the first time in their adult lives, from endless waged labor and overtime. (When they first arrived in Fayetteville, in 1974, they had worked as nursing home orderlies.) At the house, Hayes also started a small house garden ("The Lavender Thumb"), which helped them put some food on the table, while selling other items to a town florist and to the food co-op. It wasn't long, though, before Mulberry House brought its socialist feminist ideology to bear through their staff role at the co-op.

As early as September 24, 1976, a co-op friend named Coralie wrote to Mulberry House, beseeching them to strike some different political notes.[6] Her letter led with her affection for them, addressing them as "Dear Friends" and acknowledged their many talents. She then clarified her love by saying "Your sexual preferences do not concern me." She continued, "What I don't like is your politics. Your choice of tactics, the way you come on." She described their approach as a leftist "dogmatism" familiar from her own childhood as a red diaper baby: a political style characterized by "catch-words, party-lines, brain-washing, public confession of our unoriginal sins, unity based on dogma—whether it's Catholic Church, Reverend Moon, or Marxist." Her letter struck the motherly tone of a seasoned radical who saw in Mulberry House a youthful leftist fundamentalism that they should quickly grow out of. Closer to her age, Williams responded to her maternal air and tone-policing with "An Open Letter to the Ozark Food Co-optation entitled *I Am Tired*."[7] His response unleashed the anger of a gay militant on the co-op hippies' heterosexist and middle-class assumptions. He had much to unburden and his tone was both exhausted *and* blistering.

The Mulberry House sissies were not alone in holding different views about what new directions the food co-op should take. They joined with a few other employees, including radical women, to issue a November newsletter titled "Cooptation Blues," echoing language from Williams's letter.[8] In many ways this newsletter brought the same participatory, collectivist ethic found in Oglesby's conference critique to the food co-op's operations and the question of the region's food supply chains, on a global and local level. The tagline read "If you don't think food is political—try living without it." The cover image was a raised red fist, composed of many tiny human figures converging into a single place, and circled by a blue wreath of vegetables and grains. In the introduction, the authors identified themselves as workers who were always derisively labeled "activists," or sometimes simply "them," and who felt that the white, straight hippie countercultural leadership of the co-op—the "Bored of Directors"—appropriated the workers' revolutionary energy only to seem edgy while carefully maintaining the status quo.

The authors referenced a recent co-op membership survey, which asked, "Do you think the co-op should reach out to blacks, gays, rurals, etc.?" Seventy percent of members had responded "No." The newsletter authors critiqued how even the language of this question underscored the leadership's very limited social imagination and confirmed their narrowly white heterosexual perspective. In response, the "activists" sought to use the newsletter to change how the co-op measured its success. They proposed the organization no longer be judged by its financial stability, its appropriate staff compensation, or quality stock—all achieved by exploitative means—but instead by its ability to feed *all* in the community while ensuring food quality and withdrawing from agribusiness. Throughout the newsletter, they cited the struggles of earlier radical movements. For example, in the opening they quoted Frederick Douglass: "Those who profess to favor freedom and yet depreciate agi[t]ation are people who want crops withou[t] plowing up the ground." With this text they pushed the metaphor of liberation-as-farming into quite literal territory. The newsletter included the following salutation: "From us, in hope, anger, and great love, [signed] Them."

"Cooptation Blues" defined the system that they were all caught in as "the economic and political chains of Amerikan agribusiness imperialism." They excerpted a *Morning Due* article that outlined the role of sugar in the slavery-based plantation economies that gave rise to the nation. They noted the place of sugar in recent US imperialist relations with Cuba and the Philippines, and in the media's targeting of children as consumers to be hooked on sweets. As if to make plain the strategic role of food in US foreign relations, they quoted the imperialist position of Secretary of Agriculture Earl Butz, who said, "Food is a weapon. It is one of the principal tools in our negotiation kit." They described Butz's career as one "married to agribusiness," claiming that, while he had since resigned his position on the boards of several major food corporations, he still maintained his sizable shares in their stock. They called the USDA the "executive committee of agribusiness corporations" and showed how the US government and major banking institutions conspired to reduce the land available to individuals—including the aggressive foreclosure of small farms in places like the Ozarks—effectively turning over agriculture to large businesses that inflated food prices, manipulated demand, risked consumer health with herbicides and preservatives, lobbied public officials, and offered shares to big banks.

Internationally, they argued that the US government strategically funded overseas regimes in exchange for trade agreements that would make whole nations dependent on US food companies. The authors argued that countries like Cuba were compelled to focus their entire economies on producing a narrow range of cheap raw goods for export to the United States, and then to import back, at high cost, the resulting processed foods that they needed to feed themselves. In other words, US foreign relations created the puppet governments necessary to cultivate world hunger and produce dependencies on US mass-produced, unhealthy foods. Reporting the alarming rates of world hunger, malnutrition, and starvation, the authors of "Cooptation Blues" insisted that hunger was *not* natural; rather, under capitalism, hunger was sewn into the very fabric and means of the global economy. Their newsletter claimed that "Hunger = Imperialism" and "Hunger is not lack of food. Hunger is lack of money." Similarly, they insisted that "Prisons *are* the crime," showing how prisons often functioned to silence any resistance to the system, as was the case for agitators for Puerto Rican independence and such Black liberationists as Assata Shakur. For the co-op "activists," crime and hunger were problems that capitalist powers cast as natural in order to prevent the public from seeing them as they were: as injustices cultivated and managed by the state.

Given this critique, their goal was to reshape the Ozark Food Co-op as a liberationist enterprise rather than the complicit, liberal, and ostensibly countercultural operation it then was.[9] They called for something other than an alternative grocery that was pitched to a hippie market. The food co-op they envisioned wasn't a place organized around shopping but, taking a note from Douglass, a site of agitation. They saw it as a platform to raise member voices against federally proposed cuts to food stamps and welfare, against food taxes, and against the neoliberal USDA. They demanded the co-op hire those most marginalized by the system—along racial, ethnic, gender, sexual, and class lines—who would then ally with each other to support causes, like international liberation movements, that, no matter how distant, were intimately connected by oppressive global foodways. They supported breaking dependence on imperialist food systems at all levels: international and federal, regional and local.

Mostly composed of regional gay and women's liberationists, the co-op activists extended automatic membership to volunteers at the university women's center and, following Laughlin and Jackson's environmental activism, they loudly decried the health problems Ozark women suffered from regional agribusinesses' use of herbicides. They encouraged the boycott of SunBelt produce—like Texas citrus, for the use of dyes and preservatives, and California grapes and wine, for their reliance on unprotected (often migrant) farm labor. They wanted to relocate the Ozark co-op closer to working-class neighborhoods, and to stock fewer boutique items in order to offer more staples: beans and rice. Such staples would be priced on a sliding scale so that middle-class members would pay the markup and others could simply pay the bulk rate or, for the poorest, simply take the food at no cost. They contended that the central goal of the co-op was to simply make sure that *everyone* in the community ate. Finally, they asked that the Ozark Food Co-op reconsider the location of its storefront in the Green Warehouse, a multi-unit shopping center with a broadly countercultural market but backed by local big-banking interests. This last item was the most recent sticking point between Mulberry House and the Co-op "Bored of Directors"; it was the stink to which Coralie primarily referred in her letter. "The Cooptation Blues" sought to upend business-as-usual at the Ozark Food Co-op.

This food activism may strike us as a sharp departure from gay liberation. However, it was a radical extension of domestic liberation that followed two key questions: (1) How can we imagine a free house when it is so shaped by what lies beyond its walls? and (2) How might we more fully share in that most basic of reproductive labor: breaking bread? Mulberry House's socialist feminist, collectivist view of domestic liberation was not exclusively focused on innovating the home's interior; it was also bent on opening to the world and uniting the tables of those least fed by the imperialist system. After all, when Oglesby urged the privileged to "MOVE OVER and share resources," he meant it quite literally. As gay liberationists, they not only critiqued institutions like psychiatry and the military; they also analyzed food systems in order to show how they served imperialist ends to cast hunger as natural or personal when privation was actually engineered in order to organize the world into regions of modulated dependency. Their systemic critique did not paralyze their local action, though. They had a quite specific plan for collectivizing the food co-op in ways similar to how they had collectivized the home. And with plans for a "fairy farm" in an Ozarks region full of affordable land, much of it collectivized by radical women, the time and place were fairly ripe to begin building a more socialist farm-to-table concept. In other words, Mulberry House was embedded in a regional network that—because it included farms, collective houses, a women's center, a co-op, a food warehouse, and a women's trucking collective—had the necessary infrastructure to begin withdrawing from imperialist food systems, to throw a monkey wrench into the wider food system, and to share the motherly labor of feeding each other. They audaciously called for a world where the (heterosexist, patriarchal) family was no longer necessary to feed each other, and they named a few concrete first steps for the co-op to take.

Just before Thanksgiving 1976, Williams wrote to a friend, inviting him to "picture five radical faggots struggling with 150–200 white heterosexist middle-class liberal hippies, and you have some idea of what we face."[10] While this suggests that Mulberry House might have been united as a collective David against the co-op's Goliath, Williams also told this friend that "My collective is a 24-hour live-in study group that is in perpetual caucus" and that due to his age and middle-class background, Williams often caucused alone. Eventually a perpetual caucus among five would have to be acknowledged as an indefinite rift. In the late spring of 1977, as their struggles with the Ozark Food Co-op became more embittered, Mulberry House would split in two. The working-class members—Thornton and Oglesby, with Duane Riddle, a Texas-born newcomer—stayed on Lawson Street. Williams and Hayes rented a second house, at 316 Watson Street. They were joined by a new middle-class collectivist, Bob Reich.

Reich was born in Troy, New York. He was Jewish, and the most formally educated of any of the Mulberry House sissies. He studied history and business—at Rutgers and then at Tulane. He also was a skilled bookkeeper. While in New Orleans he worked with the lesbian feminist collective Atlantis, and when Hayes sent an inquiry to Atlantis, Reich became intrigued about the Arkansas collective's work. Their co-op projects appealed to him, as someone freshly entrenched in the whole-foods movement. Soon after, he relocated to Fayetteville. (Williams remembered first meeting Reich the previous fall, 1976, when their agitation at the Ozark Food Co-op began.) Because he was solidly middle class and because he secured work in distribution at the Green Warehouse across the street, he naturally moved into the Watson Street house. Because Reich had fewer political bones to pick with the co-op's existing hippie leadership, and because Williams sometimes became jealous of Reich's attentions toward Hayes, the Watson Street house often itself felt splintered along ideological and affectional lines, rather than class lines.

Grim Fairy Tales: Children in Regional White Christian Supremacist Violence

I emphasize, though, that the timing of this split wasn't random. The spring of 1977 was when the Florida Save Our Children campaign was launched, with Anita Bryant as its spokesperson. Bryant—the former Miss Oklahoma, then living in the Miami area with her children and husband-manager Bob Green—was alarmed when it came to her attention that Miami-Dade County had passed an ordinance to protect homosexuals from discrimination in employment and public services. In the 1960s Bryant had established herself as a recording artist who performed on USO tours in Vietnam with Bob Hope. Toward the end of the decade she was a household name. She became the face of Florida citrus, appearing in widely seen commercials as a wholesome mother promoting the healthful joys—the "sunshine"—in a daily glass of orange juice. Her virtuous media image was expanded in the early 1970s when she began publishing Christian books (some with her husband) and continued recording religious and patriotic songs. She and Green attended a Baptist church in the Miami area and sent their children to a religious school. The new ordinance put her on the offensive.

What concerned Bryant most was that the ordinance would allow homosexuals to teach children—*her* children. She felt that this would not only infringe on her parental rights to raise her kids within her own moral frame; it would also expose vulnerable, innocent children to militant homosexuals who plotted to "recruit" kids because they couldn't reproduce any of their own. Following the January 1977 passage of the ordinance, a coalition of conservative, religious leaders formed Save Our Children—with Bryant as their spokesperson—to overturn the law. Largely due to Bryant's media reach in a campaign conducted over the first half of 1977, Save Our Children successfully flipped the ordinance in a landslide vote, making anti-gay discrimination legal again in Miami by the month of June. Their success was so widely televised that other cities followed the Florida strategy as a template to reverse their own ordinances.

Historians of the New Right have uncovered the processes that yoked a surprising range of US conservative religious, political, and economic institutions into a new and powerful bloc, and how central homophobic disinformation was to achieving their ends. It is important to draw upon these historians' findings to understand the full context of Save Our Children. For example, David Cunningham has shown how, in the 1960s, the FBI fabricated or exaggerated charges of homosexuality in order to smear New Left leadership and dismantle their fledgling alliances. This practice was particularly aimed at any potential solidarity between leftist, anti-war, and Black movements. Cunningham cites a particular example with a folkloric reference that is uncannily resonant with Bryant's horror stories about the nation's children being whisked away by homosexuals. In 1968, FBI agents provided the *New York Daily News* with information on anti-war agitator David Dellinger's 1949 arrest for alleged homosexual activity in a men's restroom, referring to Dellinger's politics as "the perversion of the Pied Piper for Protesters for Peace."[11] This imagery suggests a US small-town Hamelin in which innocent parents wake to find all their children taken, conjured away by the piping of sexual and political dissidents.

Cunningham shows how the FBI used similar tactics against white supremacists, but unevenly. Regarding various ideologically oriented US Nazi groups, they sowed rumors of homosexuality and even took out subscriptions to gay magazines in leaders' names in order to plant the division necessary to tear their organizations apart. However, they handled Southern white supremacist groups, like the vigilante Ku Klux Klan and the established Citizens Councils, differently. FBI leadership was concerned about the Klan's more combustible violence, so instead of eliminating Southern chapters by turning them against each other with homosexual smear campaigns, they tended to infiltrate the Klan groups and route their numbers into the more stabilizing but equally racist Citizens Councils, where oppression of Black Southerners was achieved more quietly and thoroughly by white control of local political and economic offices.[12]

Gillian Frank has described how latter-day clusters of local white leaders—quite similar to Citizens Councils—backed Save Our Children. In Miami, Anita Bryant was merely the spokesperson for a more complex set of Florida Save Our Children political actors who were just as busy fighting desegregationist busing initiatives and the Equal Rights Amendment as they were gay rights. Mostly composed of professionals—politicians, ministers, and businesspeople—they carefully expressed their opposition to busing initiatives, as Frank shows, in "color blind" ways that shifted the racial discourse to parents' rights, child protectionism, and neighborhood schools. Their arguments were specious, and often retained language that invited fears around how racial and gendered mixing could lead to rape. This strategy enabled

Save Our Children to deploy their "color blind" messaging to build cross-racial coalitions with conservative churches while also referencing racist tropes familiar to the most overt white supremacists in their networks. For example, Frank traces how Save Our Children child protectionism drew on the model of the publicity around Florida governor Hayden Kirk's 1970 decision to stop forced busing, an act somewhat made possible by its wide base of supporters—composed of purportedly "race-neutral" *and* openly racist parents.[13] Instead of withholding inflammatory homophobic and racist rhetoric as FBI counterintelligence did, Save Our Children centered it, thereby courting regional white supremacists like the Klan into their base of supporters.

The choice of Bryant as a spokesperson, however, was strategic. That she was a white Christian mother, a gospel singer who couched her own homophobic positions in fundamentalist contexts, was important. Jennifer Dominique Jones has shown how, of the main US white supremacist groups, the Ku Klux Klan was most prone to melding their racism and homophobia within a Christian rhetorical context. Specifically, Jones points to the Klan's 1967 pamphlet *God Is the Author of Segregation*, where the "curse of Ham"—a biblical passage used to explain the origin of darker-skinned peoples as a curse from God—was interpreted as God's retaliation on Ham for committing the "crime" and "sin of sodomy."[14] This revision, as Jones shows, was recycled in Klan literature into the 1970s, linking Blackness, same-sex sex, and gender nonconformity even more intensely after the 1967 *Loving v. Virginia* case rendered miscegenation a less viable tool for smearing desegregationist causes.[15] Bryant's white Christian homophobia would have spoken most to 1970s Klan groups, frothing them into action. And act, they did.

The June 1977 victory of Save Our Children would not only lead to other cities overturning their antidiscrimination laws; it would also spark homophobic violence—from the stabbing of Robert Hillsborough in San Francisco ("Here's one for Anita!") to gay liberationist suicides in Miami and New Orleans. These tragedies in coastal Sun Belt cities are poorly remembered by historians of the New Right. However, even less attention has been paid to the Ozark dynamics of Save Our Children. Carol Mason, however, frames Anita Bryant's own ideology by her early political formation in Oklahoma.[16] Born in 1940, the future 1958 Miss Oklahoma grew up in a state that had quickly disavowed its recent socialist history and its racially diverse background. Mason cites the influence of George Benson, the Oklahoma-born president of Arkansas's Harding College. By 1941 Benson was an outspoken anti-communist, both nationally and regionally, who criticized area New Deal programs and advocated in their place an ideology based on his own trust in free-market enterprise, fundamentalist Christianity, and segregationist policies. Mason points out that, by 1957—just before Bryant won the Miss Oklahoma title—Benson had assumed the role of chancellor at Oklahoma Christian College, too, allowing him to influence the cultural and political minds of a generation of young people across the Arkansas-Oklahoma state line, which formed the lumbar region of the Ozarks. Mason makes the case that Bryant was an indirect product of Benson's conservative "curriculum." Although all the Mulberry House sissies came to the area from elsewhere, after the height of Benson's regional influence, his cultural legacy would have been palpable in the 1970s Ozarks. If Mason's implications are correct, then the Arkansas gay liberationists would have recognized that Bryant's homophobia was expressed in the register of a white Christian supremacist femininity scarily resonant in the Ozarks where they lived.

Bryant clearly represented a vigilantly guarded *white* femininity. Mason reminds us that Bryant openly shared with the media her intent to adopt specifically white children. Therefore, it was apparent to many (especially Southern) viewers that the children her campaign intended to save were decidedly white. Because they *saw* a woman committed to her racial purity while *hearing* her speak so desperately about sexual vulnerability, the racist Jim Crow fear of white women being raped by Black men, which led to so many Southern lynchings, was reanimated by Bryant's audiovisual rhetoric. This surely primed the more vigilante-minded white supremacists in the Save Our Children audience for action. When Bryant stoked fears about homosexual teachers' "recruiting" children, she both raised white supremacist fears about integrated classrooms *while* she reinforced Save Our Children propaganda that sought to implicate homosexuals as agents in widespread pedophilia rings. The word "recruit," then, was loaded, ushering in several possible things at once: wartime seduction, kidnapping, brainwashing, or rape. Such media rhetoric raised fears in order to compel voter support from a spectrum of white supremacists, but it also knowingly risked triggering Klan violence. Mulberry House would have seen Anita Bryant's spectacle as a largely gestural, but nevertheless clear, call to arms against liberationist homosexuals, women, *and* Blacks.

For this rallying cry to be raised by a mother must have given the sissies pause. Many in the wider faggot culture had discarded their fathers' names in favor of their mothers'. They had taken up goddess worship in the context of faggot witchcraft. However, as socialist feminist sissies they must have refined their own sense of motherhood—away from the white supremacist sense of mothering as parental control of pure children that were *hers*, like property. Instead, they would have emphasized the collectivized role of sissies'

Cover of *The Torch*, July 1977.

mother*ing* in order to break the cycle by which women are compelled into unrewarded reproductive labor. They would have resisted seeing the home as a site of enforced isolation from any and all difference. They would have redoubled their efforts to build a cross-class, cross-generational collective that would offer a functional alternative to Bryant's white supremacist motherhood. They would have continued their project of transforming the Ozark Food Co-op into an operation to feed the whole community and resist the imperialist system that weaponized food.

Jones's attentive analysis exposes how the Klan's Christian rhetoric, after 1967, increasingly linked and vilified queerness and Blackness. In the Ozarks that rhetoric would also include misinformation, triggering hyperbole and apocalyptic tropes to incite Klan violence. For example, *The Torch: The* REVOLUTIONARY *Newspaper of* WHITE *Christianity* was published in Bass, Arkansas, and edited by Thomas Arthur Robb, the current director (since 1989) of the Knights of the Ku Klux Klan. The issue pictured appeared one month after the June 1977 victory of the Save Our Children campaign, and the main headline echoes the campaign slogan. The bottom of the page recycles Bryant's claims that homosexuals "recruit" children, both echoing the midcentury Pied Piper motif and amplifying claims of violence without reference to evidence, only forceful authority: "Homosexual attacks on children are ... unleashing a whirlwind of tragedy that sometimes ends in the murder of the young victims, police warn." The placelessness of this alleged tragedy, instead of prompting its readers to question the story's validity, more likely triggered an apocalyptic sense that the threat was omnipresent, that it would come with the suddenness and devastation of a tornado. A photograph on the front page features three Los Angeles men in drag. The caption refers to them as "three degenerate queers" and prophetically asserts that "in the days to come they will be executed by law." On this Ozark front page we see Save Our Children homophobia wielded in the name of the Klan's white Christianity: While proclaiming the inevitability of homosexuals being executed *by law*, the writer uses unfounded accusations of child kidnapping, rape, prostitution, and murder in order to create an urgent, ambient fear that might generate reasons for vigilante violence to preempt a slower act of law.

Such tactics did not exclusively focus on homosexuals. Bethany Moreton has shared how, in the years after *Roe v. Wade*, conservative Christians linked homosexuality and abortion as outright assaults on the sacred, reproductive family unit. Therefore, when Jerry Falwell asked audiences to imagine dumpsters overflowing with the bodies of aborted babies, he introduced images of direct violence, pounding pulpit and pews with horror and urgency.[17] Such speech-acts demonstrate how liberated women came under the white supremacist fire of New Right assemblages like that of Save Our Children. As a popular gospel singer and the spokesperson for the campaign, Anita Bryant evangelistically orchestrated emotions in ways similar to would-be televangelists, priming them for violence.

It is easy for us to read such rhetoric as an empty gesture made for a dwindling audience. However, this was not altogether the case in the Ozarks of the late 1970s. It was an example of hate speech that led to concerted violence. Mason lists several specific instances of KKK support for Bryant in Texas, West Virginia, and Oklahoma, between June 1977 and January 1978. She further drives home this regional salience by reporting that, in a frightening reversal, the Klan began *recruiting* teenagers in Oklahoma City high schools to launch "a campaign of terror against homosexuals."[18] She further reports that the Associated Press ran a national story about Oklahoma Klan recruitment in January 1978 and that by that point the Klan had attracted over one hundred teens who staged a cross-burning and launched a letter-writing campaign to shut down homosexual establishments. In the spring 1978 issue of *RFD*, Mulberry House, signing their letter as the "Arkansas Sissies," would plead with the West Coast faggot editors to imagine "living in an area of the U$A where the KKK is very entrenched and has alot of support for its evils—the enslavement and or genocide of 3rd world people. . . . In Oklahoma City, the KKK is invading gay bars and beating people with baseball bats."[19]

Living in the midst of this Ozark geography possessed of a white Christian supremacist culture that predated its more recent hipbilly culture, Mulberry House would have watched the Ozark pot boil as soon as Save Our Children launched in January 1977. The more ordinary interpersonal and class-based tensions of that spring would have been intensified by their clenched anticipation of the coming violence. It is possible that the countercultural hipbilly networks of the region had even absorbed some of the white supremacist ideology already there. Over the summer of 1977, Mulberry House weathered threats of violence from co-op hippies, and they knew it was not purely homophobic but interwoven with racist and sexist associations, too. Williams recorded the summer's escalations in his journal.

In June, Williams wrote that "the Anita Bryant backlash is gaining momentum in F'ville, it seems. Third-hand rumor at warehouse meeting this morning has it that a petition is being circulated to purge the queens from the Co-op."[20] Then in July he commented, "It's coming down, kids. Anita has made queer-baiting the in sport among the self-righteous of all ages. Two years ago a young lawyer in the co-op said he had every right to discriminate against gay people.

A year ago an elderly co-op member resigned from the board, calling us 'moral problems.' Two weeks ago the current president of the Board said he hated queers & thought homosexuality was 'fucked' (his verb). And today a teenage stranger, as far as I know, threatened to rape me. It's coming down."[21]

Note how the lapsed time between each event shortened as the threat of violence became more imminent, physical. This entry is a textual document of a quickened pulse, an ensuing panic—accelerated by Save Our Children. The phrase "it's coming down" might even be said to evoke an apocalyptic tenor—something like the biblical ten plagues of Egypt—which Williams might have internalized from the white Christian supremacist rhetoric around him—like a tornado, an herbicide cloud, or a pestilence. And then, shortly after, he writes, "[An] incredibly homophobic flyer showed up in the Co-op yesterday. It accuses us of 'acting like storm troopers.' . . . And the three hets on the staff quit this week—the last today: a liberal Quaker woman who is scared of strong women. So now the Board . . . will have 'virtuous' excuse to fire the dykes & faggots . . . as well as the black woman & black man (Roger) hired this week. A purge of all undesirables: women, queers, & blacks."[22]

We here see the recognition of a linked anti-Black, anti-feminist, and anti-queer agenda that Jones notes in Klan rhetoric and Frank sees in Save Our Children literature. If after returning from the Wolf Creek conference, Mulberry House recommitted itself to its regional domestic liberation characterized by a socialist feminist collectivism that centered both internal consciousness-raising and regional food justice efforts, then they also, by their own admission, focused less on the witchcraft ritual that might have bonded them more closely as sissies or raised their militant fire in collective defense. Just four months after they returned from Oregon, their need for collective defense would be great, as the early 1977 Save Our Children campaign ignited a terror of white Christian supremacist violence in the Ozarks—a violence launched from entangled racism, sexism, and homophobia. While their interpersonal and class differences were certainly factors in their spring 1977 split into two houses, I contend that the mounting violence fomented a crisis of collective defense, making a forked path all the more necessary. Williams's personal journal most closely documents the details of that crisis.

Coming Down and Feeling Beyond: The Edges of Their Collective Defense

They launched a few small-scale, collective defense initiatives that overlapped with their 1977 co-op activism. Also in 1977, Mulberry House adopted a form of collective defense designed to provide housing for gay prisoners upon release. This was a special political focus for Williams. As the writer and publisher of the Koch Farm newsletter, he had connected with incarcerated subscribers and discovered, through sustained letter writing, that several of these prisoners were eager to discuss their same-sex sexuality. This correspondence had not only catalyzed his own identification as a gay liberationist before moving to Fayetteville; it also amplified the importance of prison abolition to liberationist politics. In 1976, with the influence of *Morning Due* and Faygele Ben Miriam, *RFD* had inaugurated a "Brothers Behind Bars" series, which in the spring 1977 issue featured its first letter from the bisexual founder of the George Jackson Brigade, Ed Mead.[23] Mead critiqued the Faggots & Class Struggle organizers for measuring their anti-racism by the number of "Third World" members at their event, arguing that the better measure would be how much anti-racist, abolitionist work they had realized. For the rest of the decade Mead would write for "Brothers Behind Bars"; far from using its letter exchange as a mere platform to network or to air critique, Mead leveraged the forum to organize queers across penal walls and to request supplies and advocate for prisoner organizations like Men Against Sexism.

In the season when Mead's *RFD* letter appeared, Mulberry House was arranging to welcome a gay prisoner named Kelly who was housed at the Cummins Correctional Unit on the opposite side of Arkansas—just outside Pine Bluff, in a Mississippi Delta geography.[24] Kelly said that he had read about the Fayetteville collective in *RFD*. In addition to a home, the sissies secured employment for him at the Green Warehouse, fulfilling a necessary condition of his parole. By June 1, 1977, Kelly's parole officer called Watson Street to let them know that he would phone to notify them when an officer would come to inspect the premises. The sissies began building a bed platform and hiding their skirts and beads. However, Lawson Street called two days later to say that Kelly had already, unexpectedly, been released and he was currently in Little Rock, hitchhiking to arrive in Fayetteville that night. The working-class sissies proposed that Hayes come stay with them indefinitely in order to make room for Kelly on Watson. It is likely that Watson Street was chosen as Kelly's address because (1) the working-class sissies deserved a break from the expectation that they give up living space, as referenced in Oglesby's conference critique, and (2) because queer abolitionist work was so important to Williams's gay liberationist formation.

Correspondence and cohabitation were quite different, though. Williams's heart sank upon hearing Lawson Street's proposal. He would miss Hayes, and from then on he was suspicious of Kelly. Not only had the field inspection not happened as arranged, but Kelly had evidently called from the Little Rock Downtown Motor Lodge, which was across the street from local FBI offices.[25] His stories about being imprisoned for "smoking pot and sucking cock" sounded suspicious to Williams, too.[26] Kelly also politically offended the feminist collectivist when he referred to women as "chicks" and enthused over girlie magazines and a seedy women's prison movie (*99 Women*).[27] Shocked, Williams wondered whether their newest housemate was actually gay, but worried far more about whether he might be a government plant. He would not be able to uproot those doubts. To escape trouble in San Francisco, Kelly said he went to Virginia, then Tennessee, and finally Arkansas, where drunk on tequila, he used a rusted-out shotgun to hold up an old man, before he was handily caught by the police in a delta swamp.[28] Kelly was clearly a storyteller, so it could be that he exaggerated some of his experiences either to mystify people or to hold sensitive truths closer to his chest. The theatrical Williams could hardly have faulted him for that; perhaps the older shoplifting femme and the young ex-convict were *too* much alike in this way to get along. It's likely, too, though, that the cultured, effeminist Williams simply did not know what to make of Kelly's working-class masculinity. Kelly may have felt like Williams interrogated him, too.

Kelly began staying at Watson Street less frequently. Sometimes he floated between there and the Lawson address. He started missing shifts at the warehouse. On June 22, $200 went missing from Watson Street, and Williams and Reich were convinced Kelly took it. The working-class sissies accused them of classism, but upon being reminded of Kelly's sexist language and porn habits, as well as his recent vanishing acts, they, too, seemed more willing to consider the possibility.[29] Not long after, Williams confronted Kelly himself, anxious that this imperfect first experience would prevent their ever hosting future prisoners.

Instead of spending all his time at either the Lawson or Watson house, Kelly, a white man, had been hanging out with a Black friend, Roger Williams. Mulberry House had entreated women at Sassafras to put Roger up at their Stone Hill House, and they had agreed. When Roger invited friends over, two of them made aggressive sexual advances on a young lesbian named Corinna, and Roger said that he had then made his friends leave. Sassafras was alarmed, though, and began to discuss the issue collectively. Immediately after that, Kelly and Roger were pulled over by Fayetteville police who fined the men $25 apiece for carrying concealed weapons (pocket knives) and an additional $64.50 for Roger, for a two-year-old traffic ticket. Williams sided with Roger and Kelly in this case, stating that when college wasn't in session, the local police turned to harassing others—hippies, queers, and Black people. However, he also pointedly admired the nice new rings on each man's hands, and when they said they had only found the jewelry, he was more convinced that Kelly had stolen the $200 at Watson Street.[30] The next day Kelly called from jail. He had been caught stealing from a couple of the stores in the Green Warehouse. Concerned, Williams took him cigarettes, consulted with his parole officer, and worked with the other sissies to convince the warehouse to give him his job back once he was released. Their first collective defense experiment had proven messier than first imagined.

In the meantime, Sassafras voted to kick Roger out. Williams fired off a letter asking them to reconsider.[31] He argued that they had not tried looking through Roger's eyes. They did not consider that a residence was a condition of his parole, so they were effectively resentencing him. He argued that Roger's friends were not in his control or his sole responsibility, and that Sassafras might consider supporting Roger with concrete ways for him to set boundaries with his friends. He angrily pointed out that, in the past, Sassafras had come to collective decisions about how to resolve issues, but in this case they didn't seem to actively involve their fellow resident, choosing to prioritize their own access to over five hundred acres at the expense of Roger's desperately needed single room. Williams closed by asking whether Sassafras continued to be a community or if they had suddenly chosen to act as landlords with the one Black man among them. This was complicated correspondence because, on the same day, he sent his old friend and Sassafras founder Diana Rivers a letter asking her to pay his dental bill and buy him bifocals because the collective couldn't afford these expenses. As he asked the favor, he pointed out her privilege, framing her resources as something she owed others like him, and then he begged her to "come out" from what he saw as her withdrawal from a politicized life. Williams danced a very fine personal-political line here.

He and Lawson Street also arranged to get Roger hired at the co-op in efforts to re-secure his parole. Reich blew up over Mulberry House's embroiling themselves further with Kelly and Roger.[32] Kelly had stolen from Reich's workplace *and* from the collective, yet they had somehow convinced the warehouse to re-employ him. Reich had, in the meantime, become closer with the women at Stone Hill House, and he was alarmed that Williams would ask them to reconsider their decision when it was Roger's friends who had come close to raping Corinna. To make matters worse, in Reich's eyes, Kelly was now asking Mulberry House to pay $250 for his bail when they couldn't even afford their own medical needs. According to Williams, Reich argued that they were getting in "too deep" with Kelly and Roger and that the collective was "headed for danger." Williams angrily skewered Reich for the liberalism that he had picked up from the racist counterculture surrounding them. Williams countered, "We are already in danger—political faggots in a state where homosexuality is against the law—& that the only way of getting 'out' of our involvement with Kelly & Roger is to drop them into the tender laps of capitalist law & racist hippies. I won't do that & I don't think the collective will either."[33] Reich flatly responded that he was "at odds" with the collective on this important issue.

Williams's own ideals were soon tested, though, when on July 25, amid proliferating gossip about stolen cash and food stamps, the straight, liberal leadership of the co-op put pressure on the sissies to call the police to arrest Roger, who was then sharing a rotation in the sissies' shift. Williams held his ground, refusing to do so, but he worried about his own racism, which led him to spend the day soothing the nerves of liberal management while awkwardly avoiding talking with Roger to understand *his* needs.[34] He must have felt the ironies in his recently pointing the finger at Sassafras for similar behavior. Shortly afterward the combined Mulberry House decided that they didn't have the $250 for Kelly's bail. Kelly promptly escaped jail anyway, around August 3, and disappeared.[35] After that, Williams reflected on just how tenuous his own political alliances could become when things grew difficult. He realized he needed to commit to careful consciousness-raising to address his own racism and classism.

It's important to remember that June and July were both the first months of Save Our Children's victory *and* when the threats from the co-op ramped up. The sissies themselves felt increasingly vulnerable to a hostility that threatened a range of homophobic retaliation—from dismissal from their job to outright physical violence. This came at a time when Mulberry House—but Williams in particular—felt increasingly unable to make good on their own values of extending collective defense to area Black people, the working class, and former inmates. At the co-op, the sissies raised their concerns about the spiking sexism, racism, and homophobia within the organization, and a mediation group was set up to address those issues. It was at those very meetings that things really escalated.

On August 15, Williams said that Diana Rivers publicly railed against the sissies and dykes, and he took his old friend's words very personally. He felt that the hippies abandoned them. The next night "Crazy John," a co-op member, publicly "threatened to murder the 'dicksuckers' & lesbians" which, Williams said, "brought home to me the fact that our very lives are in danger & there is no one we can count on for support but ourselves."[36] Four days later,

John cornered Williams and another new collectivist in the smokehouse and repeated his threat to murder them, and when they reported it to others, co-op colleagues dismissed it, telling the sissies to just leave. On August 25 someone posted another ominous flier. This time it "showed a T-shirt bearing the legend SAVE COAL—BURN A FAGGOT & implied that the shirts could be ordered from the Mulberry House Collective % the Ozark Food Co-Op."[37] Williams simply noted in his journal that by the end of the month, the sissies and dykes were fired.

The collective took steps to protect themselves. One of the women, a friend, was being stalked by a rapist in her neighborhood, so they set up a team, a watch, to help keep her safe. Once their lives were openly threatened, the sissies acquired a tear gas canister, which they carried with them whenever traveling at night.[38] Later that fall a prospective sissie visited from Kansas and reported that the arrangements were "very cloak and dagger," that Mulberry House insisted on meeting him at the university campus and took him blindfolded, in the back of a van, to their address—seriously fearful of possible violence from area bigots, government plants, and vigilantes alike. Given the heightened interpersonal emotions involved, some may now see their reactions as a social hysteria—understandable, but exaggerated. However, such an interpretation forgets the material consequences of the Save Our Children rhetoric in the white Christian supremacist ley lines of the Ozarks.

Where they lived, the violence that resulted from Save Our Children was not theoretical or mere media spectacle. Threats could not be taken as posturing. As old friends and hippie networks abandoned them, they increasingly looked for support at home. When they did so, they desperately hoped that they were really *there* for each other. Reviewing his own experience of their collective defense with Kelly and Roger, Williams realized just how underdeveloped his own alliances along class and racial lines actually were. Oglesby and Thornton suggested that the middle-class sissies work through the dynamics of their own racism. Reviewing his own responses to Kelly and Roger, Williams did wonder how much his brothers and sisters could rely on him in a pinch. They were up against a lot. Obviously, the New Right assemblage of powers that mobilized conservative politicians, businesspeople, fundamentalist families, and unabashed white supremacists worked like a well-oiled machine. It even neutralized the support of liberal, white, straight hippies, leaving Black people, liberated women, and homosexuals especially vulnerable. Could their small gay liberationist collective answer such a force? As that summer of 1977 came to a close, Williams felt less and less confident about safety within their houses, and about his own place within the collective.

In September he was briefly hopeful about the prospects of a reunited Mulberry House. The sissies continued to strategize with the two Black women who remained employed at the co-op, briefly imagining that a relocation of the co-op to a working-class Black neighborhood might be possible. The women shared, though, that co-op tensions were still mounting.[39] Mulberry House planned to formally withdraw any relationship with the co-op and stake its home economics on an expanded academic indexing service. Williams started teaching radical women and sissies how to do the job, and they planned a promotional flier to send to all those in his old publishing networks. Sissies also took to the road, attending Anita Bryant protests (in Joplin, Missouri) and rallies to support Dessie Woods, a Black Georgia woman arrested for killing her would-be rapist.[40] They began facing the broader Southeast, and in the process felt more gelled with each other.

Mulberry House did not reunite, though; they split further. Oglesby and Thornton moved to another house, on Nettlespit. Reich decided not to return to Watson, Lawson, *or* Nettlespit. He sought some autonomy from the sissies, with whom he increasingly disagreed. Williams worked to acknowledge that any romantic affair that might have existed between Hayes and himself was over. In mid-September he further worried that the sissies were "escaping into our own isolation." He began updating his journal roughly every week: "ten days? Nay—ten lifetimes at least, w/ each day a little death."[41] As their internal distances grew, Williams's mood darkened.

He returned to thoughts of ageism, speculating that, being mostly in their twenties, faggot revolutionaries didn't often extend their radical concerns to those older or younger than that. He began to wonder what a coalition of young and old might look like. That summer Bryant had said to the press, "I would rather my child be dead than Homosexual."[42] To some radical lesbian feminists and gay liberationists, her stark statement made it plain just how physically dangerous the New Right home was to queer children. At best, it was like a prison; at worst, it was a minefield, a torture. In some cases, collective defense was extended to queer runaways in need of a safe place to live. Yellowhammer opened their doors to a young lesbian.[43] The previous winter Williams had met a thirteen-year-old sissie named Randy in the food stamp office. As Randy was trying to come out of the closet, Williams spoke to him periodically over the phone and even agreed to meet Randy once at the movies on the university campus, with the rest of Mulberry House present—acutely aware of the moral panic around gay pedophilia. Williams worried that Randy was in danger at home from his homophobic parents, and he asked the others if they might take him in for his own protection. They waffled, declined. When

Randy's mother later eavesdropped on a phone conversation and angrily forbade Williams and Randy to ever communicate again, Williams wrote in October that "it was too late" and Mulberry House had failed to make good on their effeminist childcare idealism, putting him *and* Randy, the young and old, in danger.[44] He framed this, and their work with Kelly and Roger, as failures of collective defense.

He felt increasingly like the odd one out, with class and age returning as the decisive wedges. He wrote that "Red China crushes its queers & so do the Red Faggots—for that's what I am: a queer among the faggots," and that "All of us are caught in the bind of our revolutionary rhetoric & none of us can feel beyond our slogans to the love we have for each other."[45] He felt that he could only turn inward as the violence around them escalated, and he was no longer just exhausted; he was "*tired* & *scared*." Still, he wondered whether his most revolutionary act might be to streamline the collective by removing the "burden" of his own struggles, by "any easing of the pressure."[46]

On the next day, October 5, his journal entry recorded a sweet goodbye to each of the remaining sissies: Oglesby, Duane, David, Hayes, and Thornton (in that order). In each note, he made his peace. He signed the entry as "Dennis"—with swirling pen strokes that seemed to place his legally given name in florid parentheses. He left the journal open in the house and headed to a nearby park to sit underneath a shade tree and take, one at a time, forty-four lye pills—one for each year in his current age.[47] His age had alienated him in the house that he had helped to create, and now he would undo it. There was no bitterness left in him, though. He took comfort in imagining that his suicide might be its own revolutionary act, freeing the others to reunite in firmer solidarity—finally, a liberationist note fit for who he was. Back at Mulberry House, his journal waited for the others to come home—an effort to remain engaged with the collective, reaching across what some would consider the most intensely private act. Their collectivist commitment was stronger than a wedding band: No death could part them.

Part II

The Louisiana Sissies in Struggle

New Orleans, 1977–79

CHAPTER FOUR

A Bus Named Desire
Turning Melba'son in New Orleans

About a week later, Terry Flaherty—Thornton's outspoken college friend—got a desperate phone call in his Uptown New Orleans apartment. At the time, Terry was a graduate student in mathematics at the University of New Orleans, and his days were long. He taught during the day and then took his grad classes at night. Nick, his partner, led a similar life. He worked in a French Quarter restaurant while he studied languages, hoping that he could someday work with impoverished New Orleans immigrant populations who did not speak English. The two enjoyed little common time in their apartment, but they had managed an Ozarks getaway together just two months before, in August. They had reconnected with Thornton and met the rest of Mulberry House. So when Flaherty answered his phone in October, he would have recognized the voice on the other end. It was Dennis Williams.

The elder sissie hadn't completed his plans for suicide under that Arkansas tree after all. Through his tears, over the lye capsules, he began to review his decades of experience. It was then that he had a sudden vision of the death mask of King Tut looking back at him.[1] He remembered that the child-pharaoh's exhibit had a scheduled stop at the New Orleans Museum of Art. He picked himself up, convinced it was a sign. He left immediately, without returning to update his journal. Mulberry House would, he knew, assume he was dead. What he did next was hitch a ride with a trucker, a Black man eager to discuss revolution, who took him as far as Little Rock. From there, an older gay couple gave him a lift to Memphis. He then found one more trucker, who followed the Mississippi River south, taking him all the way to New Orleans in exchange for a blow job. His life took such a sharp turn that it was *akin* to death, something too haphazard to be called a rebirth—at least yet. Up to that fateful day in early October, his Ozark journal had been a record of his efforts to become a true sissie, a revolutionary who could live up to a new name he'd only begun to try out: *Melba'son*—after his mother rather than his father.[2] Like Faygele Ben Miriam. In the deeper south he would compose a sissie figure to match this new name. To do so, he would immerse himself in New Orleans.

After Terry hung up the phone, Nick came immediately, by the St. Charles streetcar, to pick Melba'son up and bring him back—about an hour's trip—to their place in Uptown. The couple said he could stay, no questions asked. Melba'son was thankful, but clear: He would not continue to lean on working-class faggots. He now realized he had needed to establish independence from Mulberry House. Knowing this, he would not simply transfer dependence onto Nick and Terry. He would get a job and his own place. And, he was set on *working-class* employment, not the clerical "shit jobs" he had resorted to in similar rough patches in his past. Nick suggested that they needed a dishwasher where he worked—the Mexican restaurant Tortilla Flats, located at 95 French Market Place, at Barracks Street. Melba'son took the job, and over the next month he began to improvise a stronger sissie figure for himself.

I will describe his process in two complex parts. For the first, I will offer a psychogeographical account of the ways Melba'son engaged New Orleans in the project of refiguring himself as a radical sissie. Psychogeographies describe the influence of a specific place on a person's psyche. As a method, psychogeography commonly harkens back to the nineteenth-century French *flâneur*, a literary figure who wandered the city—observing it closely, relating richly to the place, and reflecting on their symbiotic relationship—often in writing. Reading such documents can inform portraits of a generative meeting of place and person.[3] In late 1977 Melba'son surveyed his new city, on public transportation and on foot. Over the month of October he journaled how his immersive encounter with New Orleans *re*oriented him and thereby produced a "deeper-south" version of the radical sissie he went there to become. His journal shows this was intentional.

In the second part, I detail how Melba'son deepened his psychogeographic experience by adapting principles of faggot witchcraft, less for group ritual than for an accelerated personal, radical conversion. Specifically, I will show how he used sex magic, soul alignment, and an improvised street heresy as vehicles for his brassy nonbinary gender expression and his leftist, gay liberationist political position. He used witchcraft practices to valorize his sissie reorientation and to improvise a recognizable persona on French Quarter streets. If in this chapter I draw heavily on Melba'son's journal and telescope the historical narrative to a single month, and to a single sissie's experience, I do so with the express purpose of panning in to see what such histories have too often overlooked: a pivotal moment of a gay liberationist life that, recently exhausted, reignited itself, sustaining its politics elsewhere.

New Latitudes: The Psychogeography of
Melba'son's Reorientation in New Orleans

Melba'son's own account of his change of heart—the vision of King Tut's death mask and the coincidence of its New Orleans exhibition—only gestures at the fuller magnetism that drew him south. Looking back, his choice might strike us as nonchalant, a whim. It's important, though, to remember how Melba'son's redirection took place in the dire context of spiking New Right violence. We have already seen how the older sissie experienced his desperation as a gay liberationist's crisis of collective defense. He had just realized how unprepared Mulberry House was to offer safe passage across race, class, sex, and age lines, and how inadequate their gay liberationist re-entry program was for the newly freed Kelly. They were none of them safe in the face of the Ozarks' rippling white Christian supremacist violence. New Orleans, however, offered another educational opportunity to Melba'son.

He took some time—about a week—to contact Mulberry House and let them know he was okay. He spoke by phone to Hayes, and to Thornton. Each sissie carefully extended his concern, which touched him. He then exchanged letters with Thornton, explaining why he had left and what he was up to in New Orleans. Melba'son revisited how, early on, he and Thornton had slept with each other, how he had felt so inspired by the gay liberationist world that Thornton had opened to him, and how afterward, Melba'son had always felt a compunction to prepare his words carefully with the younger liberationist, wanting to impress him. It was clear that Thornton, and Oglesby, had so moved and influenced their fellow collectivist that he struggled with feeling he had disappointed them with his stubbornly middle-class ways. However, in his letter he assured Thornton that his departure for New Orleans was ultimately not a rift but a process of growing, and then working his way back to his working-class brothers. In fact, he commented that, as time passed, he felt even more a part of Mulberry House than he had when he was in Fayetteville. He floated the theory that, whereas San Francisco may be a good place for the working-class sissies to be, New Orleans was *the* laboratory for his fellow middle-class sissies to sharpen their revolutionary practice. Later addressing Thornton directly in his journal, Melba'son wrote, "It has something to do w/ my learning how to care about you."[4]

This language is important. We have already seen how Melba'son felt about Mulberry House's anger. He felt their righteousness ("slogans") had stymied their love for each other. Melba'son felt this was a masculinist failing, and from the distance of New Orleans he was determined to exercise solidarity in a register of care, rather than shared anger. He felt this project was more firmly feminist in that it resisted masculinist intellectual argument as the dominant mode of collectivization. Early in his New Orleans education he mused, "We need to be strong *and* compassionate. We must learn to struggle *with love*."[5] To connect across class divides, though, required some shared or similar experiences, and this was a key reason Melba'son took the dishwashing job at Tortilla Flats. His journal documents how he struggled to somatically reorient himself, at different geographic scales, to his new classed position.

Much of his time was spent over the Tortilla Flats sink, at the downriver corner of the French Quarter. As a Marxist, he trusted that a totally different mode of labor would slowly begin to shape him, inside and out. Plunging himself into washing dishes in late-1970s New Orleans, he paid careful attention to how Melba'son began to emerge from his everyday life around the restaurant. He paid attention to how he began to hold his body, when certain emotions surfaced, and the people he turned to or away from. His journal entry for October 10 captured how he felt that class, gender, and sexuality—within a US imperialist context—defined even the smallest of moments. More than anything, he developed a habit of shrinking from straight, masculine sociality: "The hardest part of my job is enduring the constant macho energy of the het cooks." Standing at the sinks, Melba'son always felt the cooks behind him, and the cooks' stoves faced out the window into Barracks. The tourists would walk by and ignore the kitchen workers, but the cooks would loudly express sexual interest, appraisals of passing women. Nick would even occasionally express a similar attraction to a passing man, performing "just like one of the boys." Melba'son's journal reflected deeply on how he felt physically and emotionally compressed by his position.

The cooks' ever-present performance drove Melba'son's shoulders tighter in over the sudsy dishwater. On October 10 he documented how he contracted further into himself, "brooding over Mulberry House as I furiously scrub off baked-on beans from fake pewter serving dishes (made in Taiwan & bearing the inscription GIVE US THIS DAY OUR DAILY BREAD—at $4.95 per serving!)." He felt a swelling fury because he felt so marginalized by the others' masculine, sexualized social interaction. Their macho world pressed in on him and forced his thoughts elsewhere. Hyper-aware of imperialist, capitalist food systems, his brooding expanded—as he washed each dish, again and again—to suggest the conditions in Taiwanese factories and the ironies of civic religion in the United States, on how he was compelled to work for survival in a system that exploited labor overseas while underwriting a Christian religious perspective. He experienced that imperialist world as anything but remote; it was so ubiquitous that it was intimate—passing through his hands with a daily rhythm—and it was paced to the loud sound of hypermasculine sexual bravado. He took careful note of how it felt to be so relentlessly shaped, in a blue-collar context, in a local political economy nested in national and global capitalist headwinds. It was also the stage from which he rehearsed a different relationship to Mulberry House. The above describes the pinched script from which he had to improvise some leftist sissie way of being. It also describes his method of doing so: a nearly autoethnographic attention to his body and social station, which he then treated to careful reflection in his journal.

In the Tortilla Flats dining area, as he maneuvered "thru the mob w/ huge trays of dirty dishes, it was interesting to note how people wld look the other way . . . rather than move. Cld it be that they didn't see me at all? Did my red apron & dirty dishes make me invisible? Eventually I began to feel like the *sudras* in India, who dare not let even their shadow fall across that of a Brahmin." In the very visible trappings of blue-collar work—the red apron, the dirty dishes, the trash—he ironically became invisible to the tourists. And this happened at the same time as he became even more alarmingly aware of his own body—the detergent burns on his arms, his exhausted mechanical movements. Interpersonally, he felt himself unplugging from the customers and the owner (Jim), throwing all his energy instead into getting the cooks and servers the utensils they needed. He never left at night before the kitchen was as clean as possible, so that the next day felt like a fresh start for his coworkers. He mused that he felt as proud of his ordered kitchen as he ever had been of his complex book indexes.

By his October 17 entry, he had rented an apartment from a coworker, at 3100 Rampart Street, at the corner of Clouet. It was small and in poor condition, but the rent was cheap. He agreed to paint the place himself. He noted that almost all of his neighbors were either Hispanic or Black, and he criticized himself for being unaware of whether the former were of Mexican, Puerto Rican, Cuban, or Central American origin. He noticed no racial tension directed toward him. In fact, he commented in his October 23 entry that Tortilla Flats coworkers who were also his neighbors helped him into his new home. Robert (a busser) gave him an old sofa bed. Dan (the head cook) helped Robert move the sofa over, and also gave Melba'son some kitchenware, towels, and a heater. Melba'son reflected on how these (apparently) straight men seemed unconcerned about his queerness, offering to help him when—aside from Nick—no gay men had pitched in. He began to question his now long-held suspicion of all straight men. He also commented that in New Orleans, downriver from the Quarter, it was impossible for him to assume that the proletariat was the white factory worker of classic Marxism. In his new world, manual and service labor were conducted by people of color.

In Fayetteville, Thornton and Oglesby had urged the middle-class sissies, particularly Melba'son, to develop their anti-racist perspective. Recognizing the de facto whiteness of his own solidarity, remembering how meager his support of Roger had been, Melba'son found in New Orleans a place that would, by everyday experience, deny him the easy presumption that any leftist revolutionary figure would simply be white. He sought wider context for this new perspective, too. At the end of his tenure in Arkansas, he not only had immersed himself in the writings of the anarchist Emma Goldman, but back in June he had also sought lessons in civil rights activist Julius Lester's autobiography. Between his anarchist and civil rights readings, Melba'son began to emphasize the importance of the individual in the collective, of finding a meaningful place for one's self in the revolution. In his June 18 journal entry, he summarized a lesson learned from Lester: "Each individual is unique & the revolutionary movement must have within it the space to allow each individual to express his uniqueness. If it does not, it is not revolutionary." He would increasingly resist the idea of diluting one's self in the name of unity.

He did not imagine his education along race and class lines would be a simple matter. A new city and a new job would never magically transform him. He set himself the homework of recording in his journal his bodily, emotional, and relational shifts so that raising his consciousness was more a matter of tuning his sensorium in a sociogeographic context that intimately challenged his white, middle-class presumptions. He often fretted that this just wasn't enough. In his October entries, he began to associate Oglesby's working-class feelings with "pain" and Thornton's with "anger," and he chastised himself for imagining that his New Orleans crash course in dishwashing could ever generate any intimacy with their affective states. Vexed, he asked whether his efforts were every bit as "liberal" and "foolish" as those of *Black Like Me* (1961) author John Howard Griffin, who had darkened his skin and traveled across the Deep South to understand Black people's experiences of racism.[6] In the end, Melba'son decided that, at worst, his leftist class analysis would be improved; however, as a sissie politically determined to build more intimate and less masculine solidarity, he was more focused on his capacity to care than on his intellect. His goal, as he had put it on October 8, was to learn to "struggle with love."

If this description emphasizes the discipline Melba'son put into his self-education, into his reorientation, we can imagine that the elder sissie also felt somewhat fit for it. First, leftist faggot politics—a significantly mobile culture—warned against the temptation to imagine that a single socialist strategy was fit for all places. At the Faggots & Class Struggle conference, attendees raised a critique of "city chauvinism," by which urban-dwelling faggots presumed they could simply transplant their political, sexual, and domestic cultures to Magdalen Farm.[7] Acutely aware of the need for nuanced rural–urban collective relations, Melba'son would have been at pains to thoughtfully navigate the uniqueness of his new city. Second, by drawing an analogy between his new classed invisibility at Tortilla Flats and the Indian *sudras*, Melba'son connected his prior travel journaling in diverse India—where locals had routinely queried him about racial relations between Blacks and whites in the States—to his psychogeographic practice in late-1970s New Orleans.

In some ways New Orleans invited Melba'son to extend, or indulge, that transnational analogy. It's a town that has been frequently defined by its exceptionalism. Because its landscape wore the fact that it was once a French *and* a Spanish city, in a Caribbean world so shaped by competing colonial plantation economies, the anti-imperialist sissie would have anticipated a town that exceeded its place in the United States. In fact, in the 1960s the city's cultural consonances extended along eastern latitudes as much as they faced a Caribbean deeper south. Because of that, Melba'son might have romantically intuited a 1970s New Orleans that made an easy home for the King Tut exhibit.

To the extent that Mardi Gras informs the mythos of the city, the krewe names of Thoth and Cleopatra alongside Zulu, Rex, Endymion, Bacchus, and Orpheus hint at the town's Hellenistic cultural orientation, defined by a meeting of African, Asian, and European cosmologies. This was a mystique New Orleans generated out of its cultural exceptionalism. *New Yorker* columnist A. J. Liebling, in his 1961 book about Louisiana politician Earl Long, observed that "New Orleans resembles Genoa or Marseilles, or Beirut or the Egyptian Alexandria more than it does New York. . . . Like Havana and Port-au-Prince, New Orleans is within the orbit of a Hellenistic world that never touched the North Atlantic. The Mediterranean, Caribbean, and Gulf of Mexico, form a homogenous, though interrupted, sea."[8] This quote was heavily recycled—enough to speak to local novelist John Kennedy Toole, who used it in *The Confederacy of Dunces*, which he drafted from Puerto Rico in 1963. The city cultivated associations, then, that were defined more by its particularly wide latitudes than by any secure national borders. In India, Melba'son had longed to visit Egypt, but his small stature and effeminacy made him worry about his safety. King Tut in New Orleans presented him, then, with an opportunity to face that mystique—both the city's and his own.

That cultural Hellenism had material roots, too. According to New Orleans historical geographer Richard Campanella, Greek sea merchants first came to the city in the colonial era and built a growing base in the Crescent City as part of the expanding cotton export industry. In the 1860s, Greek New Orleanians established the first known Eastern Orthodox church in the Western Hemisphere. Although not centralized in any particular neighborhood, Greek residents multiplied in the port town. Even as late as the 1970s, there was not only a newer orthodox church but also a knot of clubs in the French Quarter— between the 100 and 200 block of Decatur Street—pitched specifically for droves of visiting Greek sailors. Campanella tells us that the clubs had names like The Athenian Room and Zorba's. The little Greek district struggled when the city's shipping industry faltered, but it was still a known feature of the Quarter's nightlife through the 1970s and into the 1980s.[9] This historical landscape also explains the New Orleans film noir *Panic in the Streets* (1950), which built xenophobic suspense about port city contagions while presenting a French Quarter that was more peopled by Greeks, Armenians, and Turks than by French people. Further, Flaherty's partner Nick was himself of this Greek heritage, and he fascinated Melba'son—in fact, all of Mulberry House—with his good looks. The literary and cinephile Melba'son had, then, ample opportunity to associate New Orleans with the panhellenism that it then exuded, and the 1977 King Tut exhibit would have fit right into this city of wide latitudes.

This psychogeographic view of Melba'son's initial encounter with New Orleans brings to light his methods of sustaining his own gay liberation. First, we see Melba'son's recognition that faggot fire/anger was only a single component of the gay liberationist repertoire, one that could too easily eclipse other crucial elements. The Wolf Creek conference had sought to foreground a complementarity between struggle *and* unity, fire *and* moon, bread *and* roses. Melba'son sought out New Orleans as a laboratory for his "learning to care," as a classroom where he might learn to "struggle *with* love." Second, as Lavender Country observed on their queer country album, the imperialist system worked to dismantle solidarity and send us all "back in the closet, again"—that is, to isolate queer revolutionaries. Devastated by a crisis of collective defense, Melba'son first saw that crisis as a result of his personal failures or flaws, but shifted to interpret it as the real-world costs of isolation. Ultimately, then, his sissie response was to increase intimacy. This included reconnecting with Mulberry House as a way to link the houses as part of a potentially wider rural-urban network.

Third, as a white, middle-class sissie, he recognized that he had been systemically oriented away from cross-class and cross-racial connection. To begin unlearning a lifetime of segregated experience, he needed to reorient, by steeping himself in a sociogeographic context of nonwhite, working-class relations. He would have to rebuild his sensorium: relearn how to move, feel, and relate. Fourth, while he accepted the discipline this would take, he also knew better than to embrace a joyless education. After all, he had arguably already remade himself through a pedagogy of depression—as "The Mole." And this time, as Melba'son, he would not repress his own or New Orleans's panhellenistic mystique but, instead, he would test it against everyday, street-level reality. Wolf Creek spirituality had encouraged faggots to "remember forgotten dreams," and in October 1977 Melba'son intended to raise those dreams as tools for forging a radical sissie figure downriver from the Quarter.[10] The next step of his psychogeography would involve adapting faggot witchery to personal practice.

Must All the Reels Be Run Fast Forward?
The Faces of Melba'son's New Orleans Witchery

The faggot witchcraft at the previous year's Wolf Creek conference had primarily taken the form of group ritual. Essentially alone in a new city, Melba'son adapted faggot witchcraft as part of a solitary practice dedicated to accelerating his radical conversion into a more fully realized revolutionary sissie figure. If New Orleans was his laboratory for learning to care—especially in an anti-imperialist mode, across race and class lines—then witchery became his tool for a leftist personal alchemy. It was how he took the shape of his reorientation and performed it to cultivate a persona more recognizable to himself, and to French Quarter publics. From his journals we can see a number of facets through which he framed this practice, and it's important to contextualize each.

First, Melba'son knew the fragility of his mental state as he left Arkansas, and he took up the West Coast witchcraft practice of soul alignment, with a camp sensibility, in order to address his dissociative tendencies. This clearly reflected a gay liberationist antipsychiatry stance. Second, Melba'son used sex magic not only to construe soul alignment as an enactment of desire, but also as a way to root his new urban domestic liberation in New Orleans. Third, building on his erotic performance of soul alignment, he staged his radical conversion as a rebirth. This move not only built on *RFD*'s tradition of linking faggot witchcraft and effeminist/faggot reproductive labor, but it also allowed Melba'son to revitalize his commitments to youth liberation. Fourth, Melba'son contextualized his rural and leftist commitments by also referring to his rebirth as *fanshen*, a Chinese word associated with Mao's rural peasant revolution. Finally, through this combination of soul alignment and sex magic—framed as processes of rebirth and *fanshen*—Melba'son improvised a specifically leftist, nonbinary, French Quarter sissie persona that was performed as what I call a *street heresy* predicated on generating wild wonder.

Earlier, on October 4, Melba'son had compared his situation to that of anarchist Alexander Berkman, who had committed suicide in his sixties. He also imagined that his absence might streamline the efforts of the younger Mulberry House sissies, who were more on the same page with each other than they were with him. His suicide might leave them more focused. It might sharpen their collective spear. At times Melba'son also found power in what others might have seen as insanity. This is in line with some gay liberationists' antipsychiatry positions. They were convinced that what liberal psychologists might label "insane" was, in truth, simply their name for a person not functional within US imperialist mechanisms of social control. As we have seen, some *RFD* readers had embraced their mad tendencies as a decisive break with complicit models of sanity and with the imperialist state that compelled its subjects. Some readers of Melba'son's journal may be concerned by the fact he didn't merely adopt a new name but cultivated "Melba'son" as another full identity with whom "Dennis" often spoke out loud. He effectively split himself. "Dennis" was the person shaped by midcentury Cold War social conditions, the one who lived entirely within history, and "Melba'son" was the fully realized radical sissie that he might someday become. Over the summer of 1977, Melba'son's journal documented the intertwined experiences of both.

The relationship between Melba'son and Dennis wasn't described as a merely mental one; it was also embodied. For example, on July 16, Dennis wrote to Melba'son that "you wld slip in & out from under my skin occasionally, so gently that I didn't even know you were there until I opened my mouth & out wld come your voice." His splitting was not just a thought; it was also dialogic, audible, and haptic. If these dissociative moments concern us, it is important to recognize that his tendencies reflected certain cultural developments of the period, and that Melba'son explicitly referenced those cultural moments in his journal. By doing so, he let his future readers know that he was *not* unmoored. One way he did this was by invoking a feminist, camp identification with female leads in classic psychological thrillers as a way to navigate his own fearful situation. When Mulberry House consciousness-raising had become more formal than revolutionary, when it seemed to demand actual anguish as proof of change, Melba'son said, on June 11, "I beg[a]n to feel like Ingrid Bergman in *Gaslight*, but I'm learning to keep my feelings inside (it's called survival)." In casting himself as an Ozark Bergman, he dramatically bolstered his sense that even feminist consciousness-raising could operate with sexist dynamics: isolate the effeminate ones, cast doubts about every little thing, and lead them to question their reality. Drawing on the 1944 Hollywood film as a lesson, he began to protect his feelings, to insist on his own feminine reality. In this practice, he echoed what Vito Russo would demonstrate in *Celluloid Closet*: how lesbians and gay men campily read their own experiences into popular film narratives that mostly excluded them.[11] In this practice, he was again much like fellow sissie Jack Kendrick, who chose his own name, Carlotta, from a character in the Cukor movie *Dinner at Eight*.

Melba'son often reflected on his life in cinematic terms—as storylines with manipulable tempos, converging characters, and staged tensions and resolutions. He was acutely aware of how the regional fears produced by the Save Our Children campaign co-opted liberal rhetoric and rendered gay life at a fever-pitched pace. On June 3 he questioned, "O! have mercy, mercy, Sweet Gentle Goddess Mother! Why do you change the movie so often & must all the reels be run fast forward?" By October, he had hurled himself into New Orleans life. On October 15 he described his travels south as a cinematic integration: "Melba'son came to life on the trip down. It felt like Joann Woodward in *The Three Faces of Eve*: all our personalities being merged at once! . . . Our name is Dennis Melba'son." Acknowledging that Dennis and Melba'son were interdependent personalities—like Woodward's Eve White and Eve Black in the 1957 film—he managed to integrate them into a composite character (Dennis Melba'son) just as Eve had done by manifesting a coordinating personality in "Jane," a persona who knew both Eves' stories. A Southerner and former theater professional, Melba'son would have been aware that the film was based on a historical case of multiple personalities that was treated by doctors in Georgia. It is also possible that he questioned the religious and racial frames implicit in the pseudonyms used in a case study situated in the Jim Crow South. Unlike Eve, the suspicious Melba'son took no doctor. Instead, his reintegration was the product of a geographic shift. He may have imagined himself delving deeper into his own psychic space as he eluded death by relocating to a deeper south.

Ian Hacking has observed how diagnoses of multiple personality disorder resurfaced around 1970, when such explanations had been essentially abandoned by the medical world.[12] It is possible that *The Three Faces of Eve* helped to circulate social concern about the complex of symptoms, making their appearance more intelligible in unfolding Cold War contexts. Feeling like Joann Woodward in 1977, Melba'son was likely tuned in to the actress's appearance in the 1976 television movie *Sybil*, but this time as the psychiatrist rather than the patient, diagnosing another woman with multiple personality disorder. The TV movie was based on a book of the same name, published in 1973. Furthermore, the real-life Eve White, Chris Costner Sizemore, published a version of her story in her own words—*I'm Eve*—in early June 1977.

This suggests that Melba'son wasn't just campily referencing a Hollywood classic; instead he engaged a complicated 1970s popular discourse—between doctor and patient, journalist and auteur—about a highly contested psychological disorder that seemed to unevenly afflict women, to feature pseudonyms and performance as survival skills, and to engage the conventions of the thriller, often simultaneously evoking mental disintegration and demonic possession. In referencing this popular discourse, he fleshed out his suspicion of the psychiatric profession. The doctors had amassed a sexist track record, after all, and psychiatry had only shifted its pathologizing stance on homosexuality four years prior. Given the obvious absence of a caring science, Melba'son would improvise his own answers. So, in brash contrast to Sizemore, who in newfound health said, "I'm Eve," the newly integrated Dennis Melba'son, like a biblical Legion, insistently referred to himself in the plural, asserting "*Our* name is. . . ." He sacrilegiously embraced a multiple demonic form, rather than a "healthily" monotheistic one.

There was a similar precedent in West Coast witchcraft practice. Both Starhawk's Reclaiming Witchcraft and the Anderson Feri witchcraft tradition which preceded it described the Self as composed of a *Triple Soul*, which roughly approximates the id, ego, and superego, but which is understood as a convening of autonomous agents to orchestrate what we take as a single person. In these witchcraft lines, *alignment* is the goal, not *integration*, and what Freudians might call the *superego* is sometimes referred to as the *Holy Daemon*.[13] This mirrors Melba'son's claims to *merge* his three selves while still holding to a plural, first-person pronoun.

Melba'son journaled on October 23 that Nick had brought him charms to place in his new Rampart apartment—to remove any "alien spirits." Melba'son followed Nick's instructions but then improvised a solo sex magic ritual, dedicating his "sacred sexuality" to "the Goddess" and declaring his home "sanctified faggot space." Doing so both pointed back to the erotic register of his soul alignment and signaled how he wished to find a place for his practice in New Orleans. Back in the Ozarks, he'd imagined not only that his own souls might enter sexual congress with each other, but that they might erotically engage with others' multiple selves. For example, on July 3 he had fantasized that both Dennis *and* Melba'son might enter an erotic relationship with Hayes: "I want to join you—a *ménage à trois* as 'twere. Perhaps if Dean's sissy learns to trust us, we can make it à *quatre*." In Melba'son's collectivist vision, split spirits entered an intimacy with each other, which was necessary to grow their shared revolutionary potential over time. And the primary relationship had to be between one's inherited historical self and one's independent, in-progress revolutionary self.

Such arcane notions wouldn't have been completely strange in 1970s New Orleans. The city had developed its own magical culture—smaller and less organized possibly than in the Bay Area, but pronounced nonetheless. Anne Rice had published *Interview with the Vampire* only the year before, so the city's courtship with gay vampires was still new. Of course, the legend of Marie Laveau and rumors of voodoo cast the longest shadow. Tourists came to see Laveau's house and pay their respects by marking her grave. In the 1970s other locals began to capitalize on this reputation for voodoo, conjure, and hoodoo. Since the release of his 1968 album *Gris Gris*, New Orleans-born musician Dr. John had infused his musical style and performance with his hometown's voodoo. In 1972 Charles Gandolfo opened the Historic Voodoo Museum in the Quarter. With a stronger emphasis on ceremonial magic, Mary Oneida Toups established the first of her two witchcraft stores in the Quarter in 1970. In 1972 she also legally registered her coven with the state of Louisiana. Although he didn't mention these establishments in his journal, it is very possible that Melba'son would have passed either Toups's or Gandolfo's shops as he commuted across the Quarter to work on Barracks. Spell craft was then a storefront feature of Vieux Carré street life.

If he came to New Orleans seeking a curriculum for "learning to care," as October progressed, as he deepened his sex magic practice and exercised his erotic soul alignment, *desire* became his watchword. If he courted the city's mystique, he did so with the purpose of refining it against his experience of the city as it was. When staying with Nick and Terry, he had traveled nearly an hour by the St. Charles streetcar to reach the Quarter, at Canal Street. From there, he walked a brisk thirty minutes to Tortilla Flats, to work. Spending so much time on the streetcar, listening to its clacking movement, he often imagined himself transported into Tennessee Williams's *A Streetcar Named Desire*. But then he had to traverse the garish Quarter that had supplanted Williams's bohemian one. The streets along Bourbon teemed with tourists—families and drunken revelers—and boomed with rock music and the cries of merchants selling cheap souvenirs. At work, as he washed dishes, he could look out the kitchen window to see the literal Streetcar Named Desire: now only an old retired car parked near Barracks Street, with the bright word "DESIRE" emblazoned on its headlamp.

When he moved to his Rampart apartment, and got off work late at night, he took the *bus* named "FLORIDA/DESIRE" twenty minutes to his home, as he noted in his October 31 journal entry, and he realized that the destination of *this* desire lay deeper in the Ninth Ward than his new apartment even, out to the intersection of Desire Street and Florida Avenue. Whether he knew it or not, this bus named *Desire* went to where, seven years earlier, local police rained bullets into the New Orleans Black Panther headquarters.[14] He couldn't help but reflect on how politics and sex, place and history had changed as he traveled. All signs pointed to a local desire that enchanted his romantic, theatrical side, but also eluded him as a newcomer, as a white middle-class sissie. His literary streetcar had gone kaput, and the newer, but more mundane, bus—which still bore the name of a nostalgic longing—took him toward a more recent violence against Black radical culture that was rarely spoken of by the Quarter's tour guides. Melba'son followed mystique to meet hard local realities.

Further, if he'd imagined a sexual liberation for himself in the libertine city, that is not what he found. He spent much time pining for Hayes, and his manual labor and long hours often canceled his libido and left him seeking sleep more than anything else. He also identified with few in the quite visible gay culture of the area, referring to most—like his boss, Jim—as "gaymen": homosexuals mostly interested in upward mobility or partying, with only a vaguely liberal political bent. His cross-racial relationships were mostly confined to routine exchanges with his coworkers or neighbors. It is telling that, when he did hazard a trip to a local bathhouse, he documented, on October 22, mixed results. He was angry about the exorbitant price for an overnight room and about the ubiquitous hypermasculine "cock rock" that they piped into the air, but he felt it was a gift to share a tender, unexpected sexual experience with a charming "Black sissie" who "asked if I wanted any company." With no further words, they "*made love.*" The bathhouse afforded him a brief, cross-racial moment of interpersonal tenderness, but Melba'son at this point seemed incapable of imagining how to transform the graced moment into a more durable solidarity, as he continued to describe New Orleans as a place with very little sissie revolutionary potential.

He didn't fully trust his judgment. After all, he was starting over. Because he had narrowly avoided death, he saw his efforts to align his souls as a process of rebirth. He conceived the erotic meeting of Dennis and Melba'son as a means to give birth to the fused Dennis Melba'son, a practically realized radical sissie—but one who was still only a child. Of course, this position reflected socialist feminist and effeminist commitments to share reproductive labor, to practice a queer mothering. In this case, though, Dennis Melba'son's aligned souls had to mother themselves. This form of soul alignment was also not a fully original one, as reader-writers in early *RFD* had poetically described multiple selves whose psychic meeting—internally or externally—also reproduced new entities.[15] We can see how Melba'son quite consciously framed himself this way, especially upon arriving in New Orleans.

On October 15 he reflected, "We [Dennis Melba'son] came into the world wearing only the clothes we were born in, lugging a pink {symbol} security blanket & a leaky {symbol?} plastic water jug." This is how he described himself in the moments just after the trucker dropped him off in New Orleans. He gently poked fun at himself—a middle-aged man standing on the corner of a New Orleans street, squinting (he'd left his glasses in Arkansas), openly femme, and admittedly lost. When New Orleanians asked him why he left Arkansas, he replied, "I ran away from home," following that with "That's the truth!"—in the voice of Lily Tomlin's Edith Ann. He contended that, at Mulberry House, he had begun to feel *so* old that he had to leave "to learn how to cross the street again on my own." In the wake of Save Our Children, Melba'son played at feeling youthful, at seeing the world with fresh wonder and comic irony, rather than with righteousness and certitude. And we know, from the color of his baby blanket, that the eyes through which he chose to see were those of an effeminate child, a sissie.

It is important to remember the Save Our Children context. Bryant's campaign defined children by their vulnerability, their susceptibility to suggestion, their capacity to be led. In the witchy context of Melba'son's own *re*birth, he did perform a temporary innocence in need of experience, but he did *not* depict youth as powerless or vulnerable. Rather, the figure that oversaw his *re*birth was King Tut. In the child protectionist context of Save Our Children, to imagine a child as a ruler—rather than as recruitable property—required a radical shift from what US families then took as the natural order of things. At the very least, this shift required seeing autonomy, an independent agency, in the eyes of young people like Randy, the boy whose liberation had so moved Melba'son back in Arkansas. Imagining a boy-king demanded a long hard look at how the New Right's white supremacist model of parenthood rendered children, elders, and childless queers as manipulable classes. And it allowed gay liberationists to see the New Right family model as *un*natural—a twentieth-century white construct designed to benefit a precious few. In his regal African personage, King Tut defied the reigning paternalistic ideology of the Save Our Children campaign. In New Orleans, Melba'son framed his rebirth not only as the occasion for an accelerated, radical education but also as a way to tap into the energy of youth liberation.

Melba'son, who had warned other queers off the notion that gay liberation necessitated a move to the (despotic) city, was also eager not to frame his own narrative in that way. Instead he doubled down on the rural leftist aspect of his rebirth, by calling it *fanshen*. On October 7 he explained that his radical conversion was an effort to "shorten the ten years that Chairperson Mao says it takes for 'intellectuals' like me to *fanshen*." Thornton had recommended William H. Hinton's 1966 book *Fanshen*, which documented the author's experiences with Maoist land reform in rural China. Although Melba'son didn't mention reading it before leaving Arkansas, he did increasingly identify with Maoism and cultural revolution. He framed his metamorphosis as an ongoing response to Thornton, and he took the book's title, *Fanshen*, as the theme of his Crescent City experience. Interestingly, *fanshen* had multiple meanings: (1) to turn oneself over from a lying position, (2) to liberate oneself, and (3) in the context of Maoist land reform, to throw off the oppression of the landlord. Mao's strategy involved relocating urban intellectuals to the countryside to facilitate peasant revolution. Evoking agrarian metaphors, *fanshen* nicely summed up Melba'son's project of cultivating his radical sissie side, turning himself over—as if in soil. That agrarian metaphor also allowed him to continue to see himself as a rural personality, even in the city, to stage a similar geographical shift as a means to infuse his intellectual perspective with care, and to understand his own socialist reorientation to prioritize a cross-racial solidarity not so available in the Ozarks. His *fanshen* was sped up, and reversed—from country to city, but still conducted in the name of a rurally oriented revolution anchored to the possibility of a faerie farm back in Arkansas.[16]

The complexity of Melba'son's witchy rebirth is clear in the several facets through which he presented it—as sex magic, as soul alignment, as antipsychiatric self-care, as an education in cross-racial and cross-class care/desire, as queer mothering, as youth liberation, and as *fanshen*. The sissie figure that ultimately emerged from this witchery was firmly committed to wearing all that complexity on his sleeve. At the same time, his nonbinary gender expression—in a leftist, socialist feminist register—was consistent. It made a marked impression on those he worked with and on those he passed on French Quarter streets. He recorded in his journal entry for October 10 that when introducing him to the rest of the kitchen at Tortilla Flats, his boss Jim had said, "Give this man some work!" The diminutive but vocal Melba'son didn't miss a beat, telling them all that he *wasn't* a man, but a sissie. The room laughed appreciatively.

This was a different reception than he would've gotten at the Ozark Food Co-op. He wrote to Mulberry House that his radical education required him to be as forward about his gender as possible. When he learned to avoid Bourbon to instead skirt the Quarter by Royal Street, he encountered shops with little baubles in the windows. He began to sport two earrings, carried a purse, and wore Maoist red stars. He highlighted his effeminacy but didn't attempt to pass as a woman, which confused many tourists, especially their children, who would bluntly ask him, "Are you a man or a woman?" Melba'son developed a standard reply, with which he sought to amplify their sense of wonder: "I am neither. I am a . . . sissie!" He enjoyed it when he heard stories whispered—in the service industry or from the gay regulars—about the Quarter's outlandish red-starred sissie. Such rumors made the sissie Melba'son socially discernible.

Having come from a college town and farm setting, Melba'son had to adapt to the Quarter streets as a new kind of stage for the figure he was then improvising. Specifically, his femme gender nonconformity was both linked to and distinct from the "proud street queens" who were already familiar there. Marlon B. Ross, using James Baldwin as his case study, describes how the street has shaped a certain complex Black "sissy liminality." First, Ross describes how, following the Great Migration and World War II, the urban-center streets of many US cities became racialized as Black, situated in or near underserved and over-policed Black neighborhoods increasingly profiled as "ghettoes." These places were often as intensely gendered and sexualized as they were racialized, and Ross explains how one of its common figures was the Black "swish"—a figure who unapologetically expressed their femme gender nonconformity in answer to the hyper-scrutiny experienced on those city streets. Second, in this period churches became a more visible presence in such areas, through storefront congregations and street ministries. Ross explains that, especially in the case of Baldwin's Harlem, these churches both offered the sissy "overt inclusion as a sign of its [own] saving graces" and also brought that sissy into the street where his proximity, and possible similarity, to the swish invited all manner of "commensurate anxieties, temptations, and fulfillments."[17] For the Black sissy brought into the streets by the work of the church, the ambient possibility of his being mistaken for a swish was a performative minefield *and* wonderland. Ross further suggests that, post-Stonewall, "it may be that the term 'swish' indicates a heightened social consciousness of the claim to occupy public space being made by queer men in the televisual era—a consciousness particularly raised among black urban men as openly gay men, both black and white, begin more militantly to occupy 'the street' in areas within or bordering the black ghettos after World War II."[18]

Melba'son clearly enters the street in this latter period, and we know that, as a white, middle-class, gay liberationist sissie, he was not brought there by the church. It is helpful, though, to consider the *possibility*, given that gay liberationist religious figures *did* minister in these districts where gay bar patrons, queer sex workers, and gender-nonconforming people shared the streets. Kevin Mumford's profile of the Milwaukee-based Catholic priest Brother Grant-Michael Fitzgerald presents a figure who articulated a specifically "Black gay liberation" through his clerical uniform, his biblical reframing of homosexuality as a gift, and his main pastoral practice working with urban youth.[19] That Fitzgerald achieved this *within* the Catholic Church is remarkable. Joey Plaster has given us portraits of gay liberationists who "established their own congregations in tenderloin districts; claimed religious titles; ordained street kids, themselves, and others; and engaged in a politics of mutual aid and care."[20] These were figures whose religious affiliations were less formal, often stemming from the opportunities suggested by earlier renegade denominations or splinter churches—like the Old Catholics—but who still adapted traditional clerical clothing and titles (often masculine), Christian ritual, and scriptural rhetoric to address the needs of queer street kids. Of Plaster's profiles, the one I find most helpful in contextualizing Melba'son's street sissie figuration is Sylvia Rivera's sainthood.

As "street transvestites," neither Rivera nor Marsha P. Johnson was likely to don the priest's collar or adopt a title like "Father" or "Brother," as Plaster shows other street ministers to do. Similarly, formal ordination in a church—traditional or splinter—would have been difficult and/or ill-fitting. Plaster describes in Rivera, however, a figure who is no less religious, just because her practice was more varied or syncretized than formal. He calls attention to Rivera's early and ongoing Santerian belief, being of Puerto Rican and Venezuelan lineage; her Pentecostal christening as "Sylvia;" and the STAR House custom of keeping an altar and saying prayers. He also holds it as significant that, in the 2010s, New York's Metropolitan Community Church memorialized her as a saint.[21] GAA cofounder Arthur Bell's description of Sylvia when he knew her best—in late 1970—confirms Plaster's: "[S]he's forthright about [her] homosexuality, and being gay, religious, and promiscuous are all mixed up and intertwined together. Of religion, [Sylvia], who is a Catholic, says, 'I have my own way of doing things. I have an altar at home and light candles and say prayers. Sometimes I promise my saints something, and then I try to follow through. I'm not a hypocrite and don't go to church.'"[22]

Similarly, in the documentary *Pay It No Mind*, STAR House cofounder Marsha P. Johnson is remembered by her friends as a "saint." They mention her impromptu visits to churches to kneel before their various altars, her habit of always giving to others even when she had little herself, her sleeping under the flower vendor stalls to be given flowers to halo her hair, and her familiar, sunny and welcoming street presence.[23] Like Rivera, Johnson is now most often associated with angry Stonewall resistance, and sometimes for her work with STAR House, but less so as a "saint" with a religious and performance background that surely informed how she composed a striking, impactful femme street figure.

That Rivera and Johnson were considered saints is relevant here for a couple of reasons. First, it is crucial to remember that Melba'son's sissie figure stemmed from a New York City faggot genealogy with an often-conflicted orientation both to queens' femme embodiment and to their street habitus. Many of GLF-NY's revolutionaries had little prior experience with everyday gay urban culture and its sites—like streets, piers, and bars—and the Flaming Faggots/Effeminists had explicitly oriented themselves on the basis of their radical feminist rejection of the gay femme and her haunts. Despite the fact that they successfully pamphleted on Christopher Street, inspiring *Fag Rag*'s genesis, they vocally oriented themselves inward rather than outward, tending to their domestic and psychic interiors, facing away from queens like Rivera and Johnson. There is an acute irony to this move, given that STAR House was itself a nearby collective whose attention was carefully attuned to the relationship between street and house, and who often conducted that work in a spiritual mode. Because of this, I find it especially important to frame Melba'son's rebirth on French Quarter streets as an opportunity for a latter-day faggot figuration—especially one expressly interested in cross-racial and cross-class connection—to reorient in relation to the street queen, the swish, and those who would be increasingly identified as transgender.

Second, Ross's description of "sissy liminality" and Plaster's of Rivera's sainthood suggests a generative lens through which to view Melba'son and the collective that would form out of his rebirth in New Orleans. Melba'son's sissie liminality did not derive, like Baldwin's, from being brought by the church to the swish's street. Melba'son also did not, like Plaster's more traditional street church ministers, take up the collar and start his own highly improvised Christian church. Melba'son did, however, like Rivera, undergo a radical conversion, take up a femme name, and embody a non-normative gender expression. Although Melba'son did not frequent French Quarter storefront churches, as Ross describes, it is possible that the Arkansas sissie felt his faggot witchcraft practice echoed in the new witchcraft shops opened only years before in the Quarter. Like Rivera and Johnson, Melba'son drew from a performance background to refine a concerted gender expression pitched for the streets where they spent so much of their time.

I propose that the figure Melba'son cut hinged on several key features. First, unresolved complexity, or multiplicity, was an overarching value. His witchy soul alignment practice did not integrate his three souls but aligned them, or orchestrated them. Similarly, his nonbinary gender expression vocally rejected the choice of "woman" *or* "man" by proposing the sissie as a third option. In practice, this meant foregrounding both femme and masculine features so that no unified gender presentation was ever arrived at, also lending the sissie look an air of the unfinished, the always-in-process. This unresolved complexity also reflected collectivist praxis. These gay liberationists were primarily concerned with the many ways they could come together to form a house.[24] Second, as we will see, the sissie figure rehearsed a disavowal of the man/woman choice as a response primarily delivered to children, especially tourist children who openly stared on French Quarter streets. Melba'son hoped this answer would evoke wonder, endless possibility, proliferating questions—rather than foreclosed answers. Underlying this mission was a deeply rooted faith in youth liberation. Third, as a sissie who wore red stars instead of clerical collars, Melba'son also projected a leftism that defied a political binarism between New Right (white Christian supremacist) homophobia and gay-friendly liberalism. If the Cold War period had conducted witch hunts for communists and homosexuals, then Melba'son's sissie strove to embody all three at once: witch, leftist, and queer. In doing so, Melba'son perhaps reimagined himself as more heretic than saint.

At the end of the month, Hayes came to visit from Arkansas, and the two shared a magical All Hallow's Eve. In his October 31 journal entry, Melba'son took care not to belittle the sacred day "when worshippers of the Great Mother came together to do her homage," and looking back, from November 8, he vowed not to take potshots at the commercial aspects of "our festival, which the patriarchy calls Halloween." He and Hayes joined Nick and Terry Uptown to have dinner and celebrate. The next day, he and Hayes went with Nick to (finally) see the King Tut exhibit.

Of that experience, Melba'son wrote, "It came as close to being a mystical experience as one can have in the midst of a mob of [middle-class] tourists."

He was disappointed that certain items that he had followed closely—an Anubis figure, for example—weren't on display. He said, though, that the statue of Selket—the scorpion goddess who guarded royalty's canopic jars in the tomb—was deeply moving, conveying the sacred importance of death, *and* rebirth, in Egyptian cosmology. He and Hayes did not stay together as they toured the exhibit. They circled parallel items, their jaws dropped open in awe, moving through the recreated Egyptian world by tandem routes. It was surprising, then, when they suddenly "came together before the great Sissie face of Tutankhamun." Melba'son fully recognized the boy-king *as* a sissie at that moment. Hayes and he fell into each other's arms, tearful. It felt as if some golden hands had guided them back to each other. Later they would process it all at Cafe Du Monde, taking mescaline that Melba'son had saved for the occasion. The two were convinced by the crescendo of their experiences that New Orleans *was* the right place for them to morph from middle-class to revolutionary sissies—but as brothers, not lovers. Hayes *would* join Melba'son in the Crescent City, along with two others. And a new sissie collective, with strong connections back to Mulberry House, would form on the heels of the elder sissie's transformative October.

CHAPTER FIVE

Sissie Majik

From Sissystories of Terror to an Unqueer Street Pedagogy

Hayes did move down to New Orleans, but Oglesby and Thornton did *not* relocate to the Bay Area. Their critique of West Coast faggots' whiteness and regional chauvinism appeared in the Spring 1978 issue of *RFD*, so while the San Francisco faggot culture of socialist feminism appealed to them, they were concerned about West Coast faggots' increasing white insularity. The "Arkansas Sissies" were not alone in this assessment. In the same issue, a reader writing from "Sticks, Minnesota," as "Arnold J. Cornbelt," drew an animal-like figure labeled "San Francisco Scene" that begged farmers to "Feed Me!" Cornbelt further referred to Bay Area faggot politics as "WHITE WEST COAST GARABAGE [sic]."[1] A couple of pages earlier, a Minneapolis writer fumed that his submission had never been published, wondering aloud whether it wasn't "'artsie fartsie' enough," or whether "it was because if faggots don't live on the 'coast' they must not be real."[2] He further expressed doubt about the working-class experience of the editors. The wider national faggot network that had helped to anchor *RFD* on the West Coast chafed at how its young editors figured the Bay Area not as a node in that circuit but as its very nucleus. They argued that this shift replaced *community* with *scene*, whitewashed the wider faggot experience, and forgot how mobile the Bay Area faggot culture really was. The Arkansas Sissies did not see themselves in such a narrowing of faggot politics and decided to stay in the Ozarks to work toward realizing their faerie farm in Madison County.

In early 1978, Hayes and Melba'son focused on New Orleans as the place where middle-class sissies could speed *fanshen*: steep themselves in working-class labor in a city with a nonwhite proletariat as they learned *how* to care across race and class lines. The pair decided to call their new collective the Louisiana Sissies in Struggle, or LaSIS. In October 1977 Williams entered a chrysalis stage resulting in a subjective transformation to become "Dennis Melba'son"—an integration composed of his lived experience *and* his revolutionary vision. As a spiritual practice, faggot politics involved—for many, at least—a very personal, radical conversion marked by taking a new name. This was also a component of what LaSIS would refer to as "sissie majik."[3] Although we don't have accounts of their conversions, we can imagine that some similar experience informed John Singer's transition to Faygele Ben Miriam and Arthur Evans's to the Red Queen. Oglesby and Thornton—although they might have considered it—never adopted new names; they mostly went by their given ones. The core members of LaSIS, on the other hand, would all assume new sissie identities.

Hayes's name had been in beta since his Mulberry House days. In the summer of 1977, in a free-writing exercise, he had jotted the word *timid*—a quality commonly attributed to him—but replaced the initial *t* with a *d*, recognizing that his and all his brothers' given names started with a *d*. From this experiment, *Dimid* was born. He remembers realizing how he wanted to amplify his role as a good listener, and how—unlike straight men who entered rooms and took up space, demanding attention—he wanted to walk "into a room and [become] open ... [be] receptive." It wasn't until he joined Melba'son in New Orleans in spring 1978 that he began to use the name with others.

Two more sissies joined Dimid and Melba'son, in May 1978, forming the four core members of LaSIS. One of these, surprisingly, was Robert Reich. Given how bitterly Melba'son treated Reich back in Arkansas, how he cast him as hopelessly liberal, and how painful their triangulation with Hayes had been, it's difficult to imagine Reich's breezily assuming a place in LaSIS less than a year later. Reich had lived in New Orleans before, though, working with the lesbian book collective Atlantis. His familiarity with the lesbian feminist networks of the city would prove invaluable. Although we know the least about his personal transformation, once in New Orleans he no longer went by Bob Reich but by his newly adopted name, Stacy Brotherlover. This moniker reflected the radically horizontal, gay liberationist intimacy that Melba'son had argued for since the inception of Mulberry House. This indicates that he and his former Watson Street roommates were dedicated to struggling together toward similar revolutionary goals.

Stacy came to New Orleans with a new lover. David Speakman had been born in Kansas City in 1954, but moved to Salt Lake City as a young child before his family resettled back in Kansas, in Lawrence, in 1964. He remembers his young childhood in the Mormon city as particularly difficult, setting a lasting sense of himself as an outsider. However, he later appreciated that "dark gift of bigotry" because it taught him to cultivate empathy as the cornerstone of his own politics.[4] As a teenager, he read about Stonewall in a newspaper in his school library and thereafter shed any sense that he was a monster. He took work as a server in the Lawrence hippie restaurant Sister Kettle, which was supplied by the Fayetteville health food warehouse Stacy worked for. On his time off, he hitchhiked with a friend. In mid-1977 they found themselves in Eureka Springs and they stopped by Fayetteville on their way back home. On the University of Arkansas campus, they were spotted by Oglesby and Thornton, who struck up a conversation. Curious about the gay liberationist collective, Speakman and his friend agreed to be blindfolded and transported in the back of a van to Mulberry House, where they also met Melba'son and Reich (Stacy).

Speakman hit it off instantly with the latter. They shared a passion for healthy food, but Speakman also appreciated Reich's wide education and his friendly relatability outside of collectivist circles. The two struck up a correspondence, and Reich invited Speakman to move into his apartment with him, as he was then no longer interested in living with the remaining Mulberry House collectivists. On January 1, 1978, Speakman did just that, becoming part of the Arkansas Sissies after Melba'son had already relocated to New Orleans. As Speakman recalls it, he and Brotherlover went to New Orleans not only as middle-class faggots intent on a *fanshen* into radical sissie subjectivity, but also at the behest of Oglesby and Thornton. They intended to send excess salary from their city jobs back to Mulberry House to help prepare the faerie farm as a rural gay liberationist hub with a link to the hived-off, urban LaSIS in New Orleans. The plan was to keep the Crescent City and Ozark sites linked within the wider gay liberationist network.

On May 3, Speakman arrived in New Orleans with Brotherlover, and he ultimately also took a new name. Back at Sister Kettle, he had gone by "House," which was his given middle name and his mother's maiden name. He would sometimes revive its use, but he welcomed another name given him on the streets of New Orleans. When walking one morning with Hayes, he saw the sun break from behind a storm cloud. In an epiphanic moment, he felt he was being offered the name Aurora Corona—and he took it, often going by "Ro" for short. Having grown his wavy hair very long, he wore his effeminacy like a flash of intuition. Perhaps it was also fitting that Aurora Corona should take up this mantle in New Orleans, near the "House of the Rising Sun."

From how Dimid evoked a connective manner of entering a room, to how Stacy Brotherlover reminded us of the intimacy of radical brotherhood, to how Aurora conveyed sudden dawning as an effeminate quality, LaSIS used their spiritual conversions to recompose their own identities in effeminate communicative, erotic, and epistemological modes. As they assumed their places alongside Melba'son as part of LaSIS, they did so as sissies who wore their effeminacy as a sign of the roles they'd assume in their new city. Also like Melba'son, they were bookish, most with some college under the belts, but chose to work in pink-collar service jobs. Dimid worked for a short time in a Frenchmen Street café, before he and Aurora started a housecleaning service. Brotherlover was the exception. He found an office job using his accounting background and had to dress accordingly. This forced him to improvise how he expressed the nonbinary gender that became a hallmark of their sissie collective.

This chapter will describe how, from early 1978 to early 1979, LaSIS articulated their sissie figure and collectivist vision into a local practice. In this chapter, I first convey how, in the spring and summer, the collective's information activism within faggot and lesbian feminist print culture allowed them to answer New Right child protectionism with what I describe as a sissie street pedagogy that was predicated on a youth liberation locally informed as much by de/segregation as it was by the shadow of Save Our Children and the Bryant-inspired California Briggs Initiative. Next, I show how in late 1978, LaSIS anatomized their own sissie liminality by reflecting, in *RFD*, on how they were shaped by their experiences on French Quarter streets. In so doing, I demonstrate how LaSIS's sissie figure posed a time- and place-specific variation on the main faggot figures that had preceded them. Specifically, I trace how, following the New York Flaming Faggots' martyrological iconography and the West Coast's armed militant femme, LaSIS improvised a sissie form that embodied child protectionists' worst fears: a cross-dressed teacher liberating children through pedagogies rooted in proliferative wonder.

On the Books: From Collectivized Indexing to the Sissie Effeminist Bibliography

It wasn't surprising that Melba'son and Hayes decided to call the collective the Louisiana Sissies in Struggle. Since the 1976 Wolf Creek conference, Mulberry House had been unanimous in embracing a sissie identity. By not formally referring to themselves as faggots, they demonstrated their alliance with the anti-racist politics of both Bay Area gay liberationists of color and the Ozark lesbian feminists' civil rights experiences. They even more emphatically rejected the masculinity of the Oregon conference's straight-identified faggots (STIFs), embracing femininity instead. After Melba'son and Hayes settled in New Orleans, Mulberry House began referring to themselves as the Arkansas Sissies. It seemed logical, then, that the new house would similarly call themselves the Louisiana Sissies, but they added "in Struggle" to mark their ongoing (if sometimes fraught) political sympathies with the Faggots &

Class Struggle conference. Hayes has shared, though, that he and Melba'son also enjoyed how the acronym *LaSIS*, when said aloud, sounded a swishy lilt that they proudly embodied as sissies.[5]

If their name conveyed a continuity with their Ozarks collectivist experience, it is important to remember that in late 1977 Melba'son had also thought deeply about how, as much as he needed to learn to care across class and racial differences, he would also like to distinguish his own sissie collectivism from that of Mulberry House. There were two main tenets that he and LaSIS would come to emphasize. The first was the insistence that feminism was better served by their learning how to communicate compassionately and empathetically, rather than by relentless, angry critique alone. Melba'son's experience with Mulberry House had led him to wonder whether crucial collective defense was even possible in a culture based almost entirely on such divisiveness.

The second difference from Mulberry House was related to LaSIS's shared middle-class backgrounds. Even though most of them took service jobs in New Orleans, they also committed their educated backgrounds and general bookishness to working in print culture—mostly, but not exclusively, with *RFD*. In doing so, they committed themselves to information activism. Back in Arkansas, Melba'son had tried to collectivize book indexing for the university presses with whom he already had connections. His efforts were unsuccessful, though. To his mind, too few of the working-class sissies and feminists would give that work a chance, seeing it as a betrayal of their blue-collar identities. It is likely, however, that many of them rejected it just as much because doing that work would position Melba'son as the expert and de facto manager. New Orleans presented new opportunities, though. Working-class Nick studied languages in order to assist poor immigrant communities, and he held formal education in high regard. Brotherlover had come to the Ozarks from New Orleans, where he worked with the lesbian feminist collective Atlantis, who distributed literature from alternative presses. Just before Melba'son arrived in New Orleans, the local gay community had started their own newspaper, *Impact*, and LaSIS would become regular writers for that publication. As we have seen, *RFD* had been a central tool for Mulberry House's networking, collectivism, and figuration, and LaSIS would volunteer editorial oversight of multiple issues in the years to come.

In the early spring of 1978, Melba'son and Hayes composed a reading list as a way to introduce themselves to others. They mimeographed copies to distribute at events, and they eventually published it in the Summer 1978 issue of *RFD*. They titled this bibliography "Sissie Effeminism."[6] This title points to how Melba'son and Hayes themselves "remembered forgotten dreams."

Although I cannot say *how* they arrived at this name, it is clear that they revisited the New York origins of their collectivist genealogy to discover a figure—the Effeminists, and the 1973 manifesto—that had fallen into the shadow of the West Coast faggot. Embracing the effeminist figure allowed early LaSIS to foreground their feminism, emphasize less-masculinized character traits, and commit themselves to sharing reproductive labor. However, by leading with "sissie," they insisted on the importance of their physical effeminacy and distanced themselves from the original Effeminists' anti-femme stance. Before the end of 1978 the collective would have to reckon with the tensions produced by this term.

Cait McKinney has modeled ways of reading the historical lesbian or gay bibliography as an "encounter." As they explain, a reading list facilitates readers' "finding [their] people" while "shaping the 'proper' subjects and stakes of social movements."[7] Queer bibliographic encounters, then, form networks, subjectivize members, and define movements in the process of sharing formative texts. McKinney's reading of Barbara Gittings's *A Gay Bibliography* lays out how that list, in its ultimate published form, avoided claiming a confrontational gay liberationist politics and has been remembered—by bibliographer and archivist alike—for how it most often introduced the youthful and/or uninitiated reader to the possibilities of a liberal gay identity and sociality. In many ways, *A Gay Bibliography* walked isolated readers out of the closet. McKinney reads against the grain, though, by pointing out the bibliography's less typical readers (like inmates) and also questions the assumption that the encounter always produced an easy identification or transformation. McKinney's reading suggests some helpful ways for us to interpret "Sissie Effeminism."

The testimonials to the life-changing impact of Gittings's bibliography enjoy a prominent place in the archive, indicating to posterity that at least one main function of the reading list was to address uniquely uninitiated readers to the identity, life, and community that coming out offered. The primary purpose of the "Sissie Effeminism" bibliography, on the other hand, was to define LaSIS, *to themselves*, so that they could coherently introduce themselves to other liberationists. Many of the entries reflected Melba'son's reading, as he not only tried to distinguish himself from West Coast faggots but also from Mulberry House. In this way the bibliography less constituted the reader, but through the act of curation, coordinated the author into a more discernible subject. As we have seen, this synthesis would have been especially useful to sissies who (1) often sought to cobble a movement from the remains of gay liberation; (2) as leftists, set themselves the task of generating a coherent revolutionary subjectivity; and (3) turned to magical or ritualistic methods to summon forth a revolutionary persona out of their complex everyday selves. Assembling bibliographies, then, facilitated their *fanshen*. "Sissie Effeminism" did not seek to initiate others so much as it tried to reanimate their own liberation from what remained.

Their bibliography was composed of four sections: "background," feminism, sissie effeminism, and periodicals. Many of the titles were expected ones. The interestingly short sissie effeminism section included both the *Morning Due* account of the Faggots & Class Struggle conference followed by *The Double F* (the journal where "The Effeminist Manifesto" was first published). The background and feminism sections included some now-canonical accounts of gay liberation alongside feminist classics, and both folded leftist and spiritual titles into the mix. Arthur Evans's *Witchcraft and the Gay Counterculture* took a high-profile position in the background section, and M. F. Beale & Friend's *Safe House*—a feminist analysis of the state's violent attack on the Symbionese Liberation Army—underscored the importance of collective defense. Melba'son's own anarchist drift was reflected by the inclusion of Emma Goldman on the list. The last section, periodicals, mostly featured bigger cities' lesbian and gay newspapers but did not mention New Orleans's *Impact*. LaSIS pointedly described San Francisco's *Join Hands* as a gay newsletter "link[ing] . . . the prisoners on the outside, and our brothers, the prisoners on the inside."[8] The description of *Join Hands* in "Sissie Effeminism" points to a possibly more intentional gay liberationist concern with connecting across institutional barriers than did Gittings's liberal bibliography. It also reflected Melba'son's and *RFD*'s past experience with prison correspondence as gay liberationist organizing.

Two other aspects of McKinney's explication of queer bibliographic encounters suggest how we can uniquely understand "Sissie Effeminism." First, McKinney writes, "Biography, and in particular memoir, is a revealing genre for considering the encounter as trope, because it asks adult narrators to remember and make sense of their own youthful identity formation."[9] Because Melba'son and Dimid Hayes were not so much trying to remember a past identity formation as to generate *fanshen*, to foment a new revolutionary subjectivity, queer memoirs, speculative fiction, and poetry were folded into their lists as ways to author their own lives under their new names. Adrienne Rich, Marge Piercy, Rita Mae Brown, Kate Millet, Quentin Crisp, Tennessee Williams, Christopher Isherwood, and Allen Ginsberg were all featured in LaSIS's bibliography, and the memoirs of the last four were expressly referred to as "Sissystories."[10] I propose, then, that sissystories, for LaSIS, referred to a writerly practice of composing the radically converted, newly gendered, and complexly aligned sissie self. Melba'son's autoethnographic journaling and Hayes's trance-like free-writing were both processes of reflectively shaping themselves across the period of transition.

Second, McKinney applies a media studies analytical lens to interrogate how print *and* digital information encounters are designed to make the interface "invisible" so that material structure and labor disappear to give the encounter itself an air of greater immediacy.[11] This is perhaps truest for institutional encounters—for example, within libraries—and their liberal social context. As leftists, LaSIS were actually eager to call attention to the limits of their bibliographic efforts. In the cover letter they explained their process and asked for feedback. They embraced the centrality of feminism, but qualified it: "This is one reason we call ourselves *ef*feminists. For us to merely adopt the theories and vision of women and call ourselves 'feminists' without directly applying them to our own lives would be a ripoff of women's energies."[12] They admitted that their project of realizing a feminist perspective within their own differently gendered lives was as incomplete as the reading list itself. They owned that in their bibliography they did not yet "attempt to reflect what we've learned from the struggles of working-class, Black, Third World, and Native peoples, or what we've learned from anarchists and those held prisoners in jails, mental institutions, schools, and nursing 'homes.'" They framed their list as a first step, a mere snapshot of the conversations they were then working through, as part of their process of growing themselves into radical sissie effeminists. In doing so, they presented themselves as incomplete, like a single puzzle piece in search of a wider picture.

McKinney's case study of Gittings's liberal gay reading list makes possible a critical hermeneutic for bibliographic encounters. In many ways, "Sissie Effeminism" differs from Gittings's *A Gay Bibliography* somewhat predictably. It is a (latter-day) liberationist/leftist bibliography as opposed to a liberal one, and it describes a nonbinary gender encounter as opposed to a gay one. However, what I find most interesting is how "Sissie Effeminism," born of activism against New Right child protectionism, strains against the tacit paternalism of any bibliographic encounter that imagines the reader as a blank slate—an innocent or neophyte who is initiated by a more experienced bibliographer. The sissies would have been especially sensitive to how such framing sets up a hierarchical, generational, and salvific narrative absolutely compatible with child protectionism. LaSIS's own flawed bibliography, on the other hand, invited lateral collaboration, and we will see how, by reading into the labor *behind* their list, they imagined revolutionized children among their coauthors, too.

At the foot of their cover letter was an illustration of two naked, winged, bearded men kissing. This drawing is attributed to Larry Hermsen. This graphical citation is telling. In the Summer 1977 issue of *Magnus*, Hermsen illustrated a children's story called "Jesse's Dream Skirt," written by Morning Star.[13] In the story, a little boy named Jesse wears a skirt to daycare, where he is at first ridiculed by his classmates. The teacher, named Bruce, consoles Jesse, sharing that he himself had been fascinated by feminine attire as a child. Pointing out that *some* of the children admired the skirt, Bruce leads the class in a discussion in which Jesse shares that he had dreamed about this skirt and how, through it, he came to identify with his mother. After this, with Bruce's guidance, the children discussed their different reactions to wearing gender-variant clothing, before experimenting with a liberating dress-up session, a joyous parade.

Magnus published "Jesse's Dream Skirt"—with Hermsen's illustrations—the same summer that Save Our Children reversed gay antidiscrimination laws in Miami by stoking homophobic fears about flamboyant school teachers recruiting children to gay lifestyles. In 1978, as John Briggs launched his own initiative to ban Californian lesbian and gay public school teachers—or *any* teachers who supported lesbian and gay rights—LaSIS continued to imagine scenarios where sissie children like Jesse would be centered in educational conversations, and where creative gender exploration would be key to the way *all* children learned. By visually citing Hermsen, LaSIS signaled commitment to such a world. Because they moved in the same circles as the Magnus Collective, they may have known that Morning Star's legal name was Bruce Mack. If so, they might have read the children's story as a fiction in which the openly gay liberationist author played out his own dream of teaching children how to author their own sissystories. This was a vision that Melba'son and Hayes clung to in the shadow of the Save Our Children campaign.

It is further telling that in 1979 a North Carolina feminist publishing collective, Lollipop Power, would publish *Jesse's Dream Skirt* as a book, with a new illustrator, Marian Buchanan, who would herself not only speculate about Mack's desire to be a teacher but also draw Bruce, the fictional teacher, as a Black man.[14] This move echoed several of LaSIS's own concerns about the entangled racial, gender, and sexual politics of the classroom that were active in the year following their formation. A grace note at the foot of their cover letter, Hermsen's drawing allows us to see LaSIS's formation—between the New Right Save Our Children campaign and the Briggs Initiative—as intricately responding to violent child protectionist rhetoric by suggesting an alternative vision for a child-empowering, liberationist pedagogy of solidarity. Their as yet incomplete bibliography, by an illustrative citation, left breadcrumbs to follow into a world where nonconformist gender was naturalized as part of the classroom and its pedagogy.

LaSIS indicated that the majority of the texts in "Sissie Effeminism" were available through the Atlantis collective. Interestingly, even before Melba'son and Hayes arrived in New Orleans, Atlantis had themselves been conversant with faggot political perspectives. Their Summer 1977 order list included *RFD*, *Morning Due*, and *Magnus* among its periodicals. Appearing the same season as *Magnus*'s "Jesse's Dream Skirt," Atlantis's own book list featured annotations for six queerly feminist children's books. It also highlighted "NEW BOOKS ON YOUTH LIBERATION" published in Ann Arbor, including one title that advised on how to organize youth "in and out of school."[15]

That pamphlet, authored by Ann Arbor teen activists, recognized how race, sex, class, and ageism intersected, and they directly proclaimed, "Whether you are gay or not, [organizing against anti-gay practices in schools] will help all students to become more aware of their sexual feelings and prejudices."[16] Written as a how-to book, the pamphlet also included a quiz for students in de/segregated schools to find out just how equitable was the learning in their institutions, across racial and ethnic lines.[17] Signing their book list with "Cheers from Bayou Country," the Atlantis women used their own information activism to stitch West Coast faggot politics and Midwest youth liberation in such a way as to allow a similar liberationist tenor to emerge in the Deep South. It would not have been lost on these bayou feminists that they hailed from the same region that had produced the Johns Committee's purge of queer teachers.[18] LaSIS clearly followed Atlantis's lead. "Sissie Effeminism" articulated a bibliographic practice that eschewed paternalistic modes and proposed, instead, an incomplete reading list that begged for collaborators. It also invited solidarity *across* generations. In so doing, it invited children *and* teachers to take a youth liberationist perspective—instead of child protectionism—as the aftereffects of Save Our Children intensified. LaSIS would have increasing reason to focus on education as the summer waned.

In Loco Parentis: Skirting Paternalism through Alternative Childcare and Teacher Solidarity

LaSIS gelled as a full collective in May 1978. Hayes, Brotherlover, and Aurora generally found, like Melba'son and Oglesby and Thornton before them, that there was little evidence of a radical, gay liberationist presence in New Orleans. This hadn't always been true. In his portrait of the "Stonewall

South," Sears contrasts the reformist "social liberalism" of Atlanta and Charlotte's GLF chapters with chapters in New Orleans and Houston that "articulated Marxist-Leninist rhetoric and engaged in revolutionary practice."[19] Lynn Miller, Dianne Kiesling, and David Solomon formed the New Orleans GLF in the fall of 1970, eventually establishing a newsletter called *Sunflower*. One of their first actions was in response to a series of January 1971 arrests by the vice squad in the Quarter's Cabrini Park, on Barracks Street. The GLF picketed city hall, openly critiqued the excesses of the vice squad, and called for a repeal of state anti-sodomy laws. Ten days later they held a demonstration in City Park, drawing local media attention. Sears tells us that in 1969 the city's vice squad had made 167 arrests for "homosexual crimes," many of which carried a five-year sentence in Angola (the Louisiana State Penitentiary). Such sweeps were spurred by District Attorney Jim Garrison's public commitments to clean up the seedier elements of the Quarter's noirish, sin-city era. In fact, Garrison operationalized vice establishments and homosexual entrapment to further his own career, including the media spectacle he drummed up around Clay Shaw as a central player in his JFK conspiracy theory.[20]

Despite this initial focus by the New Orleans GLF on the entrapment of gay men, Sears tells us that the New Orleans GLF "emerged from the canopy of feminist organizing."[21] The early liberationist efforts in the city were primarily lesbian feminist ones. Before they moved to Arkansas, Suzanne Pharr and Barbara Scott were part of this lesbian feminist heyday. Like many post-Stonewall liberationist cultures, though, their season was short, and Pharr and Scott left for the Ozarks around 1972, worn by a backlash that included Garrison's homophobic vice district practices. Radical lesbian feminists who remained politically active in the city after this time tended not to be separatists and found easier partners in liberal feminist organizations like NOW than did lesbians elsewhere in the United States.[22] This fact must be considered alongside the city's wider anti-radical practice, though. Just before the city's GLF formed, the New Orleans police, alarmed by community projects like free breakfast and sickle-cell programs, used their "Red Squad"—a unit formed to suppress leftist activity—to infiltrate the city's Black Panthers, and on the morning of September 15, 1970, deployed roughly one hundred local and state officers to open fire, for over twenty minutes, on the Panther headquarters—located in the Ninth Ward, in the Desire neighborhood.[23] As a result, New Orleans gay liberationists and Black Panthers had little chance to learn from each other, as they had in the Bay Area described by Emily Hobson.

In April 1971, Jefferson Parish officer Dwight Crews was tapped to go undercover to gather intelligence on New Orleans radicals. His infiltration would ultimately go so far that he was chosen, along with Dolores Fernandez, to represent the city on the March 1972 Venceremos Brigade to Cuba. He delivered his report, as an informant, before the October 1972 hearing by the federal Committee on Internal Security.[24] At the hearing he reported that his undercover work in New Orleans led him to identify a local Trotskyite group, and that the original five candidates for the Venceremos Brigade together represented the following local organizations: Vietnam Veterans Against the War, the Black Workers Congress, the Student Liberation Front at Louisiana State University New Orleans, the Workers Militant Action Committee, the Community Alliance for Radical Education, the Free School in New Orleans, the Prisoners Solidarity Committee, and Youth Against War and Fascism. Regional leftists chose brigadiers to convey such local revolutionary activity to Cubans. Crews was specifically selected to represent radical factions among local veterans and students while Fernandez, a Black woman, was to represent the Panthers and the Black Workers Congress. Leftist activity was substantial enough in early-1970s New Orleans for police to dedicate intelligence efforts to it. It also seems reasonable to presume, from such examples, that local police were often successful at using intelligence to expose radical activity and then leveraging militant force to decimate it. Many gay liberationists and lesbian feminists had been inspired by the Venceremos Brigades, but in New Orleans the consequences of that identification would have had some widely known and serious stakes.

Following the 1971 New Orleans GLF protest in City Park, lesbian and gay leaders met with police chief Giarusso to insist that he halt all vice squad entrapment and conduct an independent review of existing police practices. When the GLF saw no follow-up on Giarusso's tepid agreement, they planned a federal class action lawsuit against the city. They found little support from the community. Sears speculates that many by then feared being targeted by police or the district attorney and that the more upper-middle-class or patrician community leaders, like Clay Shaw, advised against associating with any radicals.[25] Shaw had seen firsthand how ruthless Garrison could be. Many must have heeded his words, because the lawsuit lost steam. In June 1973 the devastating Upstairs Lounge Fire amplified gay residents' fears, and gay liberation appeared to go dormant, or seriously dispersed, after that.[26]

In May 1978, however, there *was* a burgeoning gay and lesbian political force in New Orleans. LaSIS's politics were so different, though, that each group was inscrutable to the other. In 1975, Alan Robinson, Bill Rushton, and Ann Gallmeyer had formed the Gertrude Stein Democratic Club, an organization that would re-energize the city's thinned gay and lesbian scene with cultural events that included local artists and media personalities—and even some national celebrities like Christine Jorgensen and Hunter S. Thompson. The longer purpose of Gertrude Stein, though, was to funnel this sociality into gay rights agendas. As Sears put it, the Gertrude Stein Society "seduced New Orleans homosexuals" with salons featuring visiting gay celebrities but also with programs interviewing local political candidates.[27] Aurora remembered Gertrude Stein as a purely social organization with "moderate conservative" values, though. On July 14, 1979, Alan Robinson would dismissively remember LaSIS as a group of gay men living like lesbians, in a collective, and accused them of bringing "a confrontation style politics that is not really applicable to the delicate internal and external politics of the New Orleans gay community."[28]

It's not true that Gertrude Stein was purely social. Rushton and Robinson were leading organizers for the Anita Bryant protest that took place on June 18, 1977, and drew to Jackson Square more than 3,000 protesters—liberal *and* radical, most contacted through Rushton and Robinson's networks. Their throng eclipsed the thirty-five Bryant supporters. The gay newspaper *Impact* was founded in the summer of 1977, just before Melba'son arrived, and Robinson and other Gertrude Stein members were regular writers for it. As LaSIS would ultimately be. The dominant political concerns in early *Impact* were (1) the police entrapment practices lingering from Garrison's tenure as D.A., and (2) defensive strategies against Anita Bryant's rumored return to New Orleans. To address the latter, Gertrude Stein leveraged its earlier social strategies, inviting celebrities to the party town in order to fundraise against Bryant's return. *Impact* copy editors objected to LaSIS's more confrontational language, and chose, for example, to delete the word *faggot* whenever the collective used it. LaSIS published some of their *Impact* pieces under the name of their political organization, the Pink Triangle Alliance (PTA); however, they began to reserve their more developed and radical writings for *RFD*.

Given LaSIS's formation under the banner of "sissie effeminism," it may not be surprising, then, that Brotherlover (writing as Robert Reich) announced in the August *Impact* LaSIS's plans to start a lesbian and gay childcare service.[29] Owning that the suggestion might surprise some readers, he cited at least twelve local gay parents interested in collectivized childcare. Not only a service for gay families, Brotherlover framed it in broader liberationist terms, too. He shared how angry he was that insidious charges of pedophilia were used to isolate lesbian and gay adults from children, especially since he himself had enjoyed having children in his life before coming out. He claimed a "political responsibility to build a community in which the care and nurturance of all is shared by all" and that, as a man, and as a sissie, he felt a special calling to ease the inordinate responsibility for childcare, which had been unevenly assigned to women. He also mentioned the need to advocate in lesbian and gay child custody cases and to vigilantly separate the issues of rape and molestation—which are matters of violence—from issues of sexuality. With this initiative, LaSIS hoped to offer an alternative to Bryant's form of oppressive family by collectivizing care work, starting with childcare.[30] Knowing that LaSIS backed such politics, it makes sense that the collective would have enjoyed signing their local political writings with the Pink Triangle Alliance's acronym *PTA*, for how it surely evoked the better known and national Parent Teacher Association. LaSIS simply believed that queer networks could parent better. Foremost in LaSIS's 1978 politics was a gay liberationist critique of the New Right family—a critique that offered radical, realizable alternatives to the violence of that nuclear family form.

Bryant and Briggs, and the Moral Majority that they represented, preferred to see teachers as reflections of idealized parents. Stemming from the concept of *in loco parentis*—according to which school personnel act with the moral authority of the absent parents—this ideal was increasingly exposed over the course of the 1960s as a fantasy propped up by normative white supremacist, patriarchal, and heterosexist family formations. Still, to the Moral Majority, the very suggestion that liberated women, homosexuals, or nonwhite teachers could ever serve as surrogates for white, gender-conforming, heterosexual parents was alarming. The very idea was an affront to their American dream. Given Brotherlover's August call for a gay childcare initiative, it is not surprising that LaSIS would also argue for a society in which *teaching* was, like childcare, shared by all. Therefore, when the largely Black United Teachers of New Orleans (UTNO) went on strike over Labor Day 1978, LaSIS understood the teachers' cause as one harmonious with gay liberation.

Like many Southern cities, New Orleans had been slow to integrate education. Bringing students of different races into the same schools was one challenge that was compounded by the parallel one of uniting teachers across the color line. Locally, there were two teachers unions—one Black and one white—that were often at odds with each other. However, in 1972 these unions merged to form UTNO, with Black teachers in the majority and in clear leadership roles. With teaching becoming more and more visibly a multiracial profession, the city's salaries remained low. Teachers had gone on strike before, in 1966 and 1969, when arguments about the pace and manner of desegregation had divided their cause. By 1978, however, UTNO had tested their cross-racial alliances, and they felt they stood a far better chance than with those past efforts. They went on strike on Labor Day, holding their ground until September 11, rebuffing insulting initial negotiations from the school board. They were confident because their union strategies were sound and they enjoyed popular support. Such good prospects led to widespread participation, with around 70 percent of city teachers striking. By September 11, the board offered more reasonable terms, and UTNO accepted, considering their bargaining empowerment one of the strike's most significant achievements.[31]

LaSIS joined the striking teachers and documented their experience in *RFD*, with a piece titled "Solidarity Forever."[32] "Solidarity Forever" established a clear and unique aesthetic tone for their collective politics. Subtitled "A Gay Playlet in One Act with Applause," the "playlet" drew upon Melba'son's theater experience, but with comic irony—simultaneously aggrandizing ("with applause") and minimizing ("play*let*") their sissie roles. They wanted to be clear: They were not leading but *joining* activism that was largely led by local Black teachers. As leftists, they didn't presume that they could map their Ozark-born liberationism onto New Orleans's unique material conditions, either. Still, they had a process for finding their place, and "Solidarity Forever" offers us insights as to what those methods were.

First, they were aware that, as a collective, they had minimal title as Southerners. As Mulberry House, they had been more regionally anchored by members who had grown up in the South—with Louisianans Oglesby and Thornton, Georgian Kendrick, and Yellowhammer's Mississippian Lawson and Kentuckian Jackson. Naming the playlet's actors "four Sissies (three ex-Yankees and one prodigal Southerner)," they owned their relative newcomer status—save the distant past of Melba'son's Texan upbringing—while reclaiming their identity as sissies. This way of joining the scene echoed Dimid Hayes's sissie way of "entering a room": not to claim that space but to remain open, to slowly engage it. Indicative of that ethos, the playlet offered no dialogue. Featuring a description of the sissies' confused efforts to find the striking teachers, "Solidarity Forever" foregrounded their imperfect, improvisational actions *over* speech—almost like a Keystone silent film. Further, the addition of the word "Forever" to the title suggested a romantic register wed to the comic one.

Second, as leftists, they *did* have a sense of how space was shaped by power. Establishing the setting as "New Orleans, historic Queen City of the South," the playlet not only feminized the place, imagining its chances of exceeding patriarchal rule, but went on to emphasize the town's origins predating the birth of the United States, formed by the intersecting colonial rule of France,

Spain, and England. Like Arthur Evans, LaSIS framed their contemporary world as the product of a capitalist imperialism that was also an extension of racist and sexist colonialism. In 1978 they described their new city as a sinking place, barely staying afloat "on fading glory and a slipping tax base." They portrayed New Orleans as putting all its chips on the tourist dollar while exploiting its majority Black population. Their focal example of this exploitation was the specific site of "Solidarity Forever," the Superdome.

Opened in 1975, inspired by Houston's Astrodome, the arena's construction displaced historic Black neighborhoods, cost the city nearly five times as much as the Houston arena, and in 1977 cost $50,000 a day to keep open (used or not) as it logged an operating loss of $5.5 million.[33] For LaSIS, the fact that the 1978 UTNO teacher strike took place in the shadow of the Superdome was painfully telling; if colonial slavery had exploited the lives and labor of Africans and if regional tourist development had similarly erased Black homes and neighborhoods while abusing their tax dollars, then the city perpetuated this oppressive tradition by exploiting the city's intellectual and care labor, substantially performed by its Black teachers. "Solidarity Forever" told the story of how LaSIS joined this local movement in its current instance of resistance to centuries-old racist oppression. They only hoped to sound an (admittedly white) gay liberationist grace note against a much longer Black freedom song. Still, if they knew their street theater performance was fallible, they hoped they could contribute something loving, something attuned.

Third, they composed their approach to the strike with highly visible political signs and smaller pamphlets. These served as a kind of political calling card. The signs communicated to the teachers how the sissies understood the strike as part of a wider project of regional racial integration. They asserted, on signs readable from a distance, that the sissies were there to support better pay for teachers but also to fight those forces, like Florida's Save Our Children, that were set against school desegregation and that blocked the cultivation of racially integrated workplaces. As newcomers, the sissies made sure they did their research. They informed themselves of the violent local landscape in which these teachers lived and worked. So, one of their signs rang a clear (all-caps) note: "GAYS SUPPORT UTNO TEACHERS STRIKE." Other of their signs put that support in further context: "GAYS AGAINST RACISM! GAYS FOR THE E.R.A.!" But one other sign may have resonated more trenchantly with local Black teachers: "FREE GARY TYLER!"

Gary Tyler was a Black teenager who in 1975 became the nation's youngest death-row inmate when he was convicted, in the absence of any compelling evidence, for the 1974 shooting death of a thirteen-year-old white boy. That thirteen-year-old had acted as part of a mob that attacked a school bus transporting Black students, including Tyler, in nearby Destrehan. No weapon was ever found, much less one linked to Tyler. Part of a too-familiar story, the racist justice system vindicated the violent white child who acted as part of a mob led by white adults, and that same system simultaneously punished a Black child, as an adult, for a crime that was most likely perpetrated by one of the white vigilantes.[34] Many of the UTNO teachers who taught only twenty-five miles downriver had surely learned to carry in their very bodies a constant fear of that vigilante violence and of the justice system that abetted it. LaSIS wanted UTNO to know that they saw the teachers' fight for higher pay as connected to recognition of the fact that navigating Louisiana educational spaces was dangerous and that too few people seemed concerned with saving *Black* children.

Another cluster of signs linked the UTNO strike to affirmative action. One shouted "DOWN WITH WEBER!" In 1974, just a little farther upriver than Destrehan, in Gramercy, a white Kaiser Aluminum employee named Brian Weber sued his employer for overlooking him for an internal training program that had instead admitted several junior Black employees. The company defended their decision. They claimed that Black workers were in the minority at the plant and that the training program operated under an affirmative action strategy of building pathways of advancement for equally qualified employees with minority status—no matter their rank. Weber had pursued an appeal to the Supreme Court by the time LaSIS arrived in New Orleans.[35] The sissies conveyed with this sign that they also saw the UTNO strike as a matter of employment discrimination. Even though the Black teachers were, in this case, in the majority within their professional union, the school board had chosen to underpay *all* public school teachers, due at least in part to the profession's no longer being seen as primarily white work. Effectively, LaSIS used their signs to honor the work of UTNO as an important local political demonstration, couched in clear response to a network of related injustices and, therefore, not an isolated or unconsidered reaction. Further, the signs would frustrate media attempts to simplify the strikers' politics. In refusing to isolate the UTNO strike, LaSIS broadly emphasized the intimacies, the familiarities, of solidarity.

Reading these messages from a distance, the New Orleans teachers welcomed the sissies into their striking ranks. Once there, LaSIS handed the teachers pamphlets protesting the California Briggs Initiative. From "Solidarity Forever" we can see the ways LaSIS wanted to implement their gay liberationist commitment to joining crucial local activism: *as sissies*, and as a way to *demonstrate*, rather than argue for, the mutual relevance of their causes. Striking teachers who might have initially been confused by LaSIS's *gay* anti-racism would have ultimately understood their shared agitation against (white, straight) child protectionism and workplace discrimination at the moment when LaSIS assembled the names of Tyler, Weber, and Briggs as linked political issues. LaSIS wanted to show, as they would assert in *Impact*, that their politics were anything but single-issue. It was this locally informed introduction as allies that won the sissies a welcome place to walk side by side with the teachers. Therefore, while LaSIS, unlike the GAA, committed themselves to multiple liberationist actions, they employed similar tactics with street theater and media performance.

"Solidarity Forever" documents that it was the mostly Black, *local* teachers who welcomed them. National union organizers questioned the sissies' place in the striking lines. They argued that only teachers could strike. The sissies responded that was clearly not the case since parents, children, and other union allies were participating. They argued that sissies were allies, too. They knew, of course, that for many, the alliance of teachers and parents was a "natural" fit by virtue of the principle of *in loco parentis* and of the similar care work embedded in the education profession. Sissies' participation—with their androgynous appearance and loud "GAY" signs—raised qualms and queered the strike, at least for the national organizers. Seeing that those organizers had stopped the sissies, the local teachers continued to invite them in: "Word spread among the teachers in front of us. Waves of energy and support came flooding back. 'You walk! Don't let them people tell you what to do! You march with us!'"

Clearly losing their ground with the rank and file, the national organizers needed to improvise a solution. They insisted that LaSIS wear the same strike placards that the teachers did. LaSIS responded with "Would we? We'd be PROUD to wear them!" In a time when Bryant and Briggs were insisting that out lesbians and gays should be fired from their teaching jobs, LaSIS marched the streets of New Orleans wearing a kind of teacher drag, assuming the mantle of protesting educators. For all intents and purposes, they became what the law increasingly told them they could *not* be: flamboyant ("PROUD") teachers. While some gay liberals elsewhere responded to Bryant and Briggs by tightening the association between gays and children ("We are your children, too") and other liberationists sought to zap Bryant's media presence (the now-famous Des Moines pie-ing of Bryant), LaSIS focused on materializing the conservative family's worst nightmares: androgynous, out teachers "recruiting" the nation's children away from violent New Right (over)protectionism. In short, they asserted that homosexuals, people of color, and liberated women could indeed do a better job as teachers and parents. "Solidarity Forever" adds this rhetorical context to LaSIS's participation in the Labor Day 1978 UTNO strike, while showing how, in New Orleans, gay liberation had to also learn how to be anti-racist in its fight against *all* school and workplace segregation. For its part, LaSIS hoped to further hone its queer art of joining the wider movement. I contend that this was a decidedly gay liberationist response to the violence that surfaced after Save Our Children.

Toward an Unqueer Street Pedagogy of Terror and Wonder

"Solidarity Forever" documented LaSIS's improvisational efforts to initiate cross-racial solidarity in New Orleans. They offered their alliance as "out front" sissies at many street demonstrations, but the UTNO strike profiles how they uniquely responded to New Right child protectionism in the era of Bryant and Briggs. Their signage also underscored that they recognized that child protectionism as a white Christian supremacist phenomenon. By joining striking New Orleans teachers, they appeared to be visibly queer teachers at a time when nothing alarmed New Right parents more. The sissies refused to see the defensive white nuclear family as natural. Liberationists like LaSIS improvised alternatives. They committed their political acts in the name of the PTA, proposed queer childcare initiatives, comported themselves as teachers, and lived in collective houses. Also material to their being "out front" was their androgynous gender expression.

LaSIS often grew their hair long. They sometimes wore skirts or dresses, but if not, they tended to wear flowing, brightly colored garments. They sported facial hair—beards, goatees, and mustaches. They often grew and painted their nails, but when they did so, it was typical for them to use different colors of polish, and/or only paint every other nail. They made strategic use of accessories. They wore earrings—usually mismatched, and often many at once. (Aurora claimed to wear as many as eight earrings at a time.) Melba'son had taken up the habit of wearing red stars—a Maoist badge—as earrings or pins. They had begun making and wearing buttons that more literally, and confrontationally, spelled out their identities: "Sissie Hippie Commie Faggot," "Cocksucker," "La Casa Maricon Commune," and "Sissie Majik." Although this button-wearing might have been a preferred practice of the outspoken Aurora, who named favorite buttons, LaSIS sold the above buttons in RFD's Winter 1978 issue, with the option for readers to request their own unique designs, or even purchase their own button machine.[36] The confrontational volume of their sissie looks could also be turned up or toned down, as, for example, when Brotherlover suited up in the business attire required by his office job but carried his earrings in his pocket to wear on the bus ride home. Further, both Melba'son and Aurora specifically described their forward sissie style as *genderfuck*.

The look was not new. Susan Stryker traces it back to the androgyny ("fairy chic") of the late-1960s countercultural style as gay liberation adapted it, and Betty Luther Hillman calls this habit of early gay liberationist men wearing beards with dresses "political drag."[37] Both scholars, however, comment that this phenomenon hit its apex in the late 1960s and early 1970s, and then fizzled out by mid-decade. This would have been when most local gay liberation chapters had dissolved and when the urban hypermasculine "clone" look—associated with leather bars and bathhouses—ascended. We already know that LaSIS—like BAGL, and Arthur Evans as the Red Queen—questioned the exclusionary practices of such gay establishments, and a couple of the "Sissie" statements discussed below took overt exception to the hypermasculinity celebrated in the recent 1978 release of The Village People's hit "Macho Man."[38] (Luther Hillman sketches how that song was consciously crafted as an anxious corrective to popular perceptions of gay men as always effeminate.) Although not new, it was surely shocking that the sissies revived and qualified genderfuck in the deeper south at the moment when the look was being disavowed by gay men in popular media and in bicoastal urban gay neighborhoods. It is important to take some time to contextualize how LaSIS came to this gender expression.

Between the Fall 1978 and Winter 1978 issues of *RFD*, LaSIS staged a form of visual historiography of the transformation of the historically isolated "sissy" to their own relationally defined *sissie*. Inserted just below the text of "Solidarity Forever" (*RFD*, Fall 1978) is a photo of a lone, formally dressed boy offering an enigmatic grin and wave to the camera.

An italicized caption provides a gloss: "From the cut of his butch disguise, we'd place our Mystery Sissy in the early 20s."[39] He works so hard to play "butch" that his effeminate thespian side overtakes his masculinity. This child seems precociously mature, even sly, like a little salesman. Published between the time of Save Our Children and the time of the Briggs Initiative, this anachronistic image captures a maturity that defies the need for child protectionism. In fact, the caption excerpts lines scribbled on the back of the photo, which celebrate "Released at last!" from "Poor Mother!" This image resonated with the New Orleans Sissies who believed in liberating young queers from violent nuclear families and collectivizing the care labor of mothering. However, they framed this young "sissy" as trapped in an earlier time, alone,

"Sissy" photo, *RFD*, Fall 1978, 3. Photo unattributed.

and the caption addresses him directly: "Hail, forgotten brother!" This framing tacitly recognized the incohesive and isolated status of the earlier identity, but by hailing him it invited him into late-1970s collectivism.

In the next issue of *RFD* we see a shift. Two photographic images appear, each vertically divided by descending text that describes the scene as "SISSIE TERROR/IN THE PHOTO BOOTH."[40] There are several important facets of this terror. The first lies in these images' insistence that the sissie is no individual threat but a collective one. LaSIS valued the collective as a sociopolitical necessity, as key to a crucial underground in a time of violence. Collectivization was also important to resist the overwhelming definition of the sissie as physically, psychically, and socially isolated. It is worth recalling here that they quite literally conceived of their subjectivity in plural terms. As Melba'son's conversion story suggests, it was not uncommon for them to experience a multiple self composed, at least, of an everyday self in dialogue with one's radicalized sissie self. These are all reasons LaSIS insisted on spelling the singular version of the plural *sissies* as *sissie*: so that the plurality persisted even in the individual form. One sissie always bodily echoed others.

"Sissie Terror in the Photo Booth," *RFD*, Winter 1978, 4–5. Photos unattributed.

Second, sissie *terror* clearly referenced the alarm experienced by vulnerable effeminate bodies, especially in the wake of Save Our Children, but the defiantly erotic, playful relation of the sissies pictured also reclaims that terror as a possible weapon for themselves. The photos suggest a threat that hovers on the flat surface of the images, ready to spring on any defensive masculinity lurking among the viewers. Some of this terrorism stems, then, from the photographic form itself. Because photo booths often take images in quick succession, produced on a long strip, they evoke film that is ready to be animated into moving pictures. These images, then, seem primed to leap into life; they evoke an imminent *now* that we can't quite be ready for. They threaten to pounce on the viewer.

Third, the photos simultaneously introduced a strange spatial magnetism. The same-sex sensuality captured is not recorded in some private domestic space, but in a photo booth—a place of only nominal privacy, found in very public and familiar spaces like streets or arcades. The photo booth, then, suggested both a familiar gateway and magical portal, threatening to suck the casual viewer into a world of illicit homosexuality. As *RFD* did from its beginnings, the photos quicken the sense that "We [sissies, faggots] are everywhere." This ubiquity meant almost anyone could stumble upon this illicit activity. This move played on New Right fears of homosexuality, but because we readers must turn the page to engage the filmic, serial quality of the images, we are also implicated in rousing these flat sissie figures.

In New Orleans, LaSIS found themselves on streets like those Marlon Ross describes, in his case study of James Baldwin. As such, the sissies would have found themselves trafficking the same spaces as latter-day swishes: the street queens remembered by Oglesby and Thornton and portrayed in John Rechy's novel *City of Night*. In the spring of 1978, Melba'son and Hayes had compiled a "Sissie Effeminism" bibliography, whose title sought to embrace sissie femme gender expression at the same time as it espoused an earlier anti-femme liberationist movement. Aurora and Brotherlover joined the collective in May, and the quartet became increasingly familiar with French Quarter streets over that summer. In the Winter 1978 issue of *RFD*, the collective was asked to be clearer about what it meant to call themselves *sissies*. What they published in response was a collection of position statements titled only "Sissie," with no reference to effeminism.[41] Their collective process and their New Orleans street experience had led to a reorientation that qualified their sissie figure for the place they now claimed as home.

With Ross's hermeneutic for reading "sissy liminality," we can cull from "Sissie" a sense of how LaSIS considered their genderfuck expression a form of interference on the audiovisual rhetoric of French Quarter streets.[42] True to their collectivist spirit, LaSIS composed "Sissie" as a textual collage of short expressions of sissie perspectives that included their own written pieces alongside those of other *RFD* readers and a few excerpts taken from opinions published elsewhere in gay liberationist print culture. Dimid, Aurora, and Melba'son consistently qualified their gender expression in genderfuck terms, which strategically demonstrated how femme gender expression could be performed in ways far more complex than earlier radical feminists had considered. This established that the dominant audience of the *text* "Sissie" was radical feminist *RFD* readers who might question LaSIS's genderfuck from a classic Effeminist point of view. LaSIS illustrated how their own gender emerged from their complex place in New Orleans street dynamics.

For example, Dimid contended that his wearing facial hair alongside feminine attire was meant to mock society's enforced definitions of *woman* and *man* and to create a productive dissonance for passersby on the street. The sissies deployed an irresolvable, high-contrast aesthetic with their genderfuck. Their carefully crafted failures to execute either femininity or masculinity and their refusals of visual consistency (by mismatching their nails and earrings) were meant as a send-up of how unnatural patriarchy's gender binary was. Aurora and Hayes coined this affect as *unqueer*. Building on their then habit of replacing /kl/ sounds with /kw/ ones, they stressed how genderfuck was adamantly *unclear*. On this point, the sissies were unanimous. Combined with the animating qualities of the sissie terrorism photos, this consensus about their femininity sought to synergize *RFD* readers around a sissie social subjectivity that hinged on a genderfuck answer to radical ef/feminist critiques of male femininities.

This was not a theoretical political stance, but a thoroughly embodied one. They experienced the French Quarter streets as an audiovisual stage for rape culture. They described the attention that their genderfuck drew on French Quarter streets. Mostly, they felt the outraged violence directed at them from men. Once sissies adopted femme aspects and/or expressed same-sex attractions, they often triggered the threat of male violence, and often these threats were themselves conveyed in sexual registers of rape. They did not equate this with what women or transgender persons felt, but they considered it "rapist energy" when men screamed "cocksucker!" at them in passing, or glared holes through them. They especially valued their genderfuck as a way to interrupt the circuit of male bonding, and they sought to use the reverse flow to direct feelings of alliance toward women, communicating to them "I am NOT a rapist." For LaSIS, the sissie figure denaturalized the male sociality of rape culture, and served as an extension of their developing anti-rape politics.[43]

As an elder sissie with Cold War life experience, Melba'son struggled the most with releasing radical ef/feminist positions in "Sissie." He reflected on the sources of his own femme orientation. As an older sissie, he offered some historical context for camp sensibility. He shared that during the Cold War, isolated sissies—before feminist and faggot witchcraft—found Goddess figures on movie screens, actresses who offered femme survival narratives that helped sissies live through the fear and pain they suffered alone, smothered in their closets. Melba'son, though, had learned not to establish a political rhetoric where sissies would merely answer women's pain with the fact of their own, forcing alliances predicated on either a neutralization or a hierarchy of different wounds caused by the same oppressors. He stressed that "pain is a powerful force, neither good nor evil. And like all such forces needs a political analysis to be effective (affective?)."[44] I take a strong reading of Melba'son's parenthetical homophone here. His tentative insertion of the word *affective* suggested that sissie political analysis might attend more closely to first responses (emotional, sensory ones) than to rational, strategic ends alone. In so doing, he proposed framing the sissie body less as a visual style than as a sensorium, a feeling-registrar, and by extension, recommended a finer description of women's *and* sissies' pain. In a way, then, "Sissie" became more about sharing individual and unresolvable feelings than boiling them down to an abstract theory. And the ambivalent (*unqueer*) form of their "Sissie" texts does reflect that impulse.

Melba'son then went on to consider the ef/feminist case against trans people. Here he foundered. He agreed with radical ef/feminist arguments, stating, "Of course my [transgender] Sissie friends on Bourbon St are oppressive to Women. They are oppressive to themselves." The agreement is troubling, confusing. He was so moved by the pain he understood radical feminists to experience that he, like New York effeminists, conceded that street queens did, in some ways, cause that pain. However, his "of course" suggested that the system was designed for this; this was simply how capitalism worked: It exploits such contradictions to set the oppressed against each other. He acknowledged his early agreement with radical ef/feminists, while in the same breath making clear his closeness to the transgender sex workers the New Orleans sissies encountered daily. Both femme groups traversed the volatile Quarter streets with their obvious nonconformism. By calling them his "Sissie friends," he refused to relinquish his intimacy with them even as he appeased their ef/feminist critics. Melba'son then described the street queens' class experiences as poor people whom neither straight nor gay employers would hire due to their highly visible femme existence. He called attention to *that* unique, classed form of pain as one that should be important to any socialist feminism.

On drag, he conceded to historical instances when female impersonation was used as a tool of the ruling order. However, he reminded readers of contemporary drag queens' pain, both as the vanguard of gay liberation but also as timeless objects of bitter treatment within gay culture. He shared that one New Orleans bar after another had turned LaSIS down when they needed a site to host their anti-Briggs ("No on 6") campaign, but it was drag queens who welcomed them to one of their establishments. He again reminded readers of the relevant pains, and the alliances that emerged from sharing them. I don't want, however, to give the wrong impression: Melba'son's statements *were* self-contradictory, digressive, and sometimes infuriating. But in the end he stated his hope that "perhaps by sharing this imperfect analysis with RFD, gaymen can begin to explore the complex nature of our relationship with Women and their symbols." Following Dimid and Aurora's coinage, he referred to his analysis as "unqueer," implying that sharing one's confusion, from within the dizzying detail of daily experience, was a way to honor the complexity of daily queer life before rushing to moralize it.

It's interesting that, in this last quote, Melba'son placed himself in the category of *gaymen*. Perhaps this softening of his usual leftist/liberal distinctions stemmed from his questioning the insensitive extremism of his own earlier politics. LaSIS's several collaborations with the Gertrude Stein group, through writing for *Impact*, may have also been a factor. The sissies' New Orleans street experiences certainly mirrored what Alan Robinson's recent investigative journalism had found. In the late summer, Robinson had begged *Impact* readers to recognize how routine physical violence had become in late-1970s New Orleans. As Robinson saw it, while the police busied themselves with entrapping gay men and while the press set about ruining those same gay men's lives and reputations, a steady flow of murders and rapes received little to no mainline journalistic attention. According to Robinson's research, in one single month, arrests were made for 106 rapes and 61 criminal homicides.[45] His figures raised the question: How many more such violent crimes did the police neglect, especially during Mardi Gras—when all was excusable—all while regularly invading gay bath houses and bars? Such was the context of sissie terror.

A vital element of their sissie majik, however, was the capacity to turn that terror on its head. In his account of Baldwin's sissy liminality, Ross vividly restages the conflicting emotions that emerged when mission work brought the "church sissy" into the hyper-public street and his proximity to the swish opened dangerous and liberating vectors. In that analysis, Ross limns a sissy anatomy shaped by an existence at the meeting of several spheres: home, church, and street. A fourth sphere was also central to Ross's sissy liminality: school. In New Orleans, LaSIS leveraged their middle-class educations, but not primarily through the jobs that schooling might have won them. They chose to work service jobs instead, and to use their print culture skills, not in formal institutions, but in alternative liberationist ones—like *RFD*, *Impact*, and *Atlantis*'s collectivized book distribution. As a result, LaSIS's information activism took place outside of school, library, or publishing house.[46] It took place in their homes, on phone lines, through the mail—*and* their information was often exchanged on the streets, as pamphlets, and as protest signs held like a disassembled bibliography.

When LaSIS put on the UTNO strike placards, donning a temporary teacher drag, they did so not in the classroom but in the streets. And as they stood with UTNO, distributing pamphlets in critique of the California Briggs initiative, they demonstrated how thoroughly they understood that the child protectionism of Proposition 6 and Save Our Children was a white Christian supremacist purity campaign set on re-entrenching segregation. These were attempts to isolate, and to indoctrinate, New Right white children. In the Ozarks, LaSIS had seen how, in response to Bryant's charge that homosexuals recruit children, it was actually the Klan that recruited teenagers to physically attack gays and lesbians. In a New Orleans paper, Bryant had confessed that she'd rather her own children be dead than gay. In truth, then, the white Christian supremacist nuclear family loomed as the institution that presented the biggest danger to all children. Save Our Children and the Briggs Initiative distracted the public's attention from these white, right-wing designs on children by raising the old specter of the Pied Piper, by raising the fairy-tale villain of the male-teacher-in-a-dress. Paul M. Renfro has observed, "Because they seemed to pose an existential threat to the white, heteronormative, male-breadwinner family, gay men shouldered much of the blame for the crises buffeting the family and the child in the 1970s and beyond," and he then adds that the era's violent rhetoric has cast a long shadow since then, contributing to "mass incarceration, the diminishing autonomy of young people, the intensifying 'war on sex' (especially underage sex), and the bipartisan fetishization of family values and child protection."[47]

As a specifically gay liberationist response, LaSIS reclaimed the figure of the male-teacher-in-a-dress. Brotherlover proposed a queer collective childcare service that would offer more considered care than dangerous New Right families could. With Atlantis, they touted Ann Arbor's youth liberation as a way to advocate for young people's agency. And in their association with the faggot journal *Magnus*'s story "Jesse's Dream Skirt," they suggested that gender nonconformity might be better understood as a vital element of a pedagogy dedicated to learning that happens in moments of wonder, through exploring dreams. "Jesse's Dream Skirt" was, perhaps, itself the indulgence of a dream—that of Bruce Mack, a queer man in the Bay Area whose longing to be a teacher would have been impossible if the Briggs Initiative succeeded. Likewise having no home in the classroom, LaSIS treated French Quarter streets as their school. They met striking teachers at their crossroads, and they inspired inquisitive tourist children in passing sidewalk exchanges.

One of Melba'son's earliest experiences had become LaSIS's collective script by late 1978. Tourist children often stopped them to ask if LaSIS were men or women. Hayes offered his own usual response in his section of "Sissie": "'I am a sissie,' I respond, and they giggle some more, eyes big like saucers as all the categories in their minds crumble and somewhere inside of them they realize there are alternatives! . . . countless ways for us to relate to each other."[48] Such exchanges turned Quarter streets into pedagogical moments for LaSIS. I suggest that LaSIS's street pedagogy is best understood as a historical form of what Nelson M. Rodriguez has called a "queer/trans pedagogy" of "generosity," in which queer/trans bodies and affect help to displace compulsory gender forms and thereby set up "the pedagogical conditions for imagining something else, for possibly cultivating a queer imaginary."[49] What is even more relevant here is how Rodriguez casts such generous pedagogy as operating in the spirit of queer utopia, as defined by José Esteban Muñoz: "a structuring and educated mode of desiring that allows us to see and feel beyond the quagmire of the present."[50]

How the sissies helped children to see "all the categories . . . crumble" in order to sense the "countless ways for us to relate to each other" certainly displaced normative gender in the process of cultivating a wonder about other futures, just as Jesse's skirt helped Jesse to materially realize his own dream. To effectively teach in this way, through wonder, LaSIS not only had to "remember the forgotten dreams" of a gay liberation that fizzled too fast, but they also had to be students themselves. On the French Quarter streets, which Black and white queers, sissies and queens brassily occupied together, LaSIS began to unlearn the Effeminists' anti-drag and anti-queen stances that were part of their complex faggot genealogy. This distantiation required sitting with the (uneven) pain experienced by all those impacted by child protectionism. It also proposed that some wonder might still grow from the terror resounding around them all.

CHAPTER SIX

Mapping Dreams
Gathering Sissie Solidarities into a Regional Network

The nonbinary sissie figure that LaSIS improvised was born of an affective liminality between terror and wonder. Those seesawing feelings arose from witnessing how the white Christian supremacist models of home and school proved increasingly dangerous, and from imagining alternatives through information activism, queer childcare, youth liberation, and witchy dreamwork. The figure that emerged embraced a heretical stance by practicing witchcraft in a tacitly Christian society and also proclaimed their leftism even as New Right forces accelerated. The sissies leaned into positively embodying the gay femme teacher and practicing a street pedagogy that simultaneously ran interference on widespread rape culture. In 1978 New Orleans, they were most shaped by the terrifying aftershocks of the Save Our Children campaign, the Bryant-inspired Briggs Initiative, and Southern re-entrenchment in de facto segregation. Although LaSIS had first flirted with reviving an earlier effeminism, they qualified and then dropped it, largely while reworking their stance on gender, as they learned to share the French Quarter with street queens. The older Melba'son struggled the most with this transition. The rest of LaSIS led an expanded sense of the group's collectivism as they galvanized a sizable regional network and honed their commitments to solidarity projects at home.

Chapter 5 more clearly defined the sissie figure that was born of LaSIS's 1978 "sissie majik." In this chapter, I describe how they quickly expanded the reach and strategy of their collectivist practice. It's helpful here to recall several points. First, LaSIS did not imagine themselves as the product of a break with Mulberry House; rather, they still thought of their houses as linked. Aurora and Brotherlover relocated to New Orleans with a charge to route funds from their city jobs back to the Ozarks, to help realize the dream of a faerie farm. Melba'son had written to Thornton that as he transformed himself in New Orleans, he felt even more strongly connected to the Arkansas Sissies. That's not to say that their relationship was easy. In fact, LaSIS would sometimes refer to themselves as the "middle-class exiles," which understandably irritated Oglesby and Thornton. After all, as they saw it, Melba'son had not been expelled; far from it, he had vanished under the hurtful guise of a false suicide. Melba'son, of course, felt like he'd had no other choice. It is also possible that

LaSIS used the word "exile" for entirely different reasons: less to sound a bitter note against the Arkansas Sissies and more to draw an affinity with their new town. The French Quarter gay bar Cafe Lafitte (opened in 1933), famed for queer clientele like Tennessee Williams, relocated a few blocks away from its original location in 1953, calling itself Cafe Lafitte in Exile.[1] If by calling themselves "exiles," LaSIS referenced the venerable New Orleans bar, then they may have instead meant to add to a story of queer persistence in their new town. In any case, they all now had experience operating as a single collective living in multiple houses, and the two groups remained psychically connected.

It is also important to remember that even though *RFD* remained a crucial platform for their most radical expression, in 1978 neither LaSIS nor Mulberry House looked to the West Coast for a faggot model. Oglesby and Thornton decided to remain in the Ozarks rather than head to the Bay Area, and several Midwest *RFD* readers had joined the Arkansas Sissies in critiquing the whiteness and class privilege they perceived in Bay Area editorial choices. LaSIS would instead orient themselves to the Southeast to grow their sissie collectivism. In a relatively short time they helped to link regional gay liberationist collectives into a network. This chapter charts LaSIS's expanding reach, so it is crucial to introduce several new key collectivists.[2]

Even as the sissies began to qualify their fleeting relationship to New York radical ef/feminism, they engaged the feminists around them more and more. We have already seen how LaSIS promoted the New Orleans lesbian feminist Atlantis collective. They also attended a New Orleans PFLAG group at an Episcopal church, befriending lesbian activists Nicki Kirby and Betty Caldwell.[3] In "Sissie," Melba'son not only distanced himself from effeminism; he also engaged with a Southeastern lesbian who had recently given her own feminist perspective in *RFD*.[4] In the Fall 1978 issue, Cathy Gross had written a letter to the West Coast *RFD* editors, critiquing their "Women's Issue" for adopting a politics of tokenistic inclusion over a radical feminist position, crowding out women's writing with too much of the editors' own words, and—most importantly—missing the opportunity to network radical rural women with rural gay liberationists.[5] She did not issue a critique, on principle, of drag or camp, but she did question editors' foregrounding those voices while neglecting to build practical solidarity between lesbians and queer men in rural areas. In "Sissie," Melba'son quoted Gross and stressed how, as a sissie himself, he felt it important to begin efforts to answer her questions, even if those answers were fated, in the early stages, to be *unqueer*.

Gross was born in Lakewood, Ohio, on the edge of Cleveland, shortly after World War II, but her family moved when she was quite young to York,

Pennsylvania. In 1969 she won early acceptance to Hofstra University on Long Island. She decided in her junior year, however, to pursue a service-learning assignment with FOCIS House in Big Stone Gap, Virginia. Founded in 1967 by forty-four former Glenmary nuns, FOCIS (Federation of Communities in Service) offered unique learning opportunities in partnership with universities like Hofstra. Gross went as an anthropology student whose studies were complemented by black lung activism, a local newspaper internship, and an NEA grant to teach an afterschool program.

The former nuns who ran the Big Stone Gap FOCIS House where she lived were interesting forebears for the young Gross. The Glenmary Sisters were an order founded by William Howard Bishop in 1941, with the mission of reaching rural populations where Catholicism was underrepresented. Recruiting posters for the order featured a nun driving a tractor. Most of the newly formed Glenmary Sisters ended up in Appalachia, and after the Vatican II of the early 1960s, Appalachian Glenmary Sisters became convinced that true service partnerships in the region required them to give up cloister and habit to live shoulder to shoulder among their mountain neighbors, as women of the world. The Church disagreed, so seventy nuns left the order and forty-four of them founded FOCIS as their new secular mission.[6]

When Gross arrived in Appalachian Virginia in 1971, she went through a similar realization. Her professors expected her to *study* Appalachians, to keep a scientific distance from her lived experience there. She saw immediately that locals especially resented outsiders' holding themselves apart in order to document the "hard facts" of area living conditions. Wanting a more immersive and interdisciplinary approach to learning, Gross transferred to Antioch College, which collaborated with FOCIS and nearby Clinch Valley College to offer a degree in Appalachian Studies. That academic program was started in 1970 by Helen Matthews Lewis, whose own recent scholarship adapted Frantz Fanon to conceptualize Appalachia as a region shaped by internal colonialism. Lewis, who would later become the director of the Highlander Research Center, led students like Gross to apply this revolutionary lens through engaged service and fieldwork.[7] So, Gross's arrival in the Southeast was auspicious in that she was introduced to the region as an early student of radical Appalachian Studies. She worked alongside former nuns, several of whom had female partners, and it wasn't long before Cathy found a partner of her own.

She is careful to point out now, though, that coming out rurally was very different. Same-sex relationships were treated as desperately guarded secrets, where a whisper of gossip could spark a chain of events leading to prison or vigilante violence. She dared not tell a soul about her relationship. That was true until, at a countercultural house party, she found herself stoned and chatting under a kitchen table with a young man named Russell Cravens, a conscientious objector five years her senior. In whispers, they came out to each other. Gross says, "That began our seventeen years of friendship." In 1977 she and Cravens decided on a change of scenery. He went west, to Denver, and she went further south, to Atlanta.

While she took full advantage of the bustling Atlanta lesbian scene, Gross just as often snuck off with gay male friends to see a drag show or go late-night dancing. She moved easily between women's and men's circles. The next year, in early 1978, she helped move Cravens from Denver to Atlanta. He drove, while she read aloud from *Even Cowgirls Get the Blues*. The two moved in together, taking a one-bedroom apartment in the Inman Park neighborhood, adjoining Little Five Points. In her autumn *RFD* letter, Gross closed with "I care about my gay brothers and hope the points I've brought up will serve to further communication between faggots and lesbians."[8] For LaSIS, who envisioned a collective network that included women, Gross's letter both sounded the familiar note of heartfelt critique *and* delivered a much-desired call for faggots and women to come together. LaSIS hoped their *RFD* statement "Sissie" was a step in her direction. Aurora further echoed her critique of *RFD*'s Women's Issue, and Melba'son cited her directly, at times seeming to invite a more regional, realizable dialogue with Gross. Little did they know that they had, effectively, already entered each other's orbits.

Running Water: Answering a Feminist Charge and Riffing on Rural Faggot Gathering

In April 1978, before Aurora and Brotherlover moved to New Orleans, Dimid took the "Sissie Effeminist" bibliography with him to the 3rd Annual Conference of Lesbians and Gay Men, in Atlanta. Gross was one of the event's organizers. The gender divide there was tense. Franklin Abbott, another organizer, who was friends with Gross, had witnessed firsthand when Atlanta gay men, mostly liberals associated with religious groups, objected to a request to have a few women-only sessions—one on female sexuality.[9] In a vote on the matter, many liberal gay men didn't even show, but Abbott and one other man cast their lot with the women. Such friction was part of a longer history. Although the original Georgia GLF had formed with the help of lesbian and Black members, it was soon dominated by liberal white men who ultimately defined the "gay ghetto" in psychological, rather than spatial or material, terms. Many left the organization, resulting in its developing an even firmer liberal gay white male perspective that took on a largely pastoral tenor due to the emphasis on the psychological angle and the remaining members' affiliations with religious groups.[10]

By contrast, Atlanta lesbians were often more radical. Several had participated in the Venceremos Brigades, and they were represented well with the local radical paper *The Great Speckled Bird*. In 1972, as gendered tensions spiked around the organization of the local Pride Parade, women left the GLF to form the Atlanta Lesbian Feminist Alliance (ALFA) in protest. Later that year a November "convention of gay militants" was held in Athens, Georgia, and a similar dynamic persisted. Liberal white male leadership leveraged Robert's Rules of Order in ways that appeared to sideline the concerns of lesbians, people of color, and leftists in favor of concentrating on reform around exclusively gay men's issues as they themselves defined them. At least that was how Lorraine Fontana reported it in *The Great Speckled Bird*.[11] Her article affronted the event's male leadership, and the men's reaction further alienated women, radicals, and people of color, so that by July 1973 the Georgia GLF, which had started with a meeting of one hundred people, was officially dissolved by the only two remaining members.[12]

Atlanta's lesbian culture thrived, though. ALFA was the political anchor for a vibrant community centered in the Little Five Points neighborhood. There were many collective households, along with lesbian musical and theatrical events, softball teams, and a bookstore (Charis) that functioned as a women's community center. These women invested in building their own institutions so that they weren't always forced to participate in patriarchal ones.[13] The realization of this rich cultural infrastructure not only paralleled the similar one in northwest Arkansas, but it likewise enamored some gay liberationist men who were primarily feminist and who did not often appreciate the exclusionary bars that gay men patronized. For example, Abbott says that he most identified with the lesbian culture of Little Five Points. There had also been a small group of gay men in Atlanta who had felt similarly, as the formation of an Atlanta "Radical Effeminists" group in 1972 indicates.[14] Those effeminists were surely a product of the split between ALFA and the Georgia GLF, which occurred that same year.

Six years later, at the Atlanta conference, lesbian feminist critique would again spark the organization of feminist gay liberationist men.[15] At the Sunday, April 2, debriefing, held at the Georgia Terrace, women critiqued men for dominating conference platforms. They recommended that the men take some time apart to work on their sexism. After delivering this charge, the women walked out, determined to hold their own discussions in private. Most of the men huffily followed shortly afterward. However, a small knot of feminist men remained to discuss the women's charge. At this point Mikel Wilson, an accomplished weaver, stood to address the others. According to Abbott, Wilson looked like "one of the wild creatures who had come down to the conference.... He wove all his own clothes. He had a long beard. He wore a tunic that he had made out of rough wool and he carried a staff, looking like an Old Testament prophet." Wilson proposed that the interested men come that summer to his Running Water Farm, in North Carolina, to start addressing the women's charge in earnest. LaSIS's Dimid Hayes immediately made plans to go.

Wilson set the event for the summer solstice, late June—around the time of his birthday. In doing so, he invited a certain kind of magic. The roughly forty attendees would have a chance to remember certain forgotten dreams. Occurring almost two years after the Oregon faggot conference, Running Water possessed certain continuities with that Wolf Creek event. Foremost of these continuities was faggot witchcraft.[16] Faygele Ben Miriam attended, having recently moved to Efland, North Carolina, to live with his radical mother. Clear Englebert remembers witchy spiral dances at Running Water. Openly gay folk singer Charlie Murphy also attended. Murphy would later record the popular feminist witchcraft ballad "Burning Times," which would revive the martyrology of the witch to inspire pagan, ecofeminist activism. Sitting on Running Water's rustic porch, he played guitar and sang, according to Hayes, while others joined in, sending choruses down the steep Appalachian mountain, like spells. Attendees like Dimid Hayes and Ben Miriam may have felt like earlier faggot fire was reignited. A second continuity was the fact that Ben Miriam had brought the struggling *RFD* with him from the West Coast. At the first Running Water gathering, he told fellow attendees that he sought collective help with the editing of the serial. Attendees agreed to that responsibility. Hayes remembers taking this news back to New Orleans, and LaSIS would be among the first to help their friend Faygele.

There were also some significant revisions to the Wolf Creek conference format. Almost as if following a note from Oglesby's working-class critique, there were no lectures. Thanks in part to Murphy, performance—particularly music—was central. However, much of the event not only followed effeminist principles of abandoning masculinist traits but also followed Atlanta's lesbian feminist charge for the men to work on their sexism by learning to relate and communicate more mutually and openly. Mindful of this, the men sat in circles, sharing their experiences of sexism and homophobia. For many, like attendee Michael Glover, this was awkward. Communicating with other men so vulnerably, allowing their emotions to surface publicly, and comforting each other verbally and physically were not only strange acts for many, but scary ones.[17] Some, like Englebert, commented how remarkable it was to see gay men engaged in healthful activities, rather than the dissipative, divisive ones that some associated with urban gay bar culture. Tennessee's Gabby Haze also brought his young children, so there was opportunity for the men to practice childcare, too—without assuming this work belonged to working-class and effeminate men, as Oglesby observed in Oregon.

Running Water was obviously less structured than Wolf Creek had been, and perhaps this was the main reason that it was called a *gathering* and not a *conference*. I suggest, though, that, more than a mere rejection of a conference's intellectual and hierarchical structure, the word *gathering* reflected another rural event model: Rainbow gatherings.[18] Begun in Colorado in 1972, in Roosevelt National Forest, that movement sought out rural space in national parks and forests, claiming them as commons, in order for countercultural sorts to collaboratively and temporarily experiment with what living a life guided by principles of peace might look like so that they could go home with learned, concrete skills for forming a better world. Although no direct overlap is mentioned by the attendees I interviewed, it is worth noting that the first annual Rainbow Gathering to occur in the Southeast was in Ozark National Forest, in 1975, just as Mulberry House was forming. Steeped in the counterculture, the members of the Southeast Network, including the Arkansas Sissies, would have had Rainbow Gatherings on their radar.

Instead of focusing on national forests and parks, the Southeastern gay liberationists—like those at Oregon's Magdalen Farm—focused their rural access on small, abandoned farms reclaimed by countercultural queers eager to host a radicalizing event. Although their focus was not peace per se, Running Water gay liberationists did go with the intention of experimenting with what relating beyond patriarchal conditioning might feel like. Both kinds of gatherings were temporally bound social experiments (not utopian settlements) meant to return attendees to the (mostly urban) everyday with the tools they needed to transform daily life in alignment with radical vision. This practice, then, networked witchy rural and urban collectives, much as Arthur Evans suggested. Also, attendees assumed that rural spaces were good places to organize and plan activism, but unlike Wolf Creek, they did not adopt overt security practices.

The sheer remoteness of Running Water helped. Mikel Wilson had owned the farm for five years. Given his rustic appearance, it is not surprising that he had looked, to Abbott, like a mountain prophet. However, at the time of the first Running Water Farm gathering, Wilson had just turned twenty-six. He was born in Miami, the youngest of four, and lost his father at the age of thirteen. The teenage Wilson and his mom moved between southern Florida, Georgia, and Appalachian North Carolina. He attended Florida State University, where he dove deeper into hippie drug culture than his studies. He left with "straight F's" and moved to Atlanta to work as a busboy at the Howard Johnson's on 10th Street. It wasn't long, though, before a beloved childhood friend convinced Mikel to join him at Guilford, a Quaker college in Greensboro, North Carolina. This time the academics resonated with his countercultural values. A set of older hippie students befriended him, and he took courses on Eastern religions and comparative arts. In 1973 he turned twenty-one and inherited a small trust from a grandmother who had died when he was a child. He took the money and went looking for a small plot of land. The first place his rural real estate agent showed him was a tiny farm angled on the side of Roan Mountain, in western North Carolina. He bought it immediately and dropped out of school.

The place was not only small (fifteen acres) and steeply appointed, at an altitude of about 3,500 feet, but it had few amenities. Wilson scoured the *Foxfire* books, *The Whole Earth Catalog*, and *Mother Earth News* for homesteading tips, eventually running a black plastic pipe from an uphill mountain spring straight into his kitchen sink so that the water ran constantly. Thus, he named the place "Running Water." The farm was beautiful. As Wilson describes it, "It had a chestnut cabin on it that had been built in the 30s. It had been abandoned, probably for decades, and it had twenty or thirty really nice old mountain-variety apple trees and . . . a garden that was almost like an acre. . . . It was just a *lovely* space, almost impossible to get to because it had been abandoned for so long."[19]

At first, two of his hippie buddies from Guilford—Phil and Terry—moved in with him, and Wilson worked as a short-order cook in a diner down the mountain. There was an elderly neighbor named Stokes Ledford who would offer the younger men advice. There was a food co-op in nearby Loafer's Glory and a spate of hippie potlucks. So, despite how remote Running Water was, Wilson plugged into the area's available counterculture. He discovered a consciousness-raising group just down the road that was hosted by a radical couple, Carol and her husband Grant. Wilson attended their group regularly, with one other member, a local hippie woman who was a friend of Carol's. In due time, the two women came out and moved together to Asheville—and Mikel divulged that he was gay, too. After, he started reading *RFD*. Possibly inspired by the women as well as by the bitter winters at Running Water, Wilson decided to board the place up and move to San Francisco. That was early 1977. He lived out west for about six to nine months before coming back to his North Carolina farm, where he took up weaving and dreamed of how he might find a place for Running Water in the gay liberationist networks of *RFD*. That dream would manifest on the summer solstice of June 1978, at the first Running Water gathering.

Franklin Abbott, an attendee who would eventually memorialize the Running Water gathering in a poem, was also quite young at the time. He'd been born in 1950, in Birmingham. He remembers his early life there as largely white, where hearing the "n- word" was normalized. His family moved to Buffalo, New York, before settling again in the South, in Nashville. Abbott then went to college at Mercer University in Macon, Georgia. The school had actively recruited Black students, and by the time Abbott enrolled, they offered Black Studies courses and hosted a vocal Black Power movement on campus. As Abbott remembers it, he left a tacitly white world for one that was significantly Black—by moving one state away. In a place once known for its slave-economy cotton industry and whose racial makeup then tilted to a Black majority, Jim Crow tensions persisted on the surface of daily life in Macon. Abbott's sense of this was amplified when, after graduation, he took work directing an area day center for the mentally ill that serviced the rural Black population. In this role he could do little to counter the legacies of segregation, which treated Black people as contagions requiring separate facilities like water fountains and restrooms, and the system did little more in terms of material support for his clients, who struggled with mental health issues. As a young director, his calls for needed funding repeatedly fell on deaf ears. He quit not long after and in 1978 moved to Atlanta, where he conducted an internship for his graduate study in social work. He was assigned to the Buckhead Mental Health Center, where he also worked with lesbian therapist Jane Gavin to establish a gay support center and helpline called Tempo. He'd come out of the closet in his sophomore year at Mercer. He had then attended the 1977 Chapel Hill regional lesbian and gay conferences that preceded the 1978 Atlanta conference.

Around that time he published in the Spring 1978 issue of *RFD* a poem he wrote just after returning from Roan Mountain. This poem records Abbott's take on the first Running Water Farm gathering. It's one of the most vital portraits of the event, and captures its unique spirit. Key, shifting emotions Abbott felt in the wake of the experience are captured in the poem's title: "Ascent, Lament, and Admonition."[20] The poem, however, began *in medias res*—not with the *ascent* but with the *lament*. The narrator slowly wakes, the morning after, to the harsh realization that he is back home in Atlanta, with "the dirt of Roan Mountain still on my feet." The city represented a suffocating heterosexist place where he was "expected to be the same" as everyone else, just as abject as he was before the liberating experience of Running Water. Abbott initially cast the little Appalachian farm as a utopia where it was impossible to stay and painful to leave.

The lament was short, though—mere lines. It is truer to say that the physical, emotional, and spiritual *ascent* that the Running Water gathering offered was psychically accessible to attendees who could revisit it in their dreams. Going there charged their spiritual batteries. To access that energy again, Abbott simply closed his eyes, "allowing the city to soften / and fade away" as, in dream-trance, he re-climbed the mountain, traveling back in time, "through honeysuckle-scented, star-silvered hems of clouds" until a "bright sun [climbed] to its solstice." The vivid sensory description brings back the geographic space where the porch hosted its musicians and the twisted apple orchard was close by: "there will my brothers hold me / turn me loose, set me free / there will I be heard, listen / and in concert sing / to the opening of hearts / and the laying down of burdens." In this stanza, Abbott most faithfully documents the activities and emotions of the gathering. Attendees practiced listening and sharing, releasing and holding, and laying down the burdens of being effeminate, queer men in the South during this particularly scary time. However, what is most telling about Abbott's "Ascent, Lament, and Admonition" is the last feeling. As we have already noted, it would be easy to understand the rural gathering as a cycle of ascent and lament, a cycle of elated connection and then painful loss, a cycle of utopian escape followed by a return to hard everyday politics. Abbott admonishes himself not to lapse into that simplistic, and ultimately self-damaging, dynamic. Instead his poem suggests two important ways the June 1978 Running Water Farm gathering can be remembered.

First, he offered his poem as a way for others—whether we attended or not—to vividly and magically travel to the Roan Mountain site in order to commune with queer fellows and to rescue us from the isolation society forces us to feel. This dream-travel was not perfect, though. Abbott knew there were harsh realities we simply could not keep at bay. He represented those poetically: "the telephone rings / I have no charm to stop" how he was "dispatched / to walk the city streets." Second, he asserted that, from the rarefied connection afforded by ascending the mountain, attendees were erotically and politically changed. He ended the poem by stating that the gathering left him "a better lover / my gentleness refined, aligned, / and dangerous."

The radical women from the Atlanta conference had tasked these gay liberationist men to chip away at their sexism, which had too often led them to take up space, physically and communicatively. At Roan Mountain, these men practiced listening and caring, opening up and making room. This required them to amplify certain qualities that were perhaps gentler than they were masculinely assertive—in the traditional (patriarchal) sense. They did this in a climate that was charged with music and song, and with ritual drawn from faggot witchcraft. If these men kissed each other as they unwound their circles and spirals, then they bolstered their same-sex eroticism in a magical context that promised to change who they had been. Many must have felt themselves able to align more easily—with each other as lovers and with the radical politics that many in the "outside" world saw as dangerous. If they shared their fears and burdens, they also held each other in support, and in awe. Their shadows melted at the edge of the apple orchard, and their voices mingled with the folk anthems belted from the high porch down the steep mountainside.

It would have been hard to go home—to aching isolation, suffocating repression, and daily physical fear. Abbott reminded them, though, that they hadn't just gone on a retreat. They had *transformed*. They had boosted their batteries and honed new skills. As a result, they were better lovers, and sharper revolutionaries. He acknowledged that they would all experience terrible lows, but they had also learned how to reach new highs, how to conduct new magic. Basically, the witchy queer mountain traveled *inside* them. This was not just Abbott's take-away. When Dimid Hayes returned to New Orleans, to LaSIS, his fellow sissies received him icily. Perhaps they suspected that he was already looking for another place to be. They likely noticed a different political tenor, too—maybe something dreamy, folksy, and pastoral, as opposed to the audacious street theater they were learning in the Quarter. Dimid felt so uncomfortable that he took his own separate apartment that summer: an echo of the split between Mulberry House and Watson House. Despite this separation, recharged by Running Water he returned to the work already underway with LaSIS—organizing New Orleans's first gay liberation rally—and he ultimately wrote "A Letter of Action" to Running Water attendees over "a cup of strong New Orleans chicory coffee and a case of the highest hopes."[21] His sissie message back to Running Water urged them to take up a collectivist practice of solidarity, which he and LaSIS learned from their earliest activism in New Orleans. LaSIS was now connected to Atlanta and Running Water—to Gross, Abbott, and Wilson—and this link began to attract many more regional gay liberationists.

At the Crossroads: Crafting Collectivist Vision from New Orleans Solidarity Campaigns

In New Orleans, LaSIS made solidarity their main queer activist practice. This would define the collectivism they would promote through *RFD* and *Running Water*, and it would distinguish them in the Crescent City's gay culture. We know that Aurora regarded the Gertrude Stein group as a social club with moderate conservative leanings, and that Stein's Alan Robinson thought LaSIS politically shrill. Both groups were, however, impactful—if with quite different aims and strategies. For their part, Gertrude Stein worked through *Impact* to catalyze a wider gay neighborhood politics which would foment significant change in the late 1970s. Lawrence Knopp has described the gay gentrification of the Marigny—just downriver from the Quarter—to include an early 1970s preservationist movement (led by a gay San Francisco architect who had bought a home in that neighborhood) followed by a later 1970s period of strategic gay development.[22] LaSIS entered, stage left, during that second phase.

There are a couple of details concerning the gay neighborhood politics of *Impact* within its first year of publication (September 1977–June 1978) that are important to establish. First, the paper extended the "salon" strategy of the Gertrude Stein Society—combining cultural coverage (an arts review) with political commentary. Second, the editors wished to avoid the gender agonism that had led to the fracturing of the New Orleans GLF in 1972. In the October 1977 issue they published a blank page titled "Women's Section" with a note from editor Gary Martin asking why no women had contributed to the newspaper: "We're just wondering where you are. Because without you, we're not complete yet."[23] Women responded. Of particular importance was Charlene Schneider, owner of the recently opened Marigny bar Charlene's, on Elysian Fields. A magnetic figure, Schneider had coordinated pool sports at the Bywater's gay lounge, The Country Club, before opening her own place. She wrote a regular events column for *Impact*, too. At Charlene's, she hosted voter registration drives and candidate debates alongside drink specials. On page and at events, Schneider not only represented lesbian New Orleans but she often led the liberal gay organizational spirit of the times.

Third, *Impact* articulated the gay vote not as a vague aspirational act but as a tangible bloc with real weight. Its writers would often cite the residential concentration of gays in the Quarter—75 percent according to one 1978 reporter—making it plain to readers and political officials alike that their organization *as* residents was a form of power.[24] In November 1977 *Impact* published a full-page ad supporting Ernest Nathan "Dutch" Morial for mayor, calling the African American and civil rights advocate "a man with a personal stake in human rights for everyone."[25] Morial would win his race, and the following June, recognizing gay support for his candidacy, he appointed Gertrude Stein member Ann Toups as representative of the gay community on the task force assigned to vet a new police superintendent.[26] This was an important placement, necessary to remove the leaders of District Attorney Jim Garrison's vice-era entrapment and extortion system, which persisted in targeting gay bars and baths. When they voted as residents, lesbian and gay New Orleanians got results, gaining an audience in city decision-making.

The newspaper's next move was to amplify their voice by articulating a visibly gay neighborhood composed of both gay establishments and residences. In the December 1977 and January 1978 issues of *Impact*, editors published a grid image of the Quarter, marking clusters of gay bars, baths, and restaurants. These maps document what geographer Richard Campanella has called the "lavender line"—five bustling gay bars clustered close to the 800 block of Bourbon Street, near the St. Ann intersection. However, *Impact's* late-1970s maps clearly also marked a gay social world that exceeded the tourist ground zero of Bourbon Street.[27] In a February 1978 article titled "Hey! Remember Decatur Street?" three new gay bars were featured alongside the older Golden Lantern to promote the sense of a new district within the Quarter that was meant to cater less to tourists than to gay residents within a few blocks' walk from the Marigny.[28] Then, in April 1978, *Impact* published a theme issue devoted to lesbian and gay real estate, full of advice on home purchase, restoration, and ownership.[29] When LaSIS fully formed—the very next month—they did so as a collectivist house, expressing a similar concern with home, but with a very different vision than the liberal gay and lesbian homeowners extending the lavender line.

Oddly, when the Gertrude Stein Society announced a June gay pride event to commemorate the one-year anniversary of the Anita Bryant protest, LaSIS volunteered their political organization, the PTA, to organize it. Although Gertrude Stein themed the festivities a "Celebration of Ourselves," the PTA implemented it as a *gay liberation* rally.[30] Hayes and Aurora worked hard to ensure that the rally included as many interested parties as possible. They secured an ACLU representative and a Unitarian minister as speakers, and invited as many leftist and progressive organizations as they could. It was also important to LaSIS—given their commitments to anti-racism, learned in Arkansas—that people of color feel welcome. Although the Jackson Square event was well attended, an *Impact* photo featuring many Black attendees tacitly disavowed the event by calling it a "gay pride rally by the Pink Triangle Alliance" and referred to those in the photograph—many of them Black—as "spectators" rather than participants.[31] The event introduced a dissonance between *Impact*'s liberal gay neighborhood politics and the PTA's liberationist approach. *Impact* readers criticized the event, arguing that the nongay content and speakers diluted the theme of "gay unity."[32]

Ultimately this critique led to the PTA clarifying their politics in the August issue of *Impact*, saying that while they did commit to supporting general gay rights, they considered that aim secondary to their primary focus on those marginalized within the gay community—for example, gay parents, older and younger gays, disabled gays, and "third world gays."[33] They framed their struggle as levied against the interwoven systems of "patriarchy and capitalism" and dedicated themselves to "devise a strategy of mutual and reciprocal support among all oppressed groups for the liberation of all. Tactically this means participation as out front gays in political events happening here in New Orleans. We have participated in Equal Rights Amendment, African Liberation Day, Philippine Independence, and the Socialist Workers Party Campaign rallies." Through the PTA, then, LaSIS concentrated their efforts on being queer allies to wider New Orleans–based political struggles. For their part, *Impact* and Gertrude Stein doubled down on their standing commitments to (1) protect lavender line residents and establishments from vice-era police harassment, such as the June 26 arrest of gay men at the Canal Baths, and (2) prevent Anita Bryant's planned return to the Crescent City. *Impact* editors also began prohibiting in their paper LaSIS's use of reclaimed epithets like *faggot*, *sissie*, and *faerie*—a parlance the sissies had become accustomed to in *RFD*.

New Orleans dates its first official Gay Pride Parade from 1980, but acknowledges the 1978 PTA-led event as a "Gay Pride *rally*," as an important precursor for the city's Pride events.[34] Aurora and Hayes both remember it specifically as a *gay liberation rally*. The political differences between the Gertrude Stein Society and LaSIS are embedded in these word choices. When Hayes returned from the first Running Water Farm gathering, planning the rally was what absorbed him. It may not be surprising, then, that it was August before he addressed his "Letter of Action" to fellow Running Water attendees, and that the letter's contents overtly reflected the solidarity focus that LaSIS had honed in Louisiana.[35] If Abbott's poem demonstrated how attendees might psychically relate themselves to the memory of Running Water as an ongoing battery for their radical transformations, Hayes urged attendees to collectivize the farm in wider regional, liberationist solidarity. His letter defined that work.

Hayes felt it was important to answer Mikel Wilson's earnest request for help in collectivizing the farm. However, he also realized this goal was easier said than done. Not everyone had the networks or mobility to simply move house to join like-minded souls. To answer such challenges, Dimid pointed to the two core vehicles for collectivization within their nascent culture: (1) a means for remote contact, which would be *RFD*, and (2) a place to come together periodically, which would be rural gatherings, like the one at Running Water. He underscored how important it was to acknowledge that they were all at different points in a *process* of entering collectivization that would be facilitated by the mobile culture posed by *RFD* information-sharing and a regular events calendar. Hayes wrote his letter to make radical collectivism seem more doable and to share what he had found valuable about collectivism since joining Mulberry House several years before. He refined sissie collectivist vision from lessons he learned from his recent experience: Mulberry House domestic liberation, Running Water care labor, *and* New Orleans street solidarities.

As with Mulberry House, he placed a special emphasis on avoiding gendered divisions of labor and the pitfalls of couplism. He made a few qualifications, too, though. He conceded how important class analysis was to collectivism before he went on to argue that, on its own, class analysis was woefully inadequate. He noted that too often the process was derailed by "fault finding"—emotional dynamics of accusation and guilt—which impeded progress to mutual support and solutions. Even though this fault finding was endemic to the Ozark socialist-feminist consciousness-raising around Mulberry House, Hayes did not, at any point, see it as endemic to feminism; to the contrary, he blamed patriarchal conditioning, especially as it manifested in "Marxist, Maoist, masculine definitions of self-transformation." He added, "I think women have shown us that revolutionary changes are more than a simplified analysis based on economics and that our analysis of reality has to become much broader."

Running Water's listening circles were meant to alchemically alter masculine ways of relating. Hayes also knew that Melba'son himself insisted, as he left the Ozarks for New Orleans, that radical sissies needed to conduct class analysis and consciousness-raising with less masculine territoriality and with more responsiveness. In fact, both sissies felt that women and feminism made this lesson abundantly clear. It is likely that it was this shared feminist vision between Hayes and Melba'son that prompted them to highlight effeminism in their April bibliography. However, Dimid—exiled, in the summer of 1978, to his Royal Street apartment—must have felt that his fellow sissies needed some reminding about how Running Water's gentler mode *was* the effeminist direction they had committed to. Hayes shrewdly used his "Letter of Action" to link LaSIS's and Running Water's politics, underscoring a shared praxis.

He also asserted, "It is very important to consciously create private spaces separate from collective spaces.... It is better to create two smaller collectives with enough private space than it is to have a larger collective without.... (Watch for this because it can be a destructive force, not giving enough respite from the rigors of collective living!)" Instead of placing a premium on all space as shared space, which had been the dominant approach at Mulberry House, Hayes recommended *designing* for privacy, as a safety valve for collective claustrophobia. This note might also reflect their more recent interest in anarchistic autonomy as a necessary complement to successful collectivism: recognition that private space supported the personal reflection and creative practice they now saw as central to collectivism.

We can also read Hayes's recommendation "to create two smaller collectives" as his coming to positive terms with the splitting of Mulberry House. By making it an element of design, he translated a painful, abject experience of "exile" into a strategy of choosing to hive off as needed. Just as a spatial plan for private and collective quarters entered Hayes's vision at this time, so did a temporal plan for seasonal commitments. He raised the possibility of signing contracts as a way to bond collectives for certain periods of time: "six months? A year?—that we will live and struggle together and it needs to be continually reaffirmed" with terms that can be "'studied' or renegotiated at any time." With these references to contracts, marriage haunted this part of the letter. Instead of a heterosexist, monogamous "til death do us part" union, though, he implicitly proposed the collective as a serial group marriage. You commit for a certain season, for the length of a certain project, and then you agree to move on. As a result, a serial form of mobile collectivism took hold as part of the network's social imagination.

Given Dimid's Mulberry House background, he was acutely aware of the importance of rural space as a sanctuary and healing space. He anticipated "a chaos of such new proportions, that we will need the security of revolutionary rural queer spaces" and that "'safe' places in the country will be needed to harbor sisters and brothers from destructive forces in the cities. City/country exchanges of individuals and energy will need to happen so that we can best use the good of both the city and country environments." It's likely that Hayes placed the word *safe* in quotes in order to demonstrate some skepticism toward any sense that rural spaces were naturally safe to them, but he also placed the word *home* in quotes, implying that queer people were uniquely un-homed, possibly necessitating their need for an accessible underground through which they could keep moving into different collectives—rural and urban homes for a season. "City/country exchanges" established a cultural norm of circulation from the urban (framed as compact) to the rural (cast as open) and back again. If Running Water featured "heart circles," then Hayes's vision connected each discrete collective as part of a wider circulatory system that passed through diastolic (open) phases in the country and systolic (compressed) phases in the city. Due to the mobility at the center of his vision, Hayes's collectivism was equal parts affective, spatial, and temporal. It was moving.

Geographically, it was conceived in regional terms. It addressed the Southeast. This choice might have been shaped by how the Arkansas Sissies had questioned the West Coast *RFD* editors' ability to represent the concerns of other regions, especially the Midwest and Southeast, where white supremacists had recently added violent attacks on lesbians and gay men to their longer Jim Crow racism. This was likely at the forefront of Dimid's mind as he wrote his "Letter of Action." Just as the Arkansas Sissies had demanded that *RFD* include images of gay liberationists of color in their photography issue, Hayes questioned any privileged suggestion that Running Water should continue as a "faggot only" space. But the most direct influence was how LaSIS were, at the very same time, sharpening their solidarity politics in New Orleans, differentiating themselves from the liberal gay focus of *Impact* and Gertrude Stein.

Hayes referred to Running Water as "'Sissiefaggot' space" to underscore how the event and site had been inclusive of multiple identities from the very beginning: faggots *and* sissies. The conversations at the event suggested to him there was an interest in future gatherings not being crafted as separate space for gay liberationist men alone but as ones that would include children and women. For him, the most fundamental work of such collectivism was to "examine the politics of a group of mostly young white gay males 'owning' land" and choose a different path: to expand intimate solidarity and share space with "other active revolutionary forces." Therefore, he did not imagine that access to rural space or the ability to circulate through its networks was accessible to all, especially those who needed it most.

He felt that any "Southeast Network" would have to contend with its Jim Crow legacies. He referenced how the issue of race was discussed at Running Water, and how he remembered at least one attendee assuming that, because there were no Black sissies or faggots present, the latter had no need of such a space or network. Hayes argued to the contrary: "If anything, I feel we need to assume [Black sissies'] needs are NOT met. I know mine aren't, and I've got it easier than most black Sissies I know. Making this assumption seems to me to be an (unconscious) attempt to totally deny the historical and contemporary facts of racism in this country." For him, gay liberationist collectivization in the Southeast required designing active forms of welcome to those whose access to the network was eroded by systemic inequalities: "We have a responsibility to actively seek out individuals and organized groups of other oppressed peoples and include them in this (specific) privilege of open rural queer space." Black Sissies were a priority, in part because LaSIS had committed themselves to amplifying their sissie identities in New Orleans as a way to chip away at the whiteness of their own middle-class backgrounds. Further, in "A Letter of Action," Dimid added that his own vision involved building relationships with the revolutionary forces for "women, children, older gays, handicapped gays, transgenderists [sic], etc.," too. This desire for an inclusive liberationist space dedicated to broad solidarity reflected how the PTA designed the June rally in New Orleans, and how they would join UTNO striking teachers come Labor Day. In the summer of 1978, LaSIS dreamed of a crossroads—rural *and* urban—where all revolutionaries met.

Cartography of a Deeper South's Sissie Networking

It seems clear that LaSIS was intent on an accelerated *fanshen*. Not only had they leveraged a variation on faggot witchcraft to perform radical conversions and reoriented themselves as heretical nonbinary street teachers, all within months, but they also flung themselves into New Orleans activism. They formed the PTA, organized a June gay liberation rally, contributed regularly to *Impact*, proposed queer childcare, volunteered in anti-rape initiatives, joined striking UTNO teachers, and gave their solidarity to a range of other local movements (the ERA, African and Philippine liberation, and the Socialist Workers Party)—all in the summer of 1978. By attending the first Running Water gathering and writing his "Letter of Action," Dimid communicated the importance of solidarity for regional gay liberationists even as he reminded LaSIS how important Running Water's affective, spiritual, and communicative praxis was for their sissie collectivism. Both groups were persuaded.

When the second Running Water gathering was held, on October 6–8, 1978, Melba'son, Aurora, and Dimid attended.[36] (Stacy did not go, presumably because of his more formal, full-time work schedule.) An urgent agenda item at this second gathering was exactly who would take responsibility for *RFD*, and the three New Orleanian sissies volunteered to coordinate the publication of the Winter 1978 issue. Other Running Water Farm attendees, intrigued by the sissies' nonbinary presentation and collectivist perspective, requested that LaSIS say more about what being a sissie meant. *RFD*'s "Sissie" (discussed in Chapter 5) was composed in response to that curiosity. This means that, in addition to reorienting themselves to New Orleans street life, LaSIS also defined themselves in dialogue with Southeastern gay liberationists—at Running Water and through *RFD*. Whereas "Sissie" more overtly described their gender expression, Dimid Hayes's "A Letter of Action" began to theorize the house's collectivism. Two other Winter 1978 *RFD* pieces developed that theory in a public-facing way.

In "Sissie Networking," Brotherlover's collectivist vision largely aligned with Hayes's but hit certain notes more emphatically. Stacy addressed logistical concerns and imagined *RFD* as a kind of circulating bulletin board.[37] For an isolated gay liberationist to collectivize thoughtfully, the existing collectives needed to be as transparent as possible. They should publish their active projects and delineate the skills and resources those projects required. Even more, he suggested that collectives share their politics, organizational structure, collective processes, social culture, and challenges. With this information, new sissies could consider which collectives resonated with them most, and what projects they might contribute to. If Hayes's letter had implied that collectivization was akin to a serial group marriage, then Brotherlover was eager to set a template for *RFD* ads as a way to prevent any unfortunate shotgun weddings. Maybe with his Mulberry House experience in mind, he wanted to develop an information-sharing mechanism that would facilitate good collectivist matches. His vision seemed predicated on an assumption that such transparency would enable creative collectivist projects, in rural and urban locales, limited only by the sissies' social imaginations. He also recognized the concrete challenges of living in the country, with no income, suggesting that urban houses host rural collectivists, especially in the winter, so that the latter could take seasonal waged work to save money for summers back in the country.

The second piece—a map that accompanied "Sissie Networking"—was sketched by a recent LaSIS collaborator, an attendee at the first two Running Water Farm gatherings: Milo Pyne. Before discussing his map, it's helpful to see how he'd entered the network. Born George Clinton Pyne III, in Durham, North Carolina, in 1950, Milo went to school for two years at Chapel Hill. He was inspired by fellow gay activist Bob Bland, and according to Sears, he quickly involved himself by "organizing student support of the mostly black female food workers, chairing meetings of the Chapel Hill Revolutionary Movement, and writing for *The Protean Radish*, a statewide alternative paper founded by a chapter of the Southern Student Organizing Committee (SSOC)."[38] Like Wilson, he grew frustrated with school and dropped out to join the third Venceremos Brigade to Cuba in 1970. There was a gay liberationist caucus in his brigade, alongside ones for Black and women brigadiers, and together they served the revolution while laboring in orchards.[39] Afterward, reflecting on his own sexuality, he came to see his leftism through the lenses of queer experience *and* rural life. Back in the United States, Pyne was determined to put his emerging politics into practice.

First he went north, meeting with a series of gay radicals. In New York he met Allen Young, whose own radical experiences in Cuba would figure so prominently in 1972's *Out of the Closets*, an anthology Young edited with Karla Jay. He also met gay activist Jim Fouratt. Next Milo went to Boston, both to join a college friend named Mike Tola—a potential love interest—and to work with the White Panthers, a group of white activists eager to make good on Huey Newton's suggestion that white anti-racists should work separately from, but in tandem with, the Black Panthers. He also met the activist and historian Allan Berube in Boston, before going even further north, to Vermont, visiting the Liberation News Service, which combined rural farm work with radical journalism. Shortly after this northern whirlwind trip, in early 1971 he moved back to North Carolina to join the rural Tick Creek collective, not far outside of Pittsboro. The collective primarily served as a way station for radicals traveling between Atlanta and DC. He cultivated an intimate, sexual relationship with a local beekeeper named Loomis, who lived close by, and then with a man named Peter, who joined the Tick Creek group. However, in 1973 the collective lost their house to a fire, and the core members of the group—including Pyne and Peter—searched for a new home.

The group eventually found Short Mountain, an abandoned farm on a couple hundred acres in rural Cannon County in Appalachian Tennessee. It wasn't terribly far, by car, from The Farm, where Stephen Gaskin had relocated roughly three hundred other San Francisco hippies in 1971, near Summertown, Tennessee. And there were other queer hippies even closer, like the gay John Harris (later Gabby Haze) and his lesbian wife Merrill Mushroom, who lived in nearby Dry Creek with their adoptive children.[40] Due to their radical pasts, Pyne and all of the Short Mountain collective were under FBI surveillance. An October 1974 FBI surveillance report out of the Memphis office indicated that informants had observed roughly twenty-five to thirty radicals living at Short Mountain. However, they closed their file on Pyne in January 1975, concluding that all the radical enclave was doing was "raising flowers and various herbs."[41] As a kind of tribute to his life under surveillance, the young radical, who had lived for years as "Milo Guthrie," ultimately kept a hybrid version of his assumed and given names, becoming Milo Pyne.[42]

By late 1976, though, Short Mountain had suffered many internal tensions—political and interpersonal—the most persistent of which stemmed from the challenge of surviving for very long in such a remote area, especially in winter, without regular wage work. Pyne was the only collectivist remaining by that second winter, save for the livestock. He published an announcement in the Winter 1976 issue of *RFD* that read, "Flying South for the Winter? Solitary faggot needs winter guests. The other (nongay) members of our group have left me with the goats and cow, on a beautiful middle-Tennessee mountain. Come and visit if you're passin' thru."[43] Mikel Wilson visited Pyne on his way out to San Francisco, and the two schemed ways to center their farms in a revived gay liberationist culture. It's no surprise, then, that the next year, Pyne went to the early Running Water gatherings. He also volunteered to partner on *RFD* editorial duties with LaSIS, contributing to "Sissie" and drawing a map for Brotherlover's "Sissie Networking."

RFD had employed maps to powerful graphic effect before. As regular reader-writers, Pyne and LaSIS would have been aware of this. In its second issue, *RFD* had printed a simple map outlining the United States, with irregularly drawn dots distributed across the forty-eight contiguous states. The caption read, "RFD COUNTRY/each dot is a known reader."[44] Scott Herring has read this map as an example of what he calls early *RFD*'s "critical rusticity."[45] Comparing it to the slick, commercial production of *The Advocate*, which shaped its readership as an equally slick and commercial male "clone" living in a coastal metropolitan area, Herring calls attention to the crudeness of the drawing as a rurally oriented send-up of an urban aesthetic of reproducible polish. He further argues that where *The Advocate* revels in its volume of purportedly very similar readers, this early *RFD* map suggests another value altogether: the intimacy that stems from connecting each unique reader and locale. Early *RFD* posed a domestic gay liberationist trans-localism as a political counterpoint to *The Advocate*'s bicoastal, cosmopolitan gay nationalism. Herring points out a couple of limitations of the 1974 map, though: It imagined itself addressing an exclusively US mainland audience, and it registered, with question marks, certain states that it still hoped to reach.

In Pyne's 1978 map, Louisiana and Arkansas were situated as the western horizon. The rest of the nation was of little concern and, therefore, was not depicted. Only the Southeast appeared.[46] This would have been important to the sissies. Of the seven to eight states to which *RFD*'s 1974 map assigned question marks, three were the adjoined Arkansas, Louisiana, and Mississippi.

Milo Pyne's "Sissie Networking" (hand-drawn map), *RFD*, Winter 1978, 20.

These three Mississippi Delta states represented a significant region that *RFD* hadn't yet embraced in 1974. However, we know that Mulberry House visited the Iowa editors in late 1975, likely aware that they were absent from the earlier map. Four years after that first map's printing, LaSIS "put itself on the map" by assuming editorial duties for the Winter 1978 issue of *RFD* and effectively addressing the magazine's 1974 question marks. In doing so, they reoriented *RFD*'s print network in the Southeast.

Lest we interpret this as mere regional agonism, it's important to remember that it was in 1978 that the Arkansas Sissies had critiqued the West Coast *RFD* editors for visually eliding gay liberationists of color in its photography issue and for appearing to be blind to the white supremacist terror raging in the Southeast. Perhaps this critique haunted the way Dimid, in his gloss for "Sissie Networking," referred to LaSIS's "daily life on the delta" as one where liberationist efforts often "dissolve into nothing."[47] We can imagine a linguistic synergy developing for LaSIS—between the queer pink *triangle* of their gay liberationist politics and the Mississippi *Delta* as a landscape of entrenched white supremacy *and* remarkable Black resistance.[48] An affective dynamic of erosion and cohesion began to inform their collectivism, and by centering this geography on the *RFD* map they insisted on the importance of confronting the region's assemblage of racist, sexist, and homophobic power.

Pyne even more powerfully anticipated Herring's second observation about the 1974 map: its squarely national parameters. At the southern and eastern edges of Pyne's new cartography, he carefully wrote (by hand, in capital letters) the names for the bordering bodies of water—in Spanish. By doing so, he fundamentally shifted our understanding of sissie collectivism's regionalism from subnational, implied by the earlier *RFD* map, to transnational, exceeding national borders and official languages. In fact, he signed his drawing, scrawling a tiny cursive "Milo" just off the tip of Florida, thereby placing his own nascent sissie identity somewhere in the vicinity of Cuba. It is crucial to remember that, whereas other gay liberationists anchored their coming out to Stonewall, Pyne owed his own to his experiences with the Venceremos Brigades. Thornton and Oglesby were similarly shaped by reading the Venceremos accounts in 1972's *Out of the Closets*. For these leftist sissies, Cuba often cast a stronger liberationist influence than did US coastal cities.

As we have seen, Ian Lekus—who interviewed Pyne for his research—has drawn comparisons between US gay liberationist experiences in Venceremos Cuba and the communal experiments that popped up afterward. Lekus has also commented on how 1960s white supremacist politicians in the Deep South deployed Cuba as a complex foil in order to link their regional anti-communist, anti-feminist, anti-civil-rights, and anti-gay agendas. What emerges from such an analysis is a sense of how the US South extended its Jim Crow white supremacy through its regional spins on national foreign policy with its especially close Cuban neighbor. Lekus uses the phrase "deeper south" to gesture toward the cultural geography cinched by this transnational rhetorical net and calls attention to the particular thread woven by gay liberationist experiences with the Venceremos Brigades. I find it a perfect phrase to describe the leftist sissie geography that Pyne sketches in "Sissie Networking," as he draws the readers' eyes down, away from dry land, and into waters where we "Americans" meet another tongue, other narratives than those commanded by the American Dream.

LaSIS—without the working-class Thornton and Oglesby—might have drifted away from any Venceremos moorings that they had once felt. However, Pyne, who had gone to Cuba himself, graphically reminded them, and other *RFD* readers, of this legacy. His map also gracefully omitted any state borders, as if suggesting to the Louisiana Sissies that they could give up naming themselves by US-defined political states. The only interior lines his map contained marked the rivers that had, in many cases, been usurped to create state borders, but whose more fundamental value was to carry travelers into the *Oceano Atlantico* or the *Golfo de Mexico*. For the environmentalist Pyne, the landscape itself had more to say to the sissie network than imposed political borders did—whether those borders faced inward or outward. His cartography was driven more by a natural and cultural geography's capacity to question nationalist geopolitics and to forge transnational relationships. As with the 1974 *RFD* issue, though, Milo's 1978 Sissie Networking map kept its unique dots, labeling them according to where Southeastern Running Water attendees lived. Importantly, this allowed the attendees to see themselves as part of a deeper-south revolution, to imagine themselves plugging in as Brotherlover and Hayes suggested. They sensed that something electrifying could take place; they could help change the face of things.

In a half year's time the sissies had radically converted themselves, improvised a nonbinary street pedagogy, centered liberationist solidarity in their politics, and thoughtfully articulated their collectivist praxis to a new regional network sprung up around *RFD* and Running Water Farm, but facing out with a deeper-south transnational orientation. Their momentum was staggering. Their voices were heard, at intersections and crossroads, at the local and regional scale. And they were poised for even broader actions.

It's crucial to remember the overt shift to an affective register of *sissie terror* that took place between the Fall and Winter 1978 issues of *RFD*, though. Melba'son had only barely survived suicide in the wake of the Save Our Children campaign, in October of 1977, and within a year LaSIS hived off from Mulberry House and remade themselves. The terror they felt did not ebb, though, as they watched other cities follow Miami's lead in stripping away recently won antidiscrimination laws protecting gays, and as Briggs picked up Bryant's baton, fearmongering with a child protectionist rhetoric that knowingly courted vigilante violence. In "A Letter for Action," Hayes proposed that rural spaces like Running Water Farm would be needed to shelter a wide array of oppressed/revolutionary groups who might find themselves in an enraged country's crosshairs.

They rolled up their sleeves to address this need. LaSIS attended the second Running Water Farm gathering, which took place in early October 1978.

Then time stopped: On the Monday after Thanksgiving, Harvey Milk, the gay San Francisco supervisor who had led the defeat of the California Briggs Initiative, was assassinated in his City Hall office, shot twice in the head.

Part III
Short Mountain
Appalachian Tennessee, 1979–81

CHAPTER SEVEN

After Milk
Performing Sissie Collectivism at New National Volumes

1977 and 1978 were terrifying years. We forget this when we remember Bryant and Save our Children through the lens of gay rights alone. We forget Robert Hillsborough's murder. We forget the activist suicides in Miami and New Orleans. We forget the emboldened violent homophobia of white Christian supremacists in Oklahoma and Arkansas. We forget how Save Our Children's rabid child protectionism was also racist and sexist (and ageist), entangled with anti-desegregation and anti-ERA entrenchments. We forget that these aggressive exclusions overlapped with a time when women of color—like Georgia's Dessie Woods—were put on trial for killing their would-be rapists and when Black children like Gary Tyler served prison sentences for white supremacists' segregationist violence. Even if Bryant was increasingly belittled by floods of gay protesters at her poorly attended concerts, Briggs borrowed her Save Our Children playbook for a homophobic California child protectionist measure, and when his Proposition 6 was defeated, Milk—the gay figurehead of his defeat—was killed. And the whole country watched this on national news. LaSIS and other Running Water gay liberationists were devastated, their momentum stalled for a season of grief during that winter of 1978.

In popular discourse, Bryant, ironically, is often credited with sparking the national gay rights movement. Before Save Our Children, gay rights initiatives had often quietly succeeded in individual cities, resulting, for example, in antidiscrimination ordinances like the one that had passed with little comment in Miami. As a New Right figurehead with media celebrity and as a white Christian mother, Bryant used her stardom to embody, synergize, and activate nationwide white conservatism against small, localized, modest gay rights advances.

In some ways, though, we can understand Bryant as she is often popularly framed, as playing into the media strategies of activists like the GAA: She broadcast a blatant homophobia that inflamed a growing number of homosexuals into activism, linking individual cities' gay rights organizations and their concentrated liberal gay voting blocs/gayborhoods (like New Orleans's Marigny) into national voices. This liberal momentum would lead to the October 1979 National March on Washington for Lesbian and Gay Rights.

This is the dominant, liberal narrative, how we primarily remember rights-based lesbian and gay progress.

However, gay liberationists were also inflamed when they watched Bryant perform her homophobia on television screens, on radio airwaves, and on newspaper pages. Some, possibly inspired by the earlier era of GAA zaps, focused on theatrical media interventions—like gay liberationist Thom Higgins' famously pie-ing Bryant at one of her television appearances. Early 1970s faggot-witch martyrology also resurged, as when *Fag Rag*'s Charlie Shively publicly burned his diploma and a Bible at the 1977 Boston Pride celebrations, performing a sacrilegious fiery sermon and issuing a threat to respond to New Right fire with a flaming faggot rage.[1] Also, over the Labor Day weekend of 1979, the first Spiritual Conference for Radical Faeries took place in Benson, Arizona. In some ways, this event presented itself as an alternative to the March on Washington, where countless lesbian and gay activists converged on the nation's capital; in Arizona, gay liberationists converged at a rural desert ashram. As a rural *conference*, with Harry Hay as one of its organizers and headliners, the event also positioned itself as a variation on the 1976 Faggots & Class Struggle conference in Oregon by suggesting another figural alternative to the faggot—the *faerie*—and framing that figure with a pointedly non-leftist form of radicalism.

In 1979 and 1980, LaSIS responded in a number of ways to this season of terror after Milk's assassination. I argue in chapter 8 that their most durable move was to articulate sissie collectivism, as they conceived it in 1978 issues of *RFD*, into a sanctuary practice anchored to Pyne's revived Short Mountain site in Appalachia. In doing so, they continued their practice of proliferating collectives across the region and across rural–urban lines. They had formed New Orleans's LaSIS out of the Ozarks' Mulberry House, and they would similarly craft an Appalachian Short Mountain with their shared New Orleans experience. In other words, they proceeded to build the underground called for in Hayes's "Letter of Action," Brotherlover's "Sissie Networking," and Pyne's deeper-south map. However, in order to adequately understand the nuances of this sanctuary practice, it is important to first look at both the sissies' own media interventions with the filming of the ABC documentary "Homosexuals" and their qualified participation in relevant events: the ongoing Running Water Farm gatherings, the March on Washington, and the Arizona Radical Faeries conference. These experiences calibrated their sissie collectivism to a wider, national scale that would inform their subsequent involvement in the Short Mountain Reinhabitation Project.

Dreaming in Circles, Inside Out: LaSIS's Sissie Performativity for ABC's *Close-Up*

In early 1979, LaSIS had the opportunity to circulate their sissie collectivism even more widely, through national media. The documentary series *ABC Close-Up* was filming an episode called "Homosexuals" in New Orleans during February and March. It was clear that producers were eager to improve upon the 1967 *CBS Reports* special called "The Homosexuals."[2] In that news feature, Mike Wallace spoke to isolated figures—all men, often obscured in shadows or behind objects—who spoke with shame or hopelessness about their "condition." The show treated them like specimens to be placed before a public who despised them, psychologists who mostly saw them as sick, and police officers who pursued them as criminals. While the program did, journalistically, tip its cap to a few doctors, religious figures, and homophile organizations that held cautiously optimistic views, these were just foils for the dominant message, which was that homosexuality was a pathological sexual compulsion. This pre-Stonewall black-and-white show adopted a noir aesthetic, with Wallace's ominous voice-over. At one point Wallace claimed, "They are attracted mostly to the anonymity that the big city gives them: New York, Chicago, Los Angeles, San Francisco. The permissiveness and the variety of the city draw them." The 1967 CBS program closed dramatically: "We end as we began—with a homosexual.... At the center of his life, he remains anonymous, a displaced person, an outsider." The show was widely critiqued by gay activists for its fear-mongering tone and its tactic of filtering gay voices through the perspective of prejudiced institutions and professionals.

In 1979, then, ABC was determined to let open gays and lesbians tell their own stories in the cities where they lived. The *Close-Up* episode, then, perpetuated an urban focus with New Orleans replacing Los Angeles in the four cities featured above. Melba'son's letters documented how LaSIS adopted a leftist collectivist strategy to prevent the earlier pathological narrative from resurfacing during the filming. This may have ultimately frustrated the film editors; the final cut included only about ten minutes of the twenty rolls of film that were recorded in New Orleans.[3] The remaining LaSIS content mostly focused on Melba'son's description of sissie pain, a topic that only barely profiled their radicalism.

However, in light of their Venceremos affinities, they called themselves, for the filming, the "Casa Maricon Commune," and the show's yellow subtitling announced them as such. This intimated, to some viewers, both their leftist leanings and their deeper-south, transnational orientation. Although contemporary TV audiences likely saw little else of LaSIS's radical side, our historical understanding of their wider work puts their appearance in clearer context. For example, one of Melba'son's bolder comments that did make the cut was how he defined "sissie" as "a term of terrorism held against any male child who doesn't conform." The sissie terror/ism profiled from the previous fall's *RFD* was as forward a component in their subjectivity as ever, following, as it did, the autumn assassination of Harvey Milk.

According to Aurora, this name also allowed them to differentiate, and modulate, their identities to different scales and to different audiences. As a result, they were most often known as the PTA in New Orleans activist circles, as LaSIS in the Southeast Network of *RFD*, and as Casa Maricon Commune to the national TV audience who watched ABC's *Close-Up*.[4] As labor-sensitive leftists, they were also eager to connect with technical crew members during filming. They actively sought to circumvent how the camera divided crew and subject. One day, as they emphasized to the set crew that homosexuality should not be construed simply as urban, or male, they learned that the largely female crew (six of the seven were women) was unionized, and one of these, a lighting technician, decided to come out on set as a "dyke." As a result, the actual filming process—the interactions with the technicians directly involved in the filming—came to feel more collaborative and personal. This was another form of leftist information activism, which demystified documentary production, pushed to make the filming process more radically inclusive and reflective, and demonstrated the relevance of feminist/gay liberationist critique to the broadcast television industry.

Marlon Ross refers to the post-Stonewall era as an increasingly "televisual" one, and he carefully reads James Baldwin's "sissy" performativity for the camera as a kind of "heroics"—as when, for example, Baldwin incorporated effeminate gesture and carriage into shots designed to foreground his literary stature or when he, with wide eyes like his mother's, or like Bette Davis's, looked back into the (white) lens, defying the code that threatened generations of Black men *not* to look directly at white people.[5] LaSIS, attempting a white sissie resistance, seemed eager to expressly resist how the 1967 *CBS Reports* special had consistently isolated gay men.

Melba'son's letters relayed how LaSIS anticipated that film crews would separate the sissies by conducting one-on-one interviews, mostly in interiors, which would isolate the sissies from each other, and from their wider community. Prepared, LaSIS hosted several gay liberationists from the wider *RFD* network, and asked for other gay New Orleanians to be on hand as often as possible during the filming. In a letter to a friend addressed as "Dav," Melba'son wrote, "At all times thr wer mor Ss [Sissies] present thn jst the four of us, whch nt only gav us spprt Bt also actd as a rlty chk."[6] On another occasion, he chuckled at how the film crew arrived to find nine men in a local courtyard, giving each other group massages and hugs. LaSIS had agreed to be outdoors as much as possible during the filming time. They also flatly refused when the crew suggested filming LaSIS strolling to shop in the French Market—something they rarely did. Not always successful with such tactics, LaSIS did manage to evade solo, talking-head interviews, a format that was common when "Homosexuals" filmed in other cities.

If the GAA's media strategy had been to zoom in on homophobia in order to spark fiery gay anger, LaSIS enacted sissie resistance by performing same-sex sociality, intimacy, and care in defiance of narratives that would reproduce homosexuals as fundamentally alone. In one scene, the four main members of LaSIS, plus Ann Arbor poet Stella Mifsud and North Carolina's Ron Lambe—sat in a circle in their Rampart house, each actively listening as Melba'son spoke, like a guru, while Lambe clasped his hand, looking at the elder sissie raptly. Mifsud, in his appearance, struck an especially spiritual tenor. He wore a roughly textured white skirt that hung down to his work boots, which when combined with his long dark hair and beard, referenced the looks of orthodox clergymen. The camera periodically zoomed in on their hands, offering glimpses of Melba'son's irregularly long fingernails. Dimid, in a head-wrap, and Aurora, his hair long and loose, sat together, their heads bowed in poses that evoked both deep listening and silent prayer. As a result, they visually presented themselves as a quasi-religious circle—cloistered in their countercultural appearance. Theirs was surely meant to profile the style of the Running Water circles in which attendees practiced receptivity, vulnerability, and care. However, it is likely that important context was missing for national viewers, and that an unexpected pastoral, therapeutic tenor ultimately eclipsed the political one.

However, their circle was not the only one featured in "Homosexuals." New York's Project Return also featured men in intimate caring circles. Counselor Jackie Garcia described Project Return as addressing the intersections of being gay and Puerto Rican or Black, without the need for a psychiatrist or anyone with "a bunch of degrees." Garcia's segment showed queer men of color sharing their feelings and providing each other intimate support, in a healing context. This would have formally resonated with the "heart circles" of Running Water, as attendees have described them, and also reflected common roots in gay liberationist antipsychiatry. The similarity is a visually remarkable element, where the whiteness of LaSIS's circle and the Puerto Rican/Black composition of Project Return's circles suggest similar collectivist strategies but little room for cross-racial dialogue among late-1970s gay liberationists. Noting this parallelism reintroduces the question of how a more inclusive sissie collectivist figure might have been realized within the context of a Southeast Network that struggled in 1979 with the persistence of white supremacy, with their own white middle-class experience, and with the sudden loss of Harvey Milk.

The sissies were not the only ones in the show to strike a similar spiritual air, either. Religious concerns were overtly taken up by John Noble, who with his partner Father Robert Clement served as clergy in New York City's gay Church of the Beloved Disciple.[7] Toward the end of "Homosexuals," the camera slowly panned through Noble's "Museum of Dreams": a room full of dollhouses, animated puppets, suspended globes, and a disco ball. It was a space that Noble likened to a ship on the sea, with lights glimmering on the walls, like stars. Noble, the "museum curator," mused, "I think when you move in a world where you are accepted, the tensions—the everyday tensions—are flaccid. For us [gay people], the everyday tensions are always tight, and immediate. I think one lives on the edge of one's life. So, I think if you are a gay person—certainly when I grew up—if you are a gay person, life is much more brilliant . . . because you are constantly at war with your surroundings."

This was consonant with how Melba'son had begun to think of the affective experience, the responsive sensorium, of sissie genderfuck. Noble also invested in a dreaminess that paralleled Abbott's and others' takeaways from Running Water: "I think that's what the dream-world is about: getting away from this harsh, fluorescent-lit plastic world into the worlds of other times and places where I feel happy." This perspective was also clearly resonant with LaSIS nonbinary street pedagogy, hinging as it did on growth through generative wonder, on a trans generosity demonstrated historically through the story of "Jesse's Dream Skirt" and Wolf Creek's theme of "Remembering Forgotten Dreams."

There is an important distinction here, though, between the use of dreams by Noble and by the Southeastern sissies. Noble's "dream museum" transported him into "the worlds of other times and places," whereas LaSIS's focused on discovering wonder in the here and now. They urged the (gender-full) performance of dreams, in traditional classrooms and in city streets—streets that were trafficked by queens, striking teachers, tourist families, street missionaries, and witch-shop clientele. Perhaps Casa Maricon Commune's most inspired move was to lead the film crew of ABC *Close-Up* out into New Orleans streets, during Mardi Gras. This set up a knowing contrast with the 1967 CBS *Special Reports* episode, which opened with a gay interviewee, Guy Larson, who confessed, "As I went down to New Orleans, and I walked around the city, particularly the French Quarter, I took a look at the homosexual world. And I was there for seven days, and I decided on the last day—without experience—that if this was homosexuality, I wanted no part of it.... The whole atmosphere was ... furtive? It was ugly."

In 1979, ABC's film crew was led to portray a different gay New Orleans. In Part One ("Oppression") a voice-over commented: "Every day when you get up in the morning, you put away your real self, and you put on the mask of someone else, which you wear. // No one is going to be in the closet on Mardi Gras Day. It's a joyful time, and it's a time to love. Mardi Gras is a gay party, and the biggest party in the world." This voice-over spliced John Noble's voice, in the first part, to Melba'son's, in the second; the initial visuals, paired with Noble's voice, captured piles of dolls, statuary, costumed mannequins, masks—a fantastic, walk-in closet—and then, through editing, the magical interior opened into a bright exterior: Mardi Gras street scenes where wild figures seemed to bring the closeted fantasy world into vibrant open life.

The camera panned the crowd, allowing the viewer to witness drag queens, leather men, and flashers—just a few examples of the celebrating multitudes. And then, just before the TV show's ten-minute mark, Melba'son appeared among the onlookers—a round face, wire-rimmed spectacles, and a wide-brimmed straw hat. His was the voice that introduced the street visuals of Mardi Gras as a messily realized here and now in which masks, performance, and costume allow us all to be more authentic, joyful, loving, free, and ... gay. This was a clearly gay liberationist message that argued that we *all* benefit from releasing our repressions, coming out of the closet—and that our dreamworld existed right in front of us: on film, on TV, *and* in our magically teeming streets. With their insistence on leading film crews out of rooms and into the streets, LaSIS strategically leveraged the mystique of Mardi Gras and the Crescent City to suggest a counterpart to Noble's private and interior "Museum of Dreams": one found in the wonder-filled crowds of New Orleans's exteriors. Even though neither LaSIS nor Noble edited the series, their hermetic interiors and jubilant exteriors made an irresistible pairing, a set of televisual bookends that so nicely illustrated the magic of coming out *and* coming together. They materially recalled the gay liberationist motto: "We are everywhere," insisting that the telos of liberation was a wondrous solidarity.

Facing the Nation after Milk: LaSIS with Running Water, the March, and the Radical Faeries

LaSIS's heightened visibility and volume didn't please everyone. Their profile as shrill New Orleans activists was clear. After the filming of ABC's "Homosexuals," local police targeted LaSIS at their Rampart rental house, leading to multiple arrests in late spring of 1979. On the morning of Thursday, May 10, Dimid and Melba'son were arrested on obscenity charges. As *The Times-Picayune* reported it, they allegedly "'paraded around'" nude on their porch, "in full view of persons in the area, including students at Charles J. Colton Junior High School."[8] The specific mention of the school deployed the alarmist child protectionist rhetoric that had proven so effective in the campaigns of Bryant and Briggs. Hayes says that, while they *had* gone on the porch that morning to collect the mail, they wore shorts, holding their coffees in their hands—a not uncommon thing to do during the hot, late spring in New Orleans. After their release, they took photos of their house from the neighboring school grounds to show that, even if they had been naked, they wouldn't have been fully visible from that distance. The official journalistic report clearly exaggerated the situation—as did the police. Ten armed, white police officers came to their Rampart house, eventually speaking to a Black couple whom LaSIS assumed were intimidated into making a statement to affirm the report of nudity. At the station, contrary to practice, their cases were separated, and Melba'son was pressured to confess his homosexuality. They were offered no lawyer, and after Brotherlover paid to have them released, Melba'son was held much longer, presumably due to his identifying himself as gay.

They—Melba'son and Dimid, plus Brotherlover—were arrested again within the week, for lewd behavior. They were put into a squad car, and the three sissies watched as the police officers went door to door, trying to find someone to make a complaint confirming the charge. Eventually they found a Hispanic woman, a neighbor whose daughter later told the sissies that her mother knew only a little English and was unable to understand what the police were asking her. According to Dimid, on the way to the station, the arresting officers told them, "We're gonna keep coming back until they lock you perverts up forever." Once downtown, they were assured that the charges would be dropped at their August court date, only if they could avoid being arrested for the rest of the summer while their house was under ongoing police surveillance. Under what amounted to an informal house arrest, LaSIS shrewdly used their regional network to build witness to their local harassment. They published accounts in *RFD*, assuring readers that all political files and mailing lists had been safely relocated away from the house, and they urged readers to reprint the story of their harassment in all the gay newspapers where readers lived. They reasoned, "Our only hope of survival is letting large numbers of gay people know what's happening."[9]

They lay low, staying close to home while they were under surveillance. That meant that LaSIS—except for Aurora—were unable to attend the June 1979 gathering at Running Water Farm. Perhaps because the sissies were under-represented, attendees decided that the farm would remain "faggot space," meaning that the inclusiveness LaSIS had argued for would not be achieved at Running Water at that time. It's likely that attendees were struggling with their sense of vulnerability and that they had not fully emerged from the grieving of the past winter. Ron Lambe, a native North Carolinian who had lived in San Francisco for the past fifteen years and was there when Milk was shot, attended the June 1979 Running Water gathering and heard Mikel Wilson's continued appeal to collectivize the farm. He asked Wilson if he could visit again, later that summer. He rounded up three other interested men to join him—John Jones, Peter Kendrick, and Rocco Patt—and the group of them established their own collective, formed the private corporation Stepping Stone, and bought Running Water as a way to realize the Southeast Network's collectivist vision for the site.

Ownership officially transferred to Stepping Stone in the fall of 1979. Around the time of the fall 1979 Running Water gathering, Ben Miriam noticed that their event mailing list included about 200 names, and this burgeoning network referred to themselves in *RFD* as the "Southeast Network." At the same time, the gatherings started to overwhelm the land. Liberationists proposed that other rural locations hold gatherings to ease the pressure on Running Water. The Stepping Stone quartet, all newcomers to the Southeast Network, were also eager to honor the previous year's activity at the Appalachian farm, even as they improvised new directions. They explained in a Running Water newsletter that their name was chosen to encapsulate their belief in respecting both "a starting point and a path [forward]."[10]

At the same time, the newsletter inaugurated a new spiritual tenor, one quite different from the previous year's faggot witchcraft. Whereas the sissies' collectivism defined inclusivity in terms of a wider liberation that sought queer solidarity with women's liberationists, Black radicals and sissies, transgender people, the disabled, revolutionaries overseas, and the young and the old, Stepping Stone seemed to prioritize including more gay men with a wide spectrum of politics and spirituality—especially centering liberal politics, traditional religion, and New Age philosophy. The newsletter offered "A Blessing," which opened with the refrain "We thank You Lord," that included the phrase "praise Your Name," and that closed with a reference to the love shared "With You and our brothers." This prayer sounded a clear Christian note, surely received by some readers as a bit dissonant alongside the witchcraft rituals of the year past. On the next page, a quote from Gautama Buddha defined Stepping Stone's view of the forest's purpose: "The forest is a peculiar organism of unlimited kindness and benevolence that makes no demands for its sustenance and extends generously the products of its life activity; it affords protection to all beings, offering shade even to the axeman who destroys it."[11] It is likely that this new, less shrill tenor served the needs of many in the growing Southeast Network, too—those who were drawn to it out of gay men's need for safety, healing, comfort, and community. Lambe himself surely sought a balm like this, having just fled a San Francisco where gay leaders were gunned down without retribution. However, the sissies' focus on feminist witchcraft, leftist collectivism, radical solidarity, and inclusive rural–urban networking quickly thinned.

The sissies found themselves similarly out of step with the planning for the October 1979 March on Washington. Milk himself recognized the need for strong local movements to be channeled into a national force, and he believed that a march on Washington could contribute to that shift. A November 1978 planning conference in Minneapolis fizzled out because there was too much disagreement among participants. Milk won some significant naysayers over to the cause, though—just before he was killed. As a result, a more committed planning conference was then slated for late February 1979, in Philadelphia. Ben Miriam went to the conference. In *RFD* he reported that cities like New York and San Francisco dominated the conversation, so he argued for the formation of a "hinterlands caucus, representing not only rural and small-town folk, but even those from [other] big cities."[12] His concerns were not merely representational, because some of these smaller groups had concrete concerns with the main plan.

For example, "19 Lesbians and Gay Men from Tennessee" wrote a letter to the march's coordinating committee and detailed their misgivings. Like Ben Miriam, they were concerned that the planning for the march had skipped crucial grassroots outreach that would lead to a richer turnout. Specifically, they felt the planners had sidelined the DC organizations who, as hosts, could speak to important logistical matters. They also noted that the intended date of the march conflicted with a Los Angeles NOW conference, a decision that might diminish the number of lesbian, feminist, and West Coast participants.

They felt that there were no real tangible demands crafted as the goals of the march, a failing that would leave the mobilized crowd little to rally around and without real sustainable outcomes to shoot for. They knew that building a grassroots base and developing common demands out of that base would take time, so they argued that the march should be put off until the following year. They also believed that a 1980 march, timed to mitigate Ronald Reagan's New Right campaign for president, had more practical benefits than a rushed 1979 march designed to commemorate the Stonewall uprising. Because the Tennesseans' letter was reprinted that summer in *RFD*, sharing a page with LaSIS's arrest update, we can assume that Milo Pyne, and Short Mountain, shared these concerns.[13]

For their part, LaSIS dug into their regional collectivist networks to quickly undertake the grassroots outreach that national organizers had skipped. They focused on groups in Arkansas, Louisiana, and Mississippi, drumming up interest in attending the October march. However, it was clear that they attended with the purpose of voicing uniquely sissie perspectives in the absence of any carefully articulated national ones to share. They marched with "Stop Rape" signs—echoing their solidarity tactics from the New Orleans teacher strike as well as their genderfuck methods of interrupting rape culture. Further, as Phillip Pendleton—who marched with the sissies—recalled, the tenor of sissie participation in the march was much more liberationist than liberal: "'No one I knew went to lobby Congress the next day. Our goal was to overthrow the government, not enter into dialogue with it!'"[14]

The first Spiritual Conference for Radical Faeries, held over Labor Day weekend, in Benson, Arizona, much more closely appealed to the gay liberationist spirit of both Stepping Stone and LaSIS. The genesis of that event can be traced to a November 1978 program at the University of Southern California.[15] Lesbian therapist Betty Berzon had invited three speakers to the Gay Academic Union conference to present on a panel called "New Breakthroughs in the Nature of How We View Gay Consciousness." The speakers were Harry Hay, Mitch Walker, and Don Kilhefner. After their presentation, the trio planned a follow-up retreat on the place of spirituality in gay consciousness. The event would be held at Desert Sanctuary, an ashram in Benson, Arizona. Hay—despite some mild static from Melba'son—had been important to sissie sociality back in Arkansas, when Oglesby and Thornton and also the two Roses had stayed with Hay and Burnside in New Mexico. Hay had recently come into his own as a gay elder, having been recognized for his political work in Jonathan Ned Katz's 1976 book *Gay American History* and in Peter

Adair's 1977 documentary *Word Is Out*. However, as we have seen, Harry Hay had run a slightly different course than that of the faggot spirituality and politics linked to West Coast *RFD* and to Wolf Creek.

Foremost, Hay had progressively distanced himself from Marxist politics since being ousted decades before from the Communist Party USA. This position did not fully flush with faggot politics, which significantly embraced a new leftism. Second, Hay flirted with quasi-essentialist theories of gay consciousness that took him further away from leftists' historical materialist explanations.[16] Third, his spirituality had tended to emphasize Indigenous gender and spiritual practice, sparked by his personal experiences in the US Southwest, rather than foregrounding faggot witchcraft.[17] It is likely that some of these differences informed why (1) West Coast *RFD* editors rejected an essay he submitted to their magazine in 1976; (2) Hay had declined to attend the 1976 Faggots & Class Struggle conference, criticizing its dearth of spiritual content; and (3) in that same year, Hay and Burnside toured Wolf Creek, briefly considering moving there, but demurred, quickly returning to New Mexico. As had been true for the sissies, Hay's subjectivity had been formed through a series of flirtations and ultimate dis-identifications with West Coast faggot culture. By 1979 he saw himself as a *faerie* more than a *faggot*.

Timmons describes Harry Hay as the political architect behind the 1979 Arizona conference. After all, Hay had been the original force behind the 1950 formation of the Mattachine Society, and in addition to his late 1970s focus on spirituality, he had also been politically active in New Mexico—writing for the radical paper *El Grito* and leading a protracted water rights campaign, in addition to forming a gay organization. As a speaker, Hay possessed a gravitas born of his long activist experience, and he easily inspired his gay audiences. For his part, the younger Mitch Walker took on a more forward Jungian-informed spiritual role at the conference, and Kilhefner a more logistical one, based on his long organizing experience.

Although Timmons's narrative traces a growing friction between Walker and Hay, it is important to note their commonalities in the early stages of Radical Faerie cultural formation. Walker was a trained Jungian psychologist, educated at San Francisco's Lone Mountain College. Like Hay, he mixed essentialist and social constructionist explanations of gay consciousness. In his essay "Visionary Love," originally published in the Winter 1976 issue of *Gay Sunshine*, he asserted the socially constructed nature of gay identity before going on to emphasize the uncovering of a "trueself" that transcends the "falseself" posited by social conditioning.[18] He ultimately brusquely dismissed Marxist analyses of gay identity, stating that "an economic analysis of gay oppression is absurd, like forming a composite animal by tacking the legs of a kangaroo onto a tuna fish."[19] This was in sharp contrast to Arthur Evans's advocating a "new socialism" but it was in line with Hay's position. As a Jungian, Walker acknowledged the *anima* as the feminine aspect of men's psyches, and worked with the sense of a multiple self that was similar to that of Anderson Feri's and Reclaiming witchcraft's tripartite soul. In the winter of 1977, though, he wrote a follow-up essay to "Visionary Love" called "Becoming Gay Shamanism," which established a stronger resonance with Hay's Indigenous spiritual leanings.

It is worth comparing the formal genealogies of the Running Water and Radical Faerie events. They were similar in that they were both men's rural events formed of gay liberationist encounters with faggot spiritual politics. There are some notable divergences, though. These events were sparked by quite different conferences. Running Water was inspired by participation at a regional activist conference, the 1978 3rd Annual Southeastern Conference for Lesbians and Gay Men, in Atlanta. The purpose of the first Running Water gathering was to respond to lesbian feminists' insistence that gay liberationists struggle with their own sexism. In contrast, the 1979 Spiritual Conference for Radical Faeries grew out of a Gay Academic Union panel focused on gay consciousness. The first Running Water event was attended almost entirely by young gay liberationists—in their twenties or early thirties. The Arizona conference was led by at least two veteran gay activists; Hay was sixty-seven at the time, and Kilhefner was forty-one. The Running Water event was billed as a "gathering," modeled more closely after the countercultural Rainbow Gatherings, and the site was an—until recently—abandoned Appalachian farm; a year later, the Arizona event was called a "conference," and at first it operated more like a spiritual retreat, taking place at a desert ashram. Timmons notes, though, that attendees at the Arizona spiritual conference quickly decided to rename their conference a "gathering," perhaps reflecting the influence of Southeastern attendees like the sissies.

LaSIS *did* go out to Benson. They got a Volkswagen van that they christened "Sissybus"—a reference, possibly, to their ongoing Sisyphean commitments to a nonbinary gay liberation, even in a time of amplified terror. In true sissie form, they arrived, as they had at Wolf Creek, late at night. Whereas steep and tiny Running Water could only comfortably accommodate about fifty campers, Desert Sanctuary welcomed close to 200 attendees that Labor Day weekend of 1979. Occurring between the winter 1978 assassination of Harvey Milk and the coming October 1979 March on Washington, the Spiritual Conference exhibited an importance of national scale. In fact, a poem documenting the retreat said that it drew gay men "from coast to coast, from North to South."[20] If the Washington March raised hopes for a national gay rights movement, the Arizona conference aimed to revive gay liberation at a similar scale.

In the improvised shift from "conference" to "gathering," though, some growing pains surfaced. At Rainbow Gatherings and at Running Water Farm, it was common for attendees to exchange contact information, create mailing lists, and offer expertise for skill-shares. This was the kind of networking Brotherlover had recommended; it facilitated a mobile culture circulating from collective to collective in between seasonal gatherings. Timmons records how Hay exploded when he came upon two attendees copying a mailing list. From Hay's McCarthy-era perspective, this practice courted the dangers of federal surveillance, infiltration, exposure, and arrest. The Mattachine Society's structure had been built on absolute secrecy and anonymous leadership hierarchies to prevent such risk. Those familiar with gathering culture used other tactics: decentralized organization, anachronistic ("rustic") and nonstandard communication formats, constant mobility, post office boxes in place of home addresses, and assumed names.[21] They so thoroughly scrambled any identifying information as to make it virtually untraceable and unintelligible to authorities. The event's primarily countercultural attendees were comfortable with such tactics, and future events would function as *gatherings*.

Two iconic events established the tenor of the first Radical Faeries conference. One was Harry Hay's Friday night address on "subject-SUBJECT consciousness," which demonstrated what the organizers meant when naming the event. In his talk Hay laid out a vision of society in which people related without objectifying each other, and he identified certain gay men as born to shift society in that direction, naming them faeries. Following his research on the visionary leadership roles assigned to certain nonbinary gender categories in Indigenous societies, this faerie identity evoked a subjectivity that appeared to be, at once, transhistorical, transcultural, and mythical. The resulting loose sense of time and place reflected his disaffection with historical materialism. So did his use of the phrase *radical as root*, by which he intended to disentangle the word *radical* from leftist politics and associate it with the depth of essence, tradition, and mythical origins.[22] He closed his speech with an injunction to his audience: "Fairies must begin to throw off the filthy green frogskin of hetero-imitation, by which disguise they managed to get through school with a full set of teeth, and discover the lovely Gay-Conscious notMAN (as the early Greeks called us) underneath."[23] The figure beneath the frogskin—his metaphor for slimy social conditioning—would, of course, be the faerie prince. Hay's speech, then, defined "radical faerie" in ways totally harmonious with Walker's Jungian frame, establishing a parallel between throwing off one's frogskin and liberating the "trueself." Hay's specific version of the gay trueself, though, was a non-assimilationist faerie with the innate, transhistorical role of transforming society to treat others as subjects rather than objects. Those in attendance discovered themselves, then, through the ecstatic lens of this sacred, timeless purpose.

The second event, the mud-bath ritual, although apparently spontaneous, materialized this faerie vision of Hay's. Near the close of the weekend, attendees dragged buckets of water to a dry arroyo, making mud to cover their naked bodies. Eventually their play centered on one man, as the group piled layer after layer of mud onto him, giving him an earthen erection and adorning his shell with foraged plant life. They lifted him into the air and carried him about the sanctuary, until they ended with a thorough washing—of him, and each other—as they laughed, embraced, and kissed. This ritual was heavily photographed, and it has been routinely and emotionally recalled as a powerful culmination of the retreat. Descriptions clearly echo Hay's faerie vision. Some reported elated sensations of being released from ordinary time. For example, one attendee said that the ritual "evoked a sensation of timelessness that I sometimes feel during especially satisfying lovemaking, that I am in touch with something thousands and thousands of years old."[24]

Another described it as being exactly like the releasing of one's trueself, a process useful to "act-out the erasing of your personality. Act-out the return to the mineral elements. Act-out the discovery of your form as the mud is washed off. Act-out the disengagement from your image."[25] This was framed as a return to an older, more authentic faerie mode of being: "We know that it [faeriespirit] is an ancient, timeless spirit. Rituals, raw image-making, primitive rituals create the images that bring associations back to our primordial sensations and functions ... unlocked spirit memories and ancient visions."[26] For others, the ritual unbound them from the earth and released them into the cosmic: "Oh, oh, I know we have left the poor planet earth far behind, I know we have soared beyond our bodies at last, understood at last we were not born there, we were not meant to 'be' there, were not meant to stay—still, yet, the final reason of our time on this planet just slipping around the corner ahead."[27] For many, the mud-bath ritual staged a rebirth in which they were first covered with earth, feeling again how confined they were in their daily lives, before rising above all earthly context, washed free of history as they knew it.

In his memories of the 1979 Spiritual Conference for Radical Faeries, Dimid expresses immense respect—awe, even—for Harry Hay. He also, like so many others, remembers the mud-bath ritual as transformative. I find it interesting, though, that in his own recounting, he lingers on the *layering* of mud—the pleasures of that stickiness, the messiness, the group cohesion. He does not mention the washing; nor does he reference a cosmic, timeless, or ancient feeling. His development as a sissie had focused on an accretive, genderfuck somatic experience that accumulated signs of solidarity through deep social engagement with the contemporary moment, the crowded crossroads. As leftists, the sissies found their hope in the dirtiness and the intimacies of the everyday: their complex moment in history. They did not find it possible, or desirable, to lift themselves out of the crossroads where their solidarities were forged. They did not dream of purifying themselves of the unities, or struggles, they held dear. These were important distinctions between the radical, magical conversions of the Southeast sissies and the earliest West Coast faeries, and these differences were similar to those between the tenors of John Noble's transporting dreamworld and LaSIS's street-anchored, nonbinary pedagogies of solidarity, wonder, and generosity. Such differences would inform how the sissies returned from the Arizona desert to the Southeast Network to build a sanctuary practice at Short Mountain. They would infuse their regionally crafted practice into bubbling national discourses.

CHAPTER EIGHT

Way Stations to Revolution
Sustaining Liberation with Short Mountain

The Labor Day 1979 Radical Faeries conference again fired up gay liberationist hope at a national scale, and both Running Water and LaSIS leaned into the faerie figure. In his editorial note for the winter 1979 issue of *RFD*, Milo Pyne referred to the "fairies of LaSIS" and declared *RFD* "now a 'fairy journal.'"[1] I argue that this identification was a partial one; it did not tell the whole story. They also subtitled that issue "Returning Forest Darlings," a nomenclature that I read to indicate that, as transformative as their time in the desert might have been, in late 1979 it was time to return to the Southeast, to the Appalachian forests of Running Water Farm and Short Mountain, to craft a course that built on their regional experience. Of course, that path would indeed be crooked. LaSIS and Short Mountain formed an axis within the Southeast Network, partnering to leverage how they edited *RFD* and repurposed Short Mountain as a means to further realize their sissie collectivism under a new faerie figural banner.

As editors of *RFD*, they sometimes took exception to the politics of the new Radical Faeries' leadership. For example, Short Mountain published the summer 1979 issue of *RFD*. In that issue, just months before the Arizona conference, the editors published Hay's second *RFD* article: "Gay Awareness and the First Americans." They prefaced it with an editorial note: "The opening paragraphs . . . propose that homosexuals represent a genotypic entity which is in exclusive possession of certain superior awarenesses. Our publishing of this article should . . . not necessarily be taken as giving assent to these or related hypotheses."[2] Short Mountain would not risk association with Hay's essentialism, especially as it co-opted Indigenous gender and sexual experience to universalize a gay exceptionalism.

Similarly, Melba'son reviewed *Visionary Love*, calling out Walker's dismissal of gay Marxists, responding bluntly, "I profoundly disagree."[3] He particularly took aim at how the Radical Faerie imagined that historical queers could simply decide to shrug off their deep social conditioning: "Mitch is asking nothing less of us than that we blast ourselves out of conditioned ways of thinking/ acting/being and join him in becoming faggot warriors."[4] Having labored so long with his own *fanshen*, still considering it an unfinished process, Melba'son resented its being reduced to a blithe decision, to a moment's shedding of skin. However, what Melba'son found most disturbing about *Visionary Love* was how it sexualized what Walker called the "Black Faggot Magickal Wand," relying on an exhausted "light/dark color dualism" to erase the spectrum of racialized (and sexual) experience. He said that Walker "romanticizes the color black in a way that seems to me, alienating to blacks and whites alike. I'm not black, so how could I ever partake of this magickal sexuality? Indeed, not all blacks are black. I wonder how a light-skinned black would react to this passage? Or a black Latino? Or an Asian? Or a Native American? In this one instance I do not hesitate to say that Mitch's way is not The Way."[5] We can read such responses as a continuation of Mulberry House's sissie critique of the West Coast *RFD* faggot culture of 1976–77. They still held to a leftist political position which also objected to gestural gay liberationist inclusivity.

Truth be told, though, the sissies struggled to realize their own vision for inclusive collectivism. They had made the case for it in the 1978 issues of *RFD*, but following Milk's assassination and their own harassment by the New Orleans police, Running Water attendees voted in the summer of 1979 to make the rural event exclusively for faggots.[6] How could they then move the needle on a regional rural-urban collectivism based on liberationist solidarity? One way they did this was through their editorial collaborations with Short Mountain on *RFD*.

Pyne and LaSIS had first partnered as *RFD* editors for the winter 1978 issue. Pyne traveled to New Orleans for that work and reflected on how it felt, as a rural countercultural liberationist, to experiment with the sissies' French Quarter street theater. We know, though, that Pyne had himself begun to gather a network of Appalachian lesbian and gay liberationists around him. Others from that network, like Clear Englebert, joined Pyne on his editorial trips to the Crescent City. Englebert remembered the witchy sacrilege LaSIS effected; for example, he said the collective kept an open Bible on the ground in back of their rental house and invited guests to urinate on it when they needed relief.[7]

A little shocked, Englebert was no stranger to liberationist culture himself. Raised in rural northwestern Alabama, in the racially mixed Colbert County of the late 1950s and early 1960s, Englebert was the son of schoolteachers. His family might have seemed unorthodox to peers. For example, his grandparents had adopted an orphaned Black boy. However, because Jim Crow business owners would not allow their son to follow his new parents into segregated establishments, they feared they caused more harm than good and ultimately felt compelled to find a Black family who could raise him. His parents also converted to Catholicism and the family had to drive quite far if they wanted to attend mass.

After graduating high school in Huntsville, where he and a girlfriend had come out to each other, Englebert felt no desire to go to college. Instead he followed his dream of opening an "alternative bookstore to get information out to the people." He and his fellow hippie brother worked and saved to open *A Good Book Store* in Huntsville in June 1971. Englebert began visibly stocking the shelves with *The Great Speckled Bird*, Black radical literature, and Eastern religious materials. He took it as a personal mission to offer alternative information to Huntsville readers. He also remembers that when his brother and sister-in-law moved to rural Alabama around the same time, the Klan burned a cross on their lawn as a warning to their new "longhair" neighbors. After a hiatus from the book industry, Englebert opened a new bookstore—*Books as Seeds*—and he added early *RFD* and many other gay and lesbian publications to his inventory. He was committed to providing a broader perspective to regional print culture, and his work with Short Mountain on *RFD* reflected that commitment.

Running Water became "faggot only" at its June 1979 gathering. Short Mountain edited the June 1979 issue of *RFD*, calling it "Roaring Fresh Decisions." The most likely inspiration for this phrase is the I Ching hexagram the Tennessee collective threw to guide their editorial hands. The results were *roaring thunder* and *wind*, which they interpreted to mean "our independence is not based on rigidity and immobility of character, but always keeps abreast of the time and changes with it."[8] This particular reading reflected their commitments to both historical materialism and a more capacious identity. They saw this impulse as "organic" and offered readers a description of the verdant Short Mountain landscape. In this spirit, the editors featured two articles authored by women—one a radical Black lesbian incarcerated in Muncy, Pennsylvania, and the other a lesbian anarchist musician. The editors' decision was radical and organic at once. While *RFD* had included women's writing in its Bay Area women's issue, the fact that that was a theme issue had cast women's voices more as an exception than the rule. It's important to remember, though, that *RFD* was a reader-written publication and that women, like Cathy Gross, had been a part of its readership for some time. Their voices had heretofore only sometimes appeared in letters to the editor but were very rarely featured as the heart of the issue. The summer 1979 issue of *RFD* broke that precedent, and did so immediately following the Running Water decision to remain "faggot only". Furthermore, they framed this move as a matter of natural course. After all, their two feature authors, in some ways, already belonged to the *RFD* network.

Since 1976, during its Wolf Creek years, *RFD* had hosted a prison letter-writing feature. Early on this had been a window on Pacific Northwest radicalism because the letters they published largely followed the struggles of Ed Mead, an incarcerated bisexual and George Jackson Brigade founder, as he sought to connect his own efforts to organize incarcerated queer men with "free" faggots on the outside. Prison administrators stymied such efforts by relocating and isolating radicalized inmates like Mead. Ironically then, as *RFD* traveled southeast with Faygele ben Miriam, some of the prisoners who read *RFD* were also routed to Southeastern prisons. It's important to remember Melba'son's own past with prison correspondence, which dated back to 1972, when as "minister of information," he had cultivated queer male inmates as a significant subscriber base for the newly formed Koch Farm newsletter. One of the bonds between Ben Miriam and the sissies had been their shared abolitionist passions. In the winter 1978 issue, edited in New Orleans, LaSIS not only continued the "Brothers Behind Bars" feature begun in Oregon with their own "Prison Rage" section, but they also made a point of including more letters from prisoners held in Southeastern prisons: two in Memphis and one in Atlanta.

In fact, it was Ed Mead who recommended that Short Mountain publish "June Boyd: A Black Strong Woman." This was a collection of Boyd's excerpted writing, composed while she was imprisoned at the Pennsylvania State Correctional Institute. Boyd framed her writing primarily as autobiography, but it shifted registers from political critique to theory to poetry. Herself a liberationist lesbian, she took aim at multiple institutions within the capitalist system of "Amerrika" and framed the prison system as white supremacist. She divulged that she was put into solitary confinement for her incendiary writing, a retaliatory act that only proved to her how powerful a thinker she was. As she put it, "I would like for people to see me as a mind rather than a body, but they are so hung up on that physical thing, that separation thing, that superior thing, they hate to respect a powerful mind, and more so when a Black Woman is controlling that mind. You [can] see deep down inside of authorities."[9] Boyd switched *RFD*'s abolitionist tenor from the voices of "brothers" alone to center a Black lesbian intellectual perspective. When "Brothers Behind Bars" returned in the winter 1979 issue of *RFD*, Ed Mead thanked the Short Mountain editors for publishing Boyd's important work. He added that he was relieved to see the queer collective was based in Tennessee, since he would soon be transferred from Leavenworth to the eastern end of their state—to Brushy Mountain Prison in Appalachia—for being a "problem," for organizing gay inmates. He wrote, "I will soon need some friends in that state."[10]

Anarchist musician Kathy Fire wrote "Nuclear Realities" in critique of nuclear power plants. To accentuate her article's relevance to Short Mountain, the editors inserted an illustration into the text of her article. It was an inverted triangle covering a map of Tennessee, with the following caption: "The biggest power project ever undertaken in America is centered in Middle Tennessee's 'Electric Triangle.'"[11] Situating Short Mountain within TVA's development agenda, the editors added, "Our layout headquarters is in a little old log cabin up in a beautiful holler. We have electricity here, a necessity for a typewriter of this kind. We burn precious few watts, but we are tied in to TVA's nuclear expansion program nonetheless. We are in the heart of an area destined for development, exploitation, and internal colonialism." With this comment, it becomes possible to see how Short Mountain had wed radical sissie collectivism to the Appalachian studies perspective of Helen Matthews Lewis, hinging as it did on applying Black radical theories of internal colonialism to Appalachia. Specifically, Short Mountain saw their region as a place exploited by the nation as a site for anchoring prison and (nuclear) energy industries. In featuring the voices of lesbians—Black and white—as leaders of such critiques, they also implicitly invited their readers to see this internal colonialism as patriarchal and white supremacist, too. When *RFD* readers from elsewhere complained about the thin relevance of nuclear power or women's views, Clear Englebert rebuffed them, saying that he lived within forty miles of the Brown's Ferry reactor, which had recently been rescued from a near meltdown, and that "considering how important wimmin are in my life, I wouldn't mind seeing more articles [by them]."[12] For him, the relevance was as obvious as his physical and social environs.

In the summer 1979 issue of *RFD*, the Short Mountain–LaSIS axis stuck to their sissie collectivism. They did so by centering radical lesbian and Black voices and applying the critique of internal colonialism to the Appalachian region where the network's rural gathering spaces were located. This was not an incidental move for them. When the editors characterized each issue of *RFD* as a gathering on the printed page, they implied that the critical inclusiveness of their *RFD* issue was just as representative of the Southeast Network as was Running Water's decision to remain faggot-only. As they put it, "Each editing becomes a gathering in itself, bringing together strands of the web, and the 'RFD collective' grows, forming and reforming."[13] Pitching no critique of the Running Water decision, the editors found a way to amplify sissie collectivism in the network's print vehicle while maintaining the regional unity that the past year's gathering culture had established. After all, they knew the terror that Milk's assassination had dialed up, they knew its white Christian supremacist roots in the South of the Save Our Children campaign, and they understood the value of care as demonstrated by the 1978 Running Water gatherings. The network was capacious enough for both responses, as long as the longer liberationist goal was remembered. And the summer 1979 issue of *RFD* was an effort to articulate that sissie collectivist vision a little more fluently. However, they still wanted to manifest a more inclusive rural event space within their wider network.

Sissies between Eff Words: Short Mountain's Reinhabitation as Sanctuary Practice

Short Mountain and LaSIS collaborated on the winter 1978 issue of *RFD*, with Pyne and Englebert traveling to New Orleans for that work. Before the Arizona Radical Faerie conference, in the spring of 1979, Milo Pyne attended the fourth annual Southeastern Conference for Lesbians and Gay Men, back in Chapel Hill. At that event, he called for assistance with a Short Mountain Reinhabitation Project. In early 1977 he and Wilson had speculated about how both their farms might contribute to gay liberation, and he felt Short Mountain was ready to follow Running Water's lead. LaSIS may have encouraged Pyne, seeing Short Mountain as a crucial node in their region's sissie networking. After all, Pyne had written a piece for "Sissie" and contributed the map alongside Brotherlover's essay. In any case, LaSIS would send Dimid to participate in the Reinhabitation Project, in the spring of 1980.

When Running Water was declared faggot space, there is evidence that the culture retained a radicalism that was at least consonant with sissie collectivism. The event mailing list urged potential attendees to boycott Nestle for pushing the use of harmful baby formula in other nations, and it promoted the Third World Gay Conference alongside the upcoming Radical Faerie conference. A handwritten note by Milo requested that news about the former be thoughtfully posted "where 3rd World people will have access to it," an active effort toward the form of inclusivity that Dimid had urged with "A Letter to Action." Underneath listed contact information was an excerpt from *The Faggots & Their Friends between Revolutions* (1977). The excerpt included an image by illustrator Ned Asta and text by author Larry Mitchell.[14]

In the winter 1978 issue of *RFD*, Aurora had positively reviewed the book, suggesting that it was designed so that radical queers could use it for "developing our own mythology from out of the stories" in preparation for a coming third revolution, which followed on the first (an attack on all women) and the second (a hoarding of all wealth by "men without color").[15] This reading was consonant with Aurora's sissie politics, which took capitalism to be both patriarchal and white supremacist at once. The excerpt on the Running Water mailing list also suggested a politics with differentiated roles. It described "fairies" who lived in the wilderness where they sometimes bonded with "faggots," who lived among men. This fairy tale offered a schema for seeing rural sites (like Running Water) as faerie-run sanctuaries for militant urban faggots.[16]

In 1979, Asta's illustrations became commonplace in the print culture of the Southeast Network. Perhaps most importantly, the title of the book would have struck the sissies as a particularly apt description of their temporal situation. In 1976, faggots had felt temporally late compared to the revolution led by Black Panthers. In 1979, sissies felt interstitial—in the sense of living between genders, living at the crossroads of their solidarities, and living between the death of gay liberation and the coming of an intensified New Right violence. Feeling between revolutions, the sissies built their underground and proliferated their alliances. They prepared. At the same time, they dreamed, like Evans, for a revolution yet to come. If Hay and Walker built a West Coast faerie figure out of shed frogskins and exposed *trueselves*, the Southeast sissies composed their own faerie figure out of Asta's illustrations and Evans's precedent.

Mitchell and Asta's book featured women as focal characters. One figure who had already captured the attention of LaSIS became even more central to the culture at this time. That person was Cathy Gross. Back in 1978, Gross had written a letter to the West Coast *RFD* editors, critiquing their "Women's Issue" for adopting a politics of tokenistic inclusion over a radical feminist position, crowding out women's writing with too much of the editors' own words, and missing the opportunity to network radical rural women with rural gay liberationists. In "Sissie," Melba'son had directly addressed Gross and her letter, suggesting that LaSIS's *ef*feminism would align more closely with regional feminisms like hers, rather than New York feminisms like Robin Morgan's. After the summer 1979 issue of *RFD*, when Short Mountain editors included June Boyd and Kathy Fire's features, Gross moved to the new rural center of sissie collectivism.

By the spring of 1980, she had moved to Gassaway, close to Short Mountain, where she contributed two pieces to the spring 1980 issue of *RFD*. One of these was a textually complex autobiographical piece, written using the name "mountain dyke." It was organized into two columns headed by the assertion "THAT I AM A DYKE. AND NOT WEIRD."[17] I argue that Gross demonstrated her place—*as a dyke*—in the liberationist network of *RFD* in two important ways: (1) she signaled her own deeper-south *fanshen* with the adoption of the name "mountain dyke," and (2) she riffed on June Boyd's autobiographical prose poetics to give momentum to how queer women wrote features for *RFD*.[18] In these ways, "That I Am a Dyke" was Gross's own dykestory unfolding alongside sissystories. In the first column, she chronicled the first chapter of her life, which was marked by an early "defiance" ("AT ONE WEEK REARED UP, HELD HEAD UP") which both cast the young Gross as a butch and led her to realize, "My mother was afraid of me." Prizing her independence but feeling isolated by her mother's fear, Gross recalled that "Depression crept in on cat's feet," and after that announcement, the first column ended abruptly with the line "I was placed in a mental hospital."

If Boyd's *RFD* piece contended in a liberationist mode with the prison system, Gross's staged a similar encounter with homophobic psychiatry. The life shared in the first column of "That I Am a Dyke" reached an end when she was institutionalized, and a new, terrifying life began. In contrast to the parallelism and forward momentum of the first column, the lines of the second blur together as one big run-on sentence meant to reflect the pain and disorientation of her clinical treatment. In the narrative, after she was released, the lines returned to a discrete, if choppier, form. One line announced that she "went South," recalling her move from New York to Appalachia, but also evoking the idiom "to go south," meaning to go wrong in some way, referring to how she had *not* been healed, but instead had been deeply injured, by psychiatry. In another turn, though, she then "moved further south" and "became political." Having entered the sociality of the Southeastern Network, she embraced her radicalism as she tried on a new name to match it. "That I Am a Dyke" ends by stating, "Now I am in my Saturn return and seeking a / refuge for awhile. The goddess within calls to me / and I must respond. I go to the mountains alone." As she deepened the defiance of her birth with a political coming of age, she followed the call to work from *within* the sissie network. As the first dyke to do so—not on the pages of *RFD* alone, but also at one of its rural sites—she certainly faced an acute form of loneliness.

Ultimately, Gross joined Dimid Hayes to participate in the Short Mountain Reinhabitation Project. There were eight total collectivists who spent the first half of 1980 transforming Short Mountain into what they would call a "sanctuary." These were Gross, Hayes, Milo Pyne, John Greenwell, Crazy Owl, a New York City couple (Jerry and David), and Pearl Sudds.[19] With one dyke among the gay liberationist men, they jokingly called themselves "Snow White and the Seven Dwarves," and Gross played along as the (un-femme) lead.[20] Their framing of the collective with a fairy tale echoed the ascendancy of the rural site as a *faerie* sanctuary for militant faggots as signaled the year before by the culture's use of the book *Faggots & Their Friends* on the Running Water mailing list. As a half-year project, Short Mountain Reinhabitation also nicely fit Brotherlover's and Hayes's concept of sissie networking, in that both suggested taking temporary residencies before circulating again within the regional underground. With Gross on board, the project also represented a first step toward the more inclusive collectivism that LaSIS had urged two years before.

It was arduous physical work conducted in rudimentary living conditions. Gross navigated the others' varied experience of working alongside women and made an early habit of clearly voicing her perspective. As a way of testing their efforts, they planned a May Day celebration, and the collective made sure to invite a number of area women. When the women protested the phallocentrism of the May Pole ritual, Gross seized the opportunity to improvise a meaningful alternative. She and Crazy Owl stood back-to-back, arms locked, at the center of the knoll. Sexual reproduction would not serve as an ill-fitting sign of their culture's generative capacities; rather, lesbian feminist and gay liberationist solidarity was affirmed as the very pulse of their creative power. Her initiative restored a sense of balance and inclusion to the event. With this inspired ritual move, Gross helped to set Short Mountain's sanctuary tone.

As Short Mountain Sanctuary emerged as a sister gathering site to Running Water, it stressed wider solidarity. In mid-1980 Pyne began writing an articulation of his political vision. He turned to the Atlanta Lesbian Feminist Alliance (ALFA) to give him feedback on early drafts.[21] Ultimately appearing in the fall 1980 issue of *RFD*, Pyne's "A Faeryist Not-Man-ifesto" used its title to sound a qualified resonance with the Radical Faerie culture growing in the West while unfurling a faery*ist* political vision descended more from regional uses of *Faggots & Their Friends*, from sissie collectivism, and from Short Mountain Reinhabitation than it did from Harry Hay's charge to shed the green frogskin of hetero-assimilation. Pyne opened the piece with a call to return to the values of gay liberation, and the bulk of the writing focused—as did Arthur Evans and LaSIS—on the magical work of forging solidarities.

Foremost, he suggested to *RFD* readers that "the time has come for faeries and lesbians to begin to talk, walk, and breathe together (con-spire) for the further development of each other's visions and dreams."[22] He drew on recent past events to illustrate what that might look like. Spiritually, his touchstone was not New Age eclecticism but political witchcraft as he cited a 1980 West Coast pagan festival at which Zsuzsanna Budapest's all-women witch ritual was buffered from a belligerent Baptist by a spiraling knot of faeries.

Pyne's vision of anti-sexist alliance thus also honored the periodic need for temporary spatial separatism. As a leftist, he also expected that their solidarity would not be merely rhetorical. He stressed the crucial work of "[sharing] our material and spiritual resources with wimmin and their movements" and "[offering] concrete support to wimmin." While he, like Wittman ten years before, wondered whether gay liberationists' anti-racism and black radicals' anti-homophobia had healed enough to facilitate the same kinds of immediate co-conspiracy, he insisted that the current moment demanded that faeries (1) offer material support to gays and lesbians of color and (2) participate as queers in direct action against white supremacy. He then referenced two recent protests that regional faeries had supported: an ecofeminist demonstration by the lesbian Spiderworts group against a Virginia nuclear plant, and faeries' marching in rallies following the 1979 Klan-incited Greensboro massacre while carrying signs that read "QUEERS AGAINST RACISM."

Pyne—as a former Venceremos Brigadier and the author of the deeper-south Sissie Networking map—did not conceive of such direct action as an appeal to the United States to elaborate a system of laws and rights to protect its citizens. Rather, he saw these anti-racist and anti-sexist protests, and even Short Mountain Reinhabitation, as part of a wider, eventual revolution to gain sovereignty from imperialist states. Therefore, he urged gay liberationist readers to support the autonomous land movements by Indigenous Americans, Puerto Rico, Chicana/o residents in Texas, and the Deep South New Afrikan movement—all of which, like Pyne's 1978 map, redefined extreme Southeastern geography as exceeding the US nationalist reach. This gay liberationist, deeper-south revolutionary perspective would gain in relevance for the mountain South, too, as, in that same fall 1980 issue of *RFD*, writers urged readers to host any of those lesbian and gay Cuban Marielitos sequestered at Fort Chaffee, outside Fort Smith, Arkansas. I argue that, in doing so, *RFD* offered not a sanctuary *city*, but a sanctuary *region* that was formed of a collectivist underground rooted in faggot witchcraft rather than formal Christianity.[23]

I find it important to note that, while Pyne argued for cross-movement alliance, he and the sissies more often dreamed of revolution as a proliferation of the difference (racial, ethnic, and gendered) already within. We see this in how they featured lesbians Boyd and Fire as already part of the *RFD* readership. We see this, too, in "A Faeryist Not-Man-ifesto," where Pyne foresees a deeper-south splintering into autonomous lands, not altogether different from how sissie houses had hived off from each other and multiplied into a vibrant network.

Pyne's "A Faeryist Not-Man-ifesto" cast the Southeast as a porous, tenuous territory primed for parceled return to the colonized and oppressed. The rural gathering sites in the sissie network should thus be understood as linked to these regional autonomous land movements. For Pyne, the rural sanctuaries were also sites especially suited for the practice of eco-feminist witchcraft: "We must create sanctuaries for ourselves, for the elves and gnomes, for the trees and flowers, birds, salamanders, frogs and little furry critters. If the planet dies, we will bear witness and sing the death song. If a species is extinguished, we will avenge it by our love. We must develop and perform ceremonies to strengthen Gaia and confound her enemies—put a hex on TVA."[24] Pyne's "A Faeryist Not-Man-ifesto" *did* also associate itself with the new Radical Faerie movement, including many quotes from Walker's *Visionary Love*, alongside references to Evans and *Faggots & Their Friends*, but did so while seeking to define "faeries" according to the politics of sissie networking. In so doing, he placed Short Mountain as a regionally specific, sissie-inspired sanctuary within a wider, emergent faerie culture. In that Pyne associated magickal practice with the actual Short Mountain Sanctuary, rendering it a deeper-south fantasy, I interpret it as a utopian geography reflecting José Esteban Muñoz's proposal that "the transregional or the global as modes of spatial organization potentially displace the hegemony of an unnamed here that is always dominated by the shadow of the nation-state and its mutable and multiple corporate interests."[25]

Likely inspired by Magdalen Farm, Elwha, and Running Water, West Coast Radical Faerie leaders had also begun to search for their own rural sites. In the summer 1980 issue of *RFD*, they called for readers to form "land trusts," which they imagined as twenty to eighty acres, owned by a nonprofit organization that would extend long-term use rights to a small set of gay male residents to host Radical Faerie events where the residents would teach attendees how to start their own land trusts.[26] There were several key differences from the early Short Mountain project. For one, these land trusts were imagined as separatist gay men's collectives. Second, instead of spiritually anchoring themselves in politicized witchcraft, they registered a shared philosophy with American Indigenous groups' anti-property stance by opening with a quote from Tecumseh: "Sell the land? Why not sell the air, the clouds, the great sea." Finally, the land movements they cited were not transnational, revolutionary independence movements but other separatist US land trusts: Oregon Women on the Land (OWL) and Georgia's New Communities, Inc. (for Black farmers). As such, their vision was inspired within a national sphere. The Faerie leaders promised that more details for land trusts would be offered at the second Radical Faerie gathering, to be held in Colorado in August 1980. At that event, though, after the call was made, a Short Mountain collectivist in the crowd responded that, in Tennessee, "this was already going on," and added that "'all you Faeries who flew away from the South because it was the South, come home.'"[27]

The Tennessee site did ultimately organize as a land trust, though, and Short Mountain, Inc., received its charter from the state the next year, in 1981. However, a drafted mission statement from a flier—with scored-out corrections—revealed lingering differences as to how they defined themselves as faeries. They stated their intentions "to create a sanctuary for all living things, to create and nourish a community of faeries on the 250 acres we live on, a community open to all faeries male and female, an environment that is ~~anti~~non-sexist and ~~anti~~non-racist, nurturing and caring.... LesbianS ~~faeries~~ are welcome at our gatherings, and are encouraged to become members. We are open to wimmin living on the land and creating their own autonomous space."[28] Not only did Short Mountain residents invite women, especially lesbians, to join them at the sanctuary, but they also (conflictingly) suggested that women *were* faeries, too. This ran counter to the developing West Coast Radical Faerie culture which assumed that only *princes* emerged from the frogskin of heteronormativity and whose leaders took care not to speak to women's separatist cultures. This also ran counter to the practice of Running Water, which decided in 1979 to remain faggot-only. However, Short Mountain's stopping short of using the phrase "lesbian faeries" suggests that there was still internal debate, across gender lines, as to whether lesbians and faeries conspiring together suggested overlapping or complementary subjectivities. The shadow of New Left organizing culture still clearly hung over Short Mountain Sanctuary.

Short Mountain maintained its solidarity position in response to racism and sexism, but their ultimate disavowal of the terms "*anti*-sexist" and "*anti*-racist" suggests their cautious hope that, within sanctuary, internal struggle and critique were less necessary. Some faeries saw this assumption as a failing of the early Short Mountain gatherings, as when, in the fall of 1981, Englebert commented that "such an emotionally self-sufficient, predominately white, exclusively male support system would hopefully be actively involved in self-analysis and self-criticism in regards to racism & sexism. I don't see that happening."[29] From this point of view, the balance between internal care, consciousness-raising, sanctuary accessibility, and political organizing—all sissie gathering features—might have come to emphasize care and organizing among existing participants more than doubling down on critique, inclusivity, and accessibility. To the degree this was so, Short Mountain risked betraying its own inclusive values to become a tacitly white and male faerie sanctuary.

In part this may have resulted from how seasonal collectivism and mobility had already been established as a feature of sissie networking. Neither Hayes nor Gross remained at Short Mountain long enough to participate in its incorporation or mission-writing. They stayed roughly six months and would both ultimately go to the high desert of northern New Mexico. This meant that LaSIS's core New Orleans membership changed, too. In many ways the nationally compelling figure of the faerie—while a subjectivity with regionally contested definitions—had eclipsed that of the sissie. In the summer 1981 issue of *RFD*, though, LaSIS did make an effort to define the culture's three primary reclaimed subjectivities: the faggot, sissie, and faerie.[30] They persistently defined the faggot figure by those details and arguments offered by Arthur Evans's *Witchcraft and the Gay Counterculture*, rendering it with a fieriness that evoked militant politics and spell-work. LaSIS defined the sissie as a gender subjectivity predicated on a "sexual terrorism" that recognized and combated the shared oppression between women and effeminate men (including all gay men, as feminized persons).[31] At this point they also celebrated sissie "drag" even more than they did in their earlier 1978 "Sissie."[32]

LaSIS explicitly traced the faerie subjectivity to the 1979 Arizona conference, rendering it the youngest of the three figures. They took some time to contrast the fire in the "faggot" epithet with how the faerie's ephemerality was reclaimed. They described faerie power mostly in terms of its airiness, or mutability—to change shape or gender, to disappear (into the background, or nature), to suddenly *re*appear, to defend the environment, and to facilitate spiritual transformation. Faeries especially focused—per Hay's SUBJECT-SUBJECT consciousness—on cultivating a more mutual, caring society. Even as this taxonomy seemed part of a LaSIS effort to maintain sissie and faggot visibility within the ascending faerie culture, LaSIS, like Pyne, simultaneously helped to raise the faerie profile even as they doggedly articulated it through sissie practice. For example, in the previous (spring 1981) issue of *RFD*, LaSIS took leadership (with Brotherlover's accounting talents) for the "Faerie Fund": a fundraising project designed to direct money to "geographically, racially, and class diverse" collectives within the "network," with a certain portion of funds marked expressly for "Prison Assistance," to get sisters and brothers out of jails.[33] They volunteered, *as faeries*, to materially support sissie collectivist projects.

After 1981, though, the word "sissie" rarely appears in *RFD*, which would thereafter colloquially be understood as shorthand for "Radical Faerie Digest."

Even though "On the Question of Names" offered a helpful indexing of the swirling subjectivities of their regional late-1970s gay liberationist movement, in retrospect it seems written for posterity rather than the moment. LaSIS and Short Mountain had already committed themselves to realizing their queer leftist practice within the contours of the faerie subjectivity and movement. Ritually speaking, that decision was put into motion with two quiet pieces of magick cast at the August 1980 Radical Faerie gathering in Colorado. First, Melba'son put his fabric art talents toward making a shawl with the image of the Horned God Cernunnos in the center. At the gathering, he tremulously and self-consciously presented it to everyone at a heart circle. Another faerie proposed that the shawl be worn by any person speaking in the full-group circles at all future faerie gatherings. Everyone agreed, and thus Melba'son's art passed into the material culture of the Radical Faeries, as a way to support the effeminist culture of thoughtful speaking and careful listening begun in the heart circles of Running Water.

Second, the founding members of LaSIS—Melba'son, Dimid, Brotherlover, and Aurora—found themselves reunited at the Colorado gathering, where they joined other faeries in dancing around a Kali Fire on the evening of Tuesday, August 12. Participants were invited to release old emotional fixations into the fire, really letting them go. Melba'son recorded in his journal the next morning, "One of the things burned in the Kali Fire last nite was the regionalism of LaSIS."[34] Standing in the Mountain West, at their second Radical Faerie gathering, selling buttons and T-shirts to raise money for the Faerie Fund, they understood their Southeastern sissie collectivism to have joined a wider cultural political stream that was galvanized most by a faerie figure. They knew that what they had started now exceeded the Ozarks, New Orleans, or Appalachia, and that it was circulating further than the region—at national and even international scales. As leftists, they never imagined that their sissie subjectivities were inherent or permanent; rather, they saw them as revolutionary social subjectivities tuned to the material and ideological conditions of the fleeting historical moment. There would always be new figures to compose, other dreams to craft.

And the sissie moment had shifted, with the wind. Pyne surely felt this ache when he commented that his final draft of "A Faeryist Not-Man-ifesto" was finished on the eve of Ronald Reagan's election. A national gay rights movement was emerging, and they all felt that the faerie subjectivity was the only gay liberationist figure with the heft to match the US gay rights narrative. What was more important to them than any sissie identity was their collectivist practice, with its repertoire for joining in solidarity, especially against the sexism and racism of the late-1970s New Right, which had sprouted from Jim Crow geographies. They knew their practice to still be *unqueer*, not yet realized. It needed time, in other hands, to come to fuller fruition. So they embraced the fey in themselves and improvised their collectivist sanctuary practice to prepare for the new decade.

Today, Radical Faeries remember the Cernunnos shawl with awe—no one quite knowing which gathering it last appeared at. The force of its message succeeded its short-lived circulation. The same might be said of the Southeastern sissie figure and the collectivism that remade itself, from Mulberry House to LaSIS to Running Water and Short Mountain, into an underground that contended with a New Right terror that wielded white Christian supremacist violence at ever wider scales. They stitched their unfinished dreams into the deltas and the hollows of that terror—for the sake of those unqueer houses yet to come.

Conclusion
Unqueer Dreams Left

LaSIS wrote that "Fairies can vanish into the woodwork of corporate paneling or forest trees."[1] In many ways, the sissies similarly disappeared from the paper record in the early 1980s. There was, of course, an afterlife for those members who had agitated in the name of Southeastern sissie collectivism. As we have mentioned, Dimid Hayes and Cathy Gross (later, Cathy Hope) went to northern New Mexico. Hayes would join a lover in Santa Fe and attend herbal medicine school in 1982. However, in an inspired send-up of the traditional family, Hayes took advantage of Louisiana's riddled Napoleonic law to adopt his former lover, Dennis Melba'son, in order to access some of those legal rights denied to those who were in queer relationships.[2] Their legal union defied the straight model of generational succession. However, just a day before the 1983 summer solstice, Melba'son's body was discovered outside a French Quarter gay bar, the Golden Lantern. There was evidence of blunt force trauma to the back of his head, but it was unclear whether this was from the fall or an attack. Some speculated that he had been mugged, since a silver pentagram pendant he had designed was missing from his neck. Whatever the case, Hayes still considers it an auspicious exit for the physically small but larger-than-life Melba'son. After all, that night was also a full moon in Capricorn, the older sissie's sun sign.[3]

Aurora often felt like he'd been left alone to steer the New Orleans sissie house through its last days. He shouldered heavy responsibilities when he set up hospice for Brotherlover, who shortly before Melba'son's death contracted an illness that would quickly take his life. Stacy first fell ill when what was then called GRID (gay-related immune deficiency) struck hard in major cities like those featured in ABC's "Homosexuals." There would be no definitive answer as to whether this disease was what took Brotherlover's life—Dimid recalls that he was misdiagnosed with meningitis—but Stacy did pass away during the first wave of that collective gay loss.[4] By Aurora's account, though, LaSIS had remained active on local and international issues to that point—even meeting the activist nun Sister Helen Prejean and sharing her activism against Louisiana capital punishment and against US imperialism in Central America. Aurora remained in New Orleans until Katrina struck. He then moved back to the Lawrence, Kansas, area, where he still lived when I interviewed him, by phone, in 2017. I regret that I never met him in person; he passed away in 2018.

Michael Oglesby and Charlie Thornton *did* move into the rural Ozarks, on land surrounded by many of the lesbian feminists whose politics inspired Mulberry House. When they graciously hosted me in the summer of 2019, they invited their neighbors to discuss my research, and I was humbled to revisit the Mulberry House days with so many local radical women, including Diana Rivers, who briefly and emotionally talked with me about the young Melba'son. The shared lesbian/sissie Ozarks community—begun in 1976—persists, vibrant, even to this day.

The refined features of the sissie figure are less clear through those lenses of gay history available today, though. The reasons are more complex than a failure of historical memory, the slim archive, or their geographic margins— although those are surely factors, too. I have shown here how sustained gay liberation was a highly dispersed and mobile culture, one that requires a (trans) regional, transnational, and networked lens to see it more fully. This story asks that its chroniclers not respond to the widespread strategic and temporary separatism of the era by assuming that these groups had an isolated, identity-based politics but instead describe their cross-movement orientations and their dreams of emergent solidarities. It asks that we not split gay from lesbian, Black from white, queer from sissie, rural from urban, vision from praxis, or culture from activism. It is also important to detail how gay liberation operated within and at the edges of the burgeoning national gay rights movement, which in the late 1970s eclipsed but never extinguished liberation.

I believe it is easy to make a case for the sissies' important contributions to LGBTQ+ history. After all, Short Mountain lives on today, arguably as the oldest of a now international network of Radical Faerie sanctuaries. It is also surrounded by related rural queer communities—an important presence in a state that is often hostile to LGBTQ+ persons. This assemblage of rural queer communities has enjoyed a remarkable gender diversity that both defies any easy profile of Radical Faerie subjectivity as a gay men's culture and also reflects the culture's roots in a meeting of femme, nonbinary, trans, lesbian, *and* gay men's collectivism.[5] With the help of Running Water and Short Mountain, *RFD* has also survived since Faygele ben Miriam brought it, on its last legs, to the Southeastern Network in 1978. The venerable magazine was published at Short Mountain through 2010, when it moved primary operations to New England. Running Water's rural retreats would morph into Gay Spirit Visions in 1990, a gay men's spiritual movement that also still meets in the

North Carolina mountains. In New Orleans, LaSIS did the lion's share of organizing for what is still remembered locally as the city's first Gay Pride event, even though their Pink Triangle Alliance purposely shaped it as a gay liberationist rally. Regional sissie collectivism was crucial to all these later developments; however, I would like not to reduce late 1970s sissie collectivism to a mere preamble for what would come after. There is so much to gather from lingering in the sunset of the 1970s, in apprehending how some proposed to survive during the early ascendance of the New Right. Only a few of those futures they dreamed have come true. This book sketches those that materialized—but also some that only survived as a doodle, or gesture. These latter dreams remain . . . unqueer.

The sissies emerged as only one of several interconnected efforts in the 1970s to sustain gay liberation's radicalism through the improvisation of queer revolutionary subjectivities. To the degree that queer movement history has focused on formal organizations, these subjectivities have remained hard to see. Looking back, the sissies remember their own figure as the product of their trying to cobble piecemeal Maoist lessons, which they received through their various networks, into a revived leftist, queer praxis. After all, the Black Panthers, which many of them had seen as the vanguard of their shared revolution, embraced Maoist tenets.[6] Maoist strategies for personal change resonated with feminist consciousness-raising techniques, and Mao's revolutionary peasant figure suggested new directions for those US counterconcultures that found themselves in rural spaces. When Williams re-emerged as Melba'son on the streets of the French Quarter in 1978, he—of course—wore red-star earrings to signal this lineage and framed his witchy radical conversion as a *fanshen*.

It has been a key argument of this book that their sissie figure also emerged out of a practice of reclaiming epithets—specifically from a sustained gay liberationist faggot genealogy. Collectivist faggotry, effeminism, sissiehood, and faeriedom improvised their figures out of their orientations to each other, to local political cultures, to historical exigencies, and to their potential allies. This proliferation of gay liberationist figures also arguably descended from when *RFD* began to riff on its eponymous acronym, suggesting an almost endless set of epithets—*eff* words and otherwise—that might be reclaimed for the revolution. The less widely espoused *fruits*, *fuzzies*, and *pansies* popped up alongside our more usual suspects: faggots, sissies, queens, and faeries. This project has looked back at the Southeastern sissies' place in this dispersed culture to understand some of their shared practices, along with the distinct ones.

Sissie embodiment was expressly nonbinary in that it disavowed an exclusive male or female script and celebrated multiplicity. While it makes sense to frame their androgyny as an extension of what Stryker has called a "'hippie/fairy' chic" rooted in the counterculture, or as what Luther Hillman has called "political drag" (a choice akin to political lesbianism), I find that, ultimately, reducing it to the sartorial or strategic hardly does sissiedom justice. Ross's hermeneutic for "sissy liminality" suggests that we can read the figure for how it navigated those uncomfortably proximate institutions that constituted it: home, church, school, and street. Creatures of their moment, pinched between Save Our Children and the Briggs Initiative, these Southeastern sissies presented themselves as nonbinary educators, wondrous Pied Pipers, information activists, radical housekeepers, and care laborers in an era when the New Right raised violent alarms about how male-teachers-in-dresses recruited the nation's (white, gender-conforming, straight) children.

In doing so, they discovered their classroom in the street. Those streets are where they found themselves actively questioning their effeminist roots as they discovered a possible femme kinship with street queens. As they renegotiated their cross-gender and cross-racial orientations, they actively registered how the transition *felt* rather than rushing to conclusive thoughts. This required them to exercise a new sensorium—one attuned to, and also *out of harmony with*, the audiovisual rhetoric of the street's saturating rape culture. It also required them to sit with the pain of the feminists and queens around them without resolving or ordering that pain, or their own. As a result, their genders were as conflicted as their stances were *unqueer*. They, and their revolutions, were decidedly unfinished, and they were increasingly convinced that remaining fully engaged, connected in solidarity, was the only path forward. As Muñoz puts it, their queerness only existed as a horizon.[7]

We can point to their documentation of this thoughtful affective exercise. Melba'son's feeling his way through dishwashing suds to find his place among global capital's Taiwanese plate-ware production, the United States' compulsory Christianity, and ubiquitous sexist catcalling is a very historical materialist version of this affective work. Pyne, sitting on the New Orleans banks of the Mississippi, imagined taking this street-oriented sensorium back to the country, to Appalachian Short Mountain, and beyond—suggesting a regional and environmentalist version. As he put it, "We might live in the country far away from the diversions and distractions of the city; [w]e might live in the bowels of the monster; [w]e might be on the road, wanderers, vagabonds, seekers, but we are one family/river. A strong river growing stronger only as we join forces. Part of RFD's purpose is to help with that flow.... Somehow sitting here sensurrounded by the city I can smile knowing that upriver there are quiet places where the water flows sweet and clear."[8] I find that the word *sensurround* nicely improvises the affective practice that was the historical condition for the sissies' nonbinary embodiment.

Feminist witchcraft was also central to their leftism. Invocation, aspecting, fire rituals, spiral dances, consecration, and spell-casting (including hexing) were all put to political purpose. Far from a New Age phenomenon, this witchery sought to draw forth revolutionary action in ways that rational lectures, discussion groups, and consciousness-raising alone could not. They trusted that performance and ritual were the surer modes for extending talk and text into lived experience. Their craft followed Evans's own definition of magic, with his fiery conflation of the collective and the coven. At Wolf Creek, the moon/fire ritual filled participants with the revolutionary audacity of a radical femme and sealed the deal by bonding them together with an intimate spiral dance or by fixating them on visions of armed femmes commandeering military tanks. Mulberry House, moved by such practice, did not manage to center it, because the Save Our Children campaign terrorized the South shortly after they returned from Oregon.

However, Melba'son—embracing the hermetic *and* the ecstatic—engaged the witch tradition of the multiple self by staging a psychic dialogue between one's everyday and radical souls as a way to perform a *fanshen*, a slow turning of the radical self into a main character. In his own practice, he did this by a psychogeographic practice—regular journaling coupled with a *flâneur's* method of finding his place in his new city. He, and the rest of LaSIS, adopted new names to signal and sustain their sissie conversions. At Running Water, witchy song and the spiral dance continued, but the "heart circle" itself—small groups of men listening, sharing, emoting, and supporting—performed its own kind of magic. As Abbott poetically suggested, these circles made better lovers—both gentler and more dangerous. In the name of the faerie figure, Pyne, like Evans, emphasized extending that connection to nature, too. Even though we don't have evidence of an actual ritual, he also suggested the practice of baneful magic: hexes on systems of oppression, like TVA.

Arguably, though, the dream became the primary vehicle for their shared political magick as the decade waned. The act of dreaming was important, since indulging it allowed them to reclaim an act that had been defined as a contrast to decisive masculine action. To the patriarchy, the dreamy belonged to a femme realm. However, since Langston Hughes asked whether a dream deferred might explode, and Martin Luther King Jr., by echoing Hughes's emphasis on dreams, famously inserted the act of dreaming into civil rights praxis, then New Left gay liberationists who had sought to learn from Black politics surely wondered how dreaming might be put to sustained political use. At the 1976 Oregon Faggots & Class Struggle conference, the theme Michael Oglesby most liked was that of "remembering forgotten dreams," a phrase the fall 1976 issue of *RFD* used for its cover. In his "Ascent, Lament, and Admonition," Abbott suggested that dreaming was a way to go back in time, to re-access the bodily and emotional connection of the rural gathering, to draw energy from it, and become a more revolutionary lover. Through their information activism, especially their sissie bibliography, LaSIS tacitly pointed regional lesbian and gay activists to "Jesse's Dream Skirt" and to youth liberation, citing how their sissie street pedagogy defied an era of violent, New Right child protectionism. They morphed themselves into the figure of the Pied Piper, or the male-teacher-in-a-dress—a figure that anti-communists and then white Christian supremacists had used to smear pinkos.

It is also important to emphasize that the Southeastern sissie subjectivity was predicated on a unique repertoire of responses to New Right child protectionism. Most of their forms of resistance reclaimed traditionally femme roles. The domestic work of maintaining radical sissie houses within the network is but one example. In an effeminist vein, they often took mothering as a form of labor that men—especially effeminate ones—were enjoined to share. Many West Coast faggots—in the shadow of military infrastructures and in proximity to the George Jackson Brigade—envisioned ways for femme men to be militants wearing skirts as they commandeered tanks or stuffed their bras with grenades; as Carol Mason has suggested, many Midwestern gay liberationists focused on media zaps, like public pie-ing; and many gay rights activists insisted to New Right mothers that "we are your children, too." LaSIS responded differently—by unabashedly assuming the roles that offended New Right families most, by performing the labor of teachers and parents—but in a genderfuck form.

The temporal applications of the period's gay liberationist dreamwork were complex and varied. In general, the sissies' practice of "Remembering Forgotten Dreams" functioned much as what Muñoz, building on Ernst Bloch, described as hope's method: "a backward glance that enacts a future vision."[9] In those years after 1973, when most GLF chapters disbanded, gay liberationists sought to affectively recall the first feelings of liberation in order to reanimate revolution in the context of new violence. Early on, faggot witchcraft did that trick. Out of that practice, in the wake of Save Our Children, the Briggs Initiative, and Milk's assassination, and in anticipation of Ronald Reagan's 1980 election, faggots, sissies, and faeries less gave up hope than they fashioned dream technologies to sustain liberation between revolutions. They recorded and shared dreams in print media, witchy ritual, street actions, rural gatherings, and televisual performances—as a way of both collectively materializing hope in the moment and leaving a crude dream that might be finished by tomorrow's liberationists.

They dreamed differently, though. The early Radical Faeries dreamed in a way that I frame as an "abstract utopia," following Muñoz and Bloch. The timeless dimensions of their dreams—often achieved by a queer appropriation of Indigenous perspectives—proposed a cosmic or primordial transcendence. There were few concrete next steps offered toward their future society based on SUBJECT-SUBJECT consciousness. John Noble's "dream museum," as framed at least in ABC's "Homosexuals," was similarly abstract, a vessel for escape, and so hermetic that it stymied any crosswalk to the collective or social. For their part, the sissies strove for a more concrete utopia in that they suggested futures built on their daily praxis. For example, they gestured toward the gender nonconforming classroom of "Jesse's Dream Skirt" through their nonbinary French Quarter street activism and pedagogy. The dream of a deeper south liberated by proliferating autonomous land movements, as envisioned in Pyne's "A Faeryist Not-Man-ifesto," seems less fantastic when we recall their specific plans for sissie networking, its map of existing collectives, their call for an underground, and their specific solidarity campaigns.

Their sense of themselves as radicals depended not only on magically remaking themselves in the name of the particular subjectivity that they embraced, but also on close dialogue with the material circumstances of the place where they lived, in the historical moment in which they were thrown. Thus, their regionalism was crucial. Despite the linking of cultures made possible by media and interstates, they knew that daily life, and the political economies that shaped it, in the South or Midwest, was incredibly different from that in the Castro or on Christopher Street. Late-1970s *RFD* readers—including Mulberry House, Gross, and Englebert—cautioned editors against a universalizing Californization of faggot subjectivity during *RFD*'s last year on the West Coast. The sissies were committed to articulating a practice conversant with the needs and cultures of *each* discrete place in the wider Southeast where they lived.

The original Mulberry House split, though, over the course of the Save Our Children campaign. They knew its child protectionism to be ideologically structured by the Jim Crow geography from which it was born. They understood its rhetoric as a defensiveness of the white supremacist family form that responded violently to racial mixing, liberated women, and same-sex relationships. They saw, then, in the vigilante violence in the murder of gay San Francisco gardener Robert Hillsborough; in the car-bombing of Latino gay liberationists in Miami; and in the Klan-incited physical attacks, by teenagers, on lesbians and gay men in nearby Oklahoma City—how all of these stemmed from late-1970s New Right child protectionism courting racist, sexist, *and* homophobic bloodshed. Mulberry House witnessed how this rhetoric emboldened the white countercultural leadership of the Ozark Food Co-op to fire and physically threaten their Black, female, and homosexual employees. Even though Anita Bryant is now dismissed as laughable, or framed as the unwitting catalyst for the gay rights movement, Hayes would have us remember just how "tenuous" life was in those days, and Thornton reminds us how one of his earliest goals was to be "open as a gay man without getting killed." In the late 1970s, Thornton's wish was seriously compromised by white Christian supremacist violence. This made solidarity with women's and Black movements a priority for the sissies, even while they honored separatist strategies as sometimes necessary components of those alliances.

This experience of regional terrorism also would inform how they came to imagine their network of rural and urban collectives as an underground. This was a form of lesbian-inspired collective defense built out of back-to-the-land movements, rural gathering culture, and *RFD* networking. If rural gathering sites were collectivized, then they might allow for radicals to circulate from site to site, for a season. In "A Letter to Action," Hayes insisted that a wider practice of solidarity was necessary to bring others than young white gay men into their collectives. Brotherlover added that using *RFD* to be transparent about each collective's practice would allow for not only better skill-sharing but for reduced dependency on local waged labor. With Short Mountain, this underground was overtly framed as a form of "sanctuary," and with his map and his "A Faeryist Not-Man-ifesto," Milo Pyne returned sissie collectivist practice to its earliest Venceremos inspirations, suggesting that it must face a deeper south, in support of revolutions in neighboring nations, but also from within: battles for independence in Puerto Rico, in the Texan Chicana/o borderlands, and in the Deep South of the New Afrikan movement. With Pyne, Southeastern sissie collectivism hearkened to how Southern white supremacy had long been entangled with anti-communism, especially in its proximity to revolutionary Cuba, and that through the anthology *Out of the Closets* (1972), gay liberation had long been entwined with Venceremos experience. This was an ambitious collectivist vision whose aims for wide solidarity across movements and political borders never really materialized; however, its influence can be seen in how, in the early 1980s, *RFD* devoted more and more pages to critique of US imperialism in Central America, and Short Mountain surely considered its own practice alongside more formal sanctuary movements that emerged in the early 1980s.

It's important to recognize, though, how the sissies were lopsidedly oriented, how some solidarities were unqueerer than others—particularly when it came to race. Gay liberation itself emerged out of a conflicted relationship to Black radicalism. It held the Black Panthers as the revolutionary vanguard, even as Carl Wittman characterized gay liberation's alliance with Black liberation as "tenuous." In turning their backs on gay streets, piers, and bars, and loudly objecting to gay femmes, the Flaming Faggots/Effeminists had implicitly oriented themselves *away from* the street queens of color understood to foment Stonewall in the first place. In 1976 the sissie figure was born out of agreement with Bay Area gay liberationists of color who critiqued the whiteness of West Coast faggotry. Thereafter, the sissies joined other regional critiques of West Coast *RFD*'s racial inclusivity as merely rhetorical. The Southeast sissies themselves tried to go further. They joined in queer solidarity with specifically Black actions like the UTNO teacher strike, Dessie Woods's defense, and the Greensboro massacre protests. They featured June Boyd, as a Black lesbian prison abolitionist, in *RFD*. Hayes called for the Southeast Network to realize regional sissie collectivism as radically inclusive, with the specific priority to actively welcome Black sissies. However, consistent, self-proclaimed Black sissie voices did not yet appear in *RFD* in the way Black faggot voices had in Boston's *Fag Rag*. According to Englebert, early Short Mountain remained largely white and male.

In his "Faeryist Not-man-ifesto," Pyne insisted that the time *had* come for gay liberationists and women to conspire together. He worried, though, that white gay liberationists' examination of their own racism and Black radicalism's analysis of homophobia might not have led to enough common ground for the same kind of collaboration in 1980. In this Pyne seemed to overlook the possibility of Black sissies, an oversight that is a testament to (1) just how white Southeastern sissie collectivism in fact remained in 1980, and (2) how early Short Mountain could so easily reproduce, and perpetuate, the rigidly parallel, identitarian model of revolutionary solidarity that had been endemic to the New Left a decade before. As we have seen, this model forced radicals into various degrees of separatism that, while not construed as permanent, proliferated endless questions over if, when, and how unity would come.

Later in the 1980s, Black queer poets like Essex Hemphill and Assotto Saint would publish in *RFD*, and some liberationists like Franklin Abbott would also become active in the National Association of Black & White Men Together.

By the turn of the century, Short Mountain would have some Black residents; and Morgensen has noted that this racial minority within the Radical Faerie community formed Faeries of All Colors Together (FACT) at a 1999 Short Mountain gathering.[10] Back in 1980, though, sissie solidarity with Black radicalism was episodic—tied to isolated street protests—but generally did not lead to multiracial sissie houses, whether in the country or the city.[11] This was one of their plans that moved according to a different timeline due to the uneven orientation of the sissie figure descended from the organizational cultures of gay liberation and the wider New Left.

Whether faggot, effeminist, sissie, or faerie, these collectivists had no other choice than to attend to the temporal and spatial elements of gay liberation. As we have seen, gay liberation in general, and faggot politics specifically, struggled with a sense of having joined in late, in relation to the wider revolution for which they regarded the Black Panthers the vanguard. This is why, according to the Lavender Country song, the gay men "brought up the rear," with grenades stuffed in their brassieres. This may also explain how Arthur Evans envisioned a long-form revolution—the first wave of which, however, was a reformist, single-issue gay movement (the GAA) intended to form a base for meaningfully contributing to the revolution down the road. This sense of belatedness may also help us understand why, almost since its inception, gay liberation obsessively checked its own pulse. Being the rear guard, gay liberation perennially worried whether it could compose its own radical analysis or revolutionary figure in time to join in. Or worse: whether they would arrive after the struggle had already been lost.

What this taught them was to build strategies for sustaining the movement as they went. They didn't just improvise a single radical figure. They developed repertoires for building new ones, attuned to changing historical and geographic conditions. Early on, these repertoires centered feminist witchcraft: group and solitary rituals, conducted in leftist tenors. Later these practices manifested as part of a wider dream technology. Later still, these figures were conceived of in complementary roles, with each contributing in varying ways to the cause—the front-line militancy of the faggot, the nonbinary street pedagogies of the sissie, and the rural sanctuary work of the faerie. And, it seems, they also learned how to retire certain figures. For a spell, that is. Because we know that they had used magick to revive gay liberation and to manage activist energy *between* revolutions. This allowed them to manage their fires in unexpected times, such as periods of mass terror or attenuated dormancy.

Equally key to this strategy was their collectivism, by which they put liberation in unexpected places: in the home, on the (abandoned) farm, in a flagging serial, in the Southeast. Establishing gay liberation in such places stymied the surveillance strategies of the time, just as their event design relied on similar tactics of diffusion, anachronism, rusticity, and obfuscation. However, in their later iterations sissies didn't turn their backs on the street and bar, but linked them to the house and farm, forming a network. This was how they established an underground for collective defense, for sanctuary—another tool for maintaining the revolution. As the national gay rights movement rose, they drew upon their leftist, mostly Venceremos inspirations, to imagine a deeper-south collectivism that might open its regional houses along transnational, anti-imperialist vectors. In a way, they tried to imagine themselves both larger and smaller than the nascent national gay-rights narrative, in order to set place-markers for alternative plotlines.

Today, New Right child protectionism flexes its own durability through "no-woke" educational bills and anti-LGBTQ+ book-banning initiatives. Such censorship must be understood as part of longer traditions of Christian white supremacist disinformation and dis-education campaigns. Further, if Save Our Children adopted queerbaiting rhetoric that courted physical violence, recent stories that falsely accuse Haitian populations of stealing and eating Americans' pets also seek to mobilize votes while tacitly inviting anti-Black and xenophobic attacks. Similar inciteful fictions are being circulated about schools forcing children into gender transitions. We should also remember that the sissystories woven in this book emerged at the time *Roe v. Wade* was being decided (1973). Bethany Moreton helpfully tells us that, during that time, televangelists circulated violence-triggering lies about dumpsters overflowing with the body parts of butchered infants. At a time when similarly gory tall tales are being spread about Haitians in Ohio, we also witness how the reversal of *Roe v. Wade* has stripped many women—and others—of their bodily autonomy, forcing them to risk their death in hospitals, all in the name of protecting the life of a future child. Many in the United States have had to forge clandestine networks to access the care they desperately need. To the degree that the current landscape looks like what Varon has called "the rarefied world of the underground—a world of extraordinary danger," the time may be ripe for sifting through earlier toolkits and repertoires.[12] Maybe, in another era's unfinished dreaming, we will find some unexpected tactics for reorienting this unqueer moment toward still sweeter tomorrows.

Acknowledgments

The questions that shaped this book have allowed me to see very differently the places I am from, to imagine other sites to which those roots might lead. The small farm where I grew up was, I now realize, only about an hour and half's drive from Short Mountain Sanctuary. When I first visited Short Mountain, in the winter of 2000, I saw that they kept goats, just as we had back home—but on the queer farm, it was common to wear drag when rising at dawn to do the milking. In the Georgia State University archives, I discovered a letter from Clear Englebert to fellow gay liberationist Franklin Abbott, and I saw that Clear's rural route number matched that of my childhood address. It was like discovering a radically parallel faerie world unfurling right alongside my own. It was like that world, equally real, lay on the other side of a queer veil.

I am honored to be trusted with the stories of so many brave souls who have helped me to better navigate that strange South. I hope I have shared your stories well. Thank you to my first oral history co-conspirator, Franklin Abbott, who so generously introduced me to the others. Looking back, it was Franklin who first mentioned "the great sissie archive" to me, and Dimid—who kept that archive, across decades—who so graciously, vulnerably introduced me to its contents. I am so grateful.

Thank you to Mikel Wilson and Douglas Caulkins for hosting me in the Atlanta area as they recalled Running Water to me. Thank you to those who spent precious hours on the phone: Clear Englebert and Jack Kendrick. I hope I didn't bend your ears too much. To Michael Oglesby and Charlie Thornton: I am so grateful that you welcomed me into your Arkansas home; introduced me to Trella Laughlin; and invited me to meet the long-standing Ozarks radical women's community, including Diana Rivers. I remember those July days with you fondly. We'll do it again. For retelling his Short Mountain adventures and sharing a meal with me in Durham, thanks to Milo Pyne. I am humbled to have won David "Aurora" Speakman's trust even as I very much regret that I wasn't able to meet him in person, at least in this life. And boundless gratitude to Dimid Hayes, Cathy Hope, and Michael Donlon. One of the greatest gifts of this research has been the time I spent with each of you. I welcome all our future adventures, my friends.

My mentor, Christina Hanhardt, has long shown faith in me and this project. I'd never have reached this stage without her spot-on advice and guidance. As a librarian myself, I am thankful to all the archivists who have supported this research: Kelly Wooten at Duke University's Sallie Bingham Center for Women's History & Culture, Morna Gerrard at Georgia State University's Women & Gender Collections, Chloe Raub at Tulane's Newcomb Archives, and Jane Klain at the Paley Center for Media. I am grateful, too, for librarian Carla Myers (Miami University), for being so assuring as you walked me through questions about permissions and images, and for Jason Tomberlin (UNC, Chapel Hill), Leanne Herman (Indiana University, Bloomington), and Kathy Lafferty (University of Kansas, Lawrence) for so swiftly coordinating image reproductions for me.

Research for the book was supported by a Mary Lilly Research Grant to Duke and by Loyola University New Orleans's Marquette Faculty Research Fellowship. Archival research is magical, and I was enabled to conduct it with the resources provided by those awards, and with the generous professional development support I received while at Loyola University New Orleans. I would also like to thank Jason Baumann at the New York Public Library. Being a recipient of the first Martin Duberman LGBT Visiting Scholarship is how I was first smitten with doing queer history, and I am thankful for Jason's advocacy through that program and with other projects since. Andreina Fernandez, my editor at the University of North Carolina Press, has been a true wonder. Your humor, care, and insights energized me through this first book project, even when I felt utterly overwhelmed. I am also grateful to my generous peer reviewers who gave my drafts such thoughtful attention, and have made this book stronger, tenfold, by that.

I was introduced to the Radical Faeries by Seth Stewart, and I then deepened that first meeting through my enchanting years with the Evelyn House River Spirits, in Memphis. Thank you all for helping me live my questions so that I could eventually chase them back in time. Spiritually, I am thankful to the makers and tenders of Short Mountain's Memorial Ridge, and to poet Michael Mason, who, as I understand it, laid the first stone there. In many ways, it was by sitting in that circle formed of tell-all trees, old names, busted dolls, bones, and vanity mirrors that I first learned how much I wanted to listen in on faerie prehistory.

Several dear old friends have been godsends across this process. Brian Isbell and Don Fox gifted me with a writing retreat with them in Hot Springs, during a crucial summer. Thank you for keeping me on my routine and bookending it with so much laughter. Stephanie Talley has gently asked for updates, while also helping me to forget the details, by asking me to join her, Chip, and Beckett for well-timed weekend getaways at their house. Matt Johnson hosted me during research trips and paced my boundless curiosity about queer history with his own. Jason Burton listened to so many of my doubts and lifted them with his thoughtful questions. Sarah Sawyer shared with me her arts in how to trumpet and share the work. The Crooked Letter poetry collective (Shine, Mary, and Beth) helped me to remember how we pass words–like cornbread. And Beth Bishop Bennett has been my queer interlocutor for so long—years of print letters, all-night phone calls, barstool conversations, scrollable emails, and even Zoom chats—that I hope she recognizes in this book an extension of so many of the threads we have woven together for literal years.

Duane Barber, my husband, has witnessed, believed in, and encouraged my work, almost daily, for going on two decades. He has kept it from growing too big, and he has stopped me when I would minimize it. He has done so even as he has juggled all kinds of other wondrous feats of his own. He's magic—and I love him for that, and for so many other reasons. Thank you for making this happen, side by side.

Out of the Stacks
Leaning into Librarianly Excess

The majority of this book was written in New Orleans, by a librarian. Historians ask to be haunted, I suppose; New Orleanians—living shoulder to shoulder with their dead, immersed in the tangible shadows of living inequities—count historiography as neither special nor casual. It's needed for getting from there to here, and that's no mean feat. Like Melba'son, I was not born in the city; I moved there. At first I rejected its mystique, avoided the Quarter, thereby proving myself an insider. Or so I thought. I was soon taught by the locals, though, that in a tourist city, mystique not only keeps the spirits up; it puts food on the table. To live in New Orleans is to commit yourself to the shared labor of mystique. It's a city remade daily by crafts that only sometimes tout themselves as witchery. But if you scratch the surface, it's all magic.

I wonder whether I could have realized myself as librarian-scholar anywhere else. The "archival turn" has, I believe, allowed scholars and archivists to re-regard each other. In 2022 the American Studies Association was in New Orleans for its annual conference, and my ears pricked up when Ann Cvetkovich (*An Archive of Feelings*) suggested, in commentary on the work of archival studies scholar Marika Cifor (*Viral Cultures*), that perhaps the time had come for interdisciplinary scholars—especially those working with archival methods—to more actively engage information studies and library science. As a practicing academic librarian, I already felt like I was undercover at the conference, so it electrified me to hear my field directly addressed. Still, because I am not an archivist or a librarian educator, I felt an orbit or two out from this still-tentative conversation. However, at another panel on scholarly practice that addressed race and the internet—a panel that featured information studies scholars Tonia Sutherland (*Resurrecting the Black Body*) and Patricia Garcia—an audience member spoke frankly about the challenges of her role as a public librarian seeking to educate in the context of uneven access and ubiquitous racial violence. As an academic librarian, I was challenged *and* validated by this fellow librarian's commentary. I felt myself homing in on the things I *might* do differently. What work did I, as a librarian, already share with fellow American Studies scholars who were regarded as teaching faculty?

From my historical research, I learned there was every reason to reconsider my place as a librarian. Gay liberationists were critical of institutions, including universities and libraries, but that suspicion did not lead them to abandon the work of those bodies. Instead, liberationists often labored twice as hard to craft alternative institutions. Information activism, as Cait McKinney terms it, was key. Sissies authored, edited, and illustrated within liberationist print culture, often following lesbian feminist models. Like Barbara Gittings, they galvanized networks through bibliographies. Melba'son tried to collectivize academic book indexing. LaSIS promoted the Atlantis collective's book distribution and also advocated pressuring libraries to add Atlantis's titles to public shelves.

Later, librarians would be focal characters in the wider Southeast Network. For example, Elizabeth Knowlton, a member of the Atlanta Lesbian Feminist Alliance (ALFA), led the careful document-keeping for the organization, making their work legible to history. Knowlton would also eventually serve as senior archivist at the Georgia Department of Archives. Cal Gough was an early regular at Running Water Farm gatherings, and he later established the circulating LGBT collection at the Ponce de Leon public library branch in Midtown Atlanta and coedited *Gay and Lesbian Library Service* (1990). Looking back, I had to ask myself: What lessons am I taking from liberationist information activism? How am I using and expanding my professional roles in service to the community?

Writing is an emotional business, and I now realize how I sought to keep my perspective as a librarian ambient, but not quite central, to this book's narrative. In retrospect, I don't so much see this as a choice as it was a reflection of academic librarians' affective training. We are conditioned as meta-beings: We are often encouraged to insert ourselves as experts in the infrastructure of scholarship while disavowing any skill or interest in actually performing it. By now I have a body memory for being *about* while refraining from ever *doing*. (Early in my career, I heard a professional development keynote where a library director shared how they had teased a political official: "Don't be silly! Real professional librarians don't *read* books. We just promote them to *actual* readers." At Loyola University New Orleans, however, I was hired as a history and social science librarian who coordinated the library instruction program. When I consulted the LGBTQ+ student organization about their needs, they said they felt generally welcomed in daily student life but wondered why their experience wasn't deemed important enough to appear in curricula. I chewed on this. How could I ever engage students with the practice of scholarship if I didn't attempt (even unevenly) to engage its queernesses myself?

Thus began a *shared* adventure. Several of my colleagues had embraced a similar leap. While I worked on the current book, fellow librarian Victoria Elmwood created and presented a digital map of historical sex work in New Orleans. Because the university's first-year seminar featured learning outcomes related to information literacy, librarians proposed and taught their own course sections; mine was on the history of US gay liberation and colleague Laurie Phillips's was on confronting misinformation. Librarians were invited to serve on panels providing feedback for students' Fulbright applications, and we increasingly framed all of our one-on-one consultations as scholar development. I volunteered to serve on the oral history committee of the LGBT+ Archives Project of Louisiana, with hopes of also finding service-learning opportunities for students. I mentored five students' LGBTQ+ thesis projects in three different disciplines, and one of them featured oral history, trained through the LGBT+ Archives Project. While some certainly saw such work as librarianly excess, in New Orleans we presented it as a *lagniappe* that demonstrated how librarians participate in the always collaborative work of scholarship. For several of us, it made instinctive sense that gathering sources was not enough; to animate a collection, we had to quicken it with our use. Dynamically connecting users with our collections involved sharing our passion and experience for engaging the material ourselves.

This book was written in that experimental New Orleans spirit. It was also written against the recurrence of a Deep South white Christian supremacy's child protectionism. In 2022, Florida passed its Stop WOKE Act in an attempt to erase education about inequities around race and gender. The law threatened that noncompliant teachers would lose their jobs and institutions their funding. In Louisiana, the state Attorney General's 2023 Protecting Innocence campaign targeted librarians, providing examples of literature for and about

LGBTQ+ experience and people of color as dangerous to children. This rhetoric knowingly inflamed public discourse falsely painting librarians as groomers and led to some public librarians receiving death threats. Objects of violence, public librarians left their jobs and looked for safety elsewhere. If the practice of librarianship and the figure of the librarian seem endangered, then both seem important not only to preserve but to redefine, with even stronger commitments to the radically democratic practice of inclusive scholarship.

As a librarian working in the train of such violent repression, I see scholarly practice as increasingly central to what I do. In 2016 the Association of College & Research Libraries issued the Framework for Information Literacy for Higher Education. One of those frames urges academic librarians to articulate "Scholarship as Conversation." I interpret that to mean that we actively initiate and stage such conversations as we strive to amplify the inherently inclusive and intimate nature of scholarship. This was also the work of early *RFD*, whose editors told reader-writers, "*You* write, sing, dance and are R.F.D." Each citation, each footnote is the record of a chemistry, a special meeting—a "bibliographic encounter," according to Cait McKinney. As queer studies scholars like Joey Plaster find professional homes in special collections, I find myself dreaming of how librarians morph our scholarly craft, too.

Notes

Introduction

1. Throughout the book, in my own writing, I will use the spellings adopted within the culture: "faeries" (plural), "faerie" (singular), "sissies" (plural), and "sissie" (singular). When referring specifically to the Radical Faeries, I will use capital letters. In quotations, I will use the spelling given in the source text.

2. Dennis Melba'son, "Excerpts from a Journal Written for a Friend in Prison," *RFD*, Fall/Winter 1980, 12–13. All the quoted passages in the first paragraph come from this source.

3. Marotta, *The Politics of Homosexuality*, 100–133.

4. See Radical Study Group member John Lauritsen's 1974 publications as a twinned representation of both strains of the group's thoughts: Lauritsen and Thorstad, *Early Homosexual Rights Movement*, and Lauritsen, *Religious Roots*. The former book framed post-Stonewall gay liberation as only the most recent wave of a longer European socialist gay liberation movement, and the latter's religious framing of homophobia included the faggot etymology also central to Evans's writing.

5. Flaming Faggots, "The Flaming Faggots."

6. Kissack, "Freaking Fag Revolutionaries," 124–25.

7. Dansky, "Hey Man," 194–99.

8. Hillman, *Dressing for the Culture Wars*, 109–10. Hillman says Morgan made the racial analogy in 1973.

9. Dansky, Knoebel, and Pitchford, "The Effeminist Manifesto," 435–38. The quoted passages in the previous sentence come from this source, too.

10. Pitchford, "Who Are the Flaming Faggots?," *motive* 32, no. 2 (Winter 1972): 16. Pitchford also states that their gentleness did not cancel their militancy, and that they did not necessarily associate their suggested anti-masculinist traits with women.

11. Serby, "Gay Liberation," 157–61. Few have considered the effeminists in much detail. Serby gives an overview of their place in a wider gay male anti-sexism, which lost steam.

12. Pitchford, "Who Are the Flaming Faggots?," 17.

13. Faderman, *The Gay Revolution*, 215.

14. Marotta, *The Politics of Homosexuality*, 134–61.

15. Marotta, *The Politics of Homosexuality*, 134–61.

16. Bell, *Dancing the Gay Lib Blues*. Bell offers contemporaneous accounts of Rivera's experiences in the GAA, witnessing how street queens like Rivera were sidelined—their gender expression framed as cultural rather than political, and their political initiatives unsupported.

17. Eller, *Living in the Lap*, 53.

18. It's important to note here that the success of these specific zaps owed more to other GAA members than to Evans—to the charismatic fearlessness of Marty Robinson and the media savvy of Arthur Bell and Kay Tobin Lahusen.

19. Evans, *Witchcraft*, 170. Martello's own political positions at the dawning of gay liberation were another animal altogether. In 1966 he espoused a somewhat libertarian, rationalist philosophy and proudly owned its similarity to that of Ayn Rand. Martello, *How to Prevent Psychic Blackmail*.

20. Pitchford, "Who Are the Flaming Faggots?," 16.

21. Arthur Evans, "Arthur Evans (1942–2011)," 2010, at Pagan Press Books website, https://paganpressbooks.com/jpl/EVANS-OB.HTM.

22. Newton, "Women's Liberation and Gay Liberation."

23. Stein, *Sisterly and Brotherly Loves*. Stein gives an account of how gay liberationists were better received at the convention than were lesbian feminists.

24. I am inspired here, in part, by how queer orientation is described in Ahmed's *Queer Phenomenology*.

25. Mumford, *Not Straight, Not White*, 92.

26. For an early example of faggot engagement with the radical figure of George Jackson, see "Behind Bars," *Fag Rag*, Fall 1971, 9.

27. Burton-Rose, *Guerrilla USA*.

28. For more on the Seattle context of the Morning Due collective, see Atkins, *Gay Seattle*.

29. Morning Due, "A Conference Report: Faggots and Class Struggle" (Wolf Creek, Oregon). Available at Michael J. Lecker's blog "It Was Curiosity," https://itwascuriosity.wordpress.com/wp-content/uploads/2012/12/conference-report-faggots-and-class-struggle.pdf.

30. Kissack, "Freaking Fag Revolutionaries," 124.

31. Vider, *The Queerness of Home*, 88.

32. Duberman, *Has the Gay Movement Failed?*, 40–41.

33. For more on STAR, see Marsha P. Johnson, "Rapping with a Street Transvestite Revolutionary." For more on the later house cultures associated with ballroom, see Bailey, *Butch Queens*.

34. Enszer, "'Stop Choking to Death,'" 180–96.

35. Gitlin, *The Sixties*.

36. Elbaum, *Revolution in the Air*.

37. Elbaum, *Revolution in the Air*; Varon, *Bringing the War Home*; Gosse, *Rethinking the New Left*.

38. Bronner, *Moments of Decision*.

39. Bronner, *Moments of Decision*; Rossinow, *The Politics of Authenticity*.

40. Hobson, *Lavender and Red*, 42–68.

41. Sears, *Rebels, Rubyfruit, and Rhinestones*, 196.

42. Herring, *Another Country*, 63–97.

43. Vider, *The Queerness of Home*, 103–4.

44. Duberman, *Has the Gay Movement Failed?*, 35; Dansky, "In Defense of Effeminism."

45. Evans, *Witchcraft*, 149–51.

46. Evans, *Witchcraft*, 1.

47. Eller, *Living in the Lap*, 53. Martello's political performance of witchcraft may have been inspired by the Women's International Terrorist Conspiracy from Hell (WITCH), a group of New York socialist feminists who, on Halloween of 1968, dressed as witches and put a pox on the stock market as they marched down Wall Street.

48. Hutton, *Triumph of the Moon*.

49. For what are now canonical overviews of US paganism, see Adler, *Drawing Down the Moon*, and Clifton, *Her Hidden Children*. Also see Salomonsen, *Enchanted Feminism*. For a primary source on Anderson Feri, see Anderson, *Fifty Years*.

50. Hanhardt, *Safe Space*, 92.

51. Evans, *Witchcraft*, 9, 9–13.

52. Evans, *Witchcraft*, 41–49.

53. Evans, *Witchcraft*, 145–46.

54. Evans, *Witchcraft*, 145–55.

55. Evans, *Witchcraft*, 120–25; Murch, *Living for the City*. Murch observes that this Bay Area military economy was an important context for the rise of the Black Panthers' militancy, too.

56. Evans, *Witchcraft*, 130.

57. Evans, *Witchcraft*, 149.

58. Evans, *Witchcraft*, 151.

59. Evans, *Witchcraft*, 155.

60. Evans, *Witchcraft*, 155.

61. Vider, *The Queerness of Home*, 100-102; 104.

62. Morgensen, "Arrival at Home."

63. Lekus, "Queer Harvests," 82.

64. For other queer transnational Caribbean frames, see Latner, *Cuban Revolution in America*; Capo Jr., *Welcome to Fairyland*; Decenes, *Circuits of the Sacred*.

65. Howard, *Men Like That*; Johnson, *Sweet Tea*.

66. Sears, *Rebels, Rubyfruit, and Rhinestones*.

67. Harker, *The Lesbian South*.

68. The critique of metronormativity in LGBTQ+ studies originates with Halberstam's *In a Queer Time and Place*, but was then significantly developed in early works by several key scholars then at Indiana University: Gray, *Out in the Country*; Herring, *Another Country*; and Johnson, *Just Queer Folks*.

69. Mims, *Drastic Dykes*.

70. Stone, *Gay Rights*; McCreery, "Miami Vice."

71. Frank, "'Civil Rights of Parents'"; Mason, *Oklahomo*; Van Cleve, "Yellow Brick Road"; Johnson, *This Is Our Message*.

72. For example, Frank is but one historian who characterizes "liberationist" Bob Kunst as playing into the hands of Save Our Children by openly espousing sexual liberation when homosexuals were being stereotyped as pedophiles. In contrast, gay rights activists are described as shrewder when they minimized gay sexuality and framed homosexuality as biological. Frank, "'Civil Rights of Parents,'" 150–51.

Chapter One

1. Dimid Hayes, interview with the author, August 3–4, 2016.

2. Williams to Lonnie, undated. This letter was likely written in the summer of 1971, given that Williams wrote two other letters to a Lonnie in June and August of that year. Dimid Hayes private collection. Hayes has since begun to transfer his private collection to Georgia State University's Special Collections, so future researchers should be able to find them there.

3. Koch Farm newsletter, November 1, 1971, and Williams to P & J in New York City, undated letter (likely 1971), Dimid Hayes private collection.

4. Williams to Lonnie, undated, Dimid Hayes private collection.

5. Unaddressed letter, June 19–28, 1970 (Chandigarh, India), Dimid Hayes private collection.

6. Unaddressed letter, August 10–25, 1970 (Pahalagam, Kashmir, India), Dimid Hayes private collection.

7. Schwartz, *In Service to America*.

8. Schwartz, *In Service to America*, 91–95.

9. Phillips, *Hipbillies*.

10. Perkins, *Hillbilly Hellraisers*.

11. Williams to Jack Tipple, November 28, 1971, and Williams to unknown addressee, July 20, 1971, Dimid Hayes private collection.

12. Williams, unaddressed letter, October 18, 1972, Dimid Hayes private collection.

13. Williams to "Dear Ones," July 12, 1973, Dimid Hayes private collection.

14. Schwartz, *In Service to America*, 93. Gorman actually reads the desire to lynch onto the Newton County locals' expressions and, disturbingly, laughs at the locals' racist helplessness, assuming that their muted rage posed no danger to the Black children present.

15. For their discussions of Morgan, see Schwartz, *In Service to America*, 159–69; Perkins, *Hillbilly Hellraisers*, 200–202.

16. Williams to Peter, April 14, 1974, Dimid Hayes private collection.

17. Allan Troxler, "A Rejection," *RFD*, Fall 1974, 15.

18. The unattributed quotes and biographical details in the rest of this chapter come from oral history interviews with the collectivists themselves. I indicate in the text who said what.

19. Oglesby, email message to author, July 14, 2019.

20. Goss, "Silencing Queers at the UpStairs Lounge," 269–77.

21. Oglesby, email message to author, November 22, 2016.

22. Edwards, "My Time on Markham Hill," Facebook post by the group Friends of Markham Hill in "Weekly Markham Hill Moment of History" (December 23, 2019), www.facebook.com/groups/239094136805594/permalink/433908253990847/.

23. Blazer, "Diana Rivers."

24. Williams to Anna, March 22, 1973, Dimid Hayes private collection.

25. Williams to Sassafras, November 15, 1974, Dimid Hayes private collection.

26. Zajicek and Lord, *Contemporary Grassroots Women's Movement*.

27. Mims, *Drastic Dykes and Accidental Activists*, 64–76.

28. Thompson, *The Un-Natural State*.

29. Pharr, interviewed by Kelly Anderson.

30. Thompson, *The Un-Natural State*, 167.

31. Sears, *Rebels, Rubyfruit, and Rhinestones*, 145–49.

32. The couples had two notable way stations in common, in fact: (1) Harry Hay and his partner John Burnside, then in rural New Mexico, and (2) Chenille, at Magdalen Farm in Wolf Creek, Oregon.

33. Editorial comment, *RFD*, Fall 1974.

34. Weeks, *The Problem with Work*.

35. Mulberry House letter, *RFD*, Fall 1976, 8.
36. Radicalesbians, "The Woman-Identified Woman."
37. Ezell, "Between F* Words," 32.
38. Wittman, "Refugees from Amerika."
39. Harker, *The Lesbian South*, 75–76.
40. Williams to Dimid Hayes, October 25, 1975, Dimid Hayes private collection.
41. Williams to Dimid Hayes, December 5, 1975, Dimid Hayes private collection.
42. In 1979 a rural community for working class women of color, Arco Iris, would be formed from parts of the dissolved Sassafras community. Arco Iris continues to exist today, even though it is no longer a women-only site. For more on Arco Iris, see Thompson, *The Un-Natural State*, and Zajicek and Lord, *Contemporary Grassroots Women's Movement*.
43. Thompson, *The Un-Natural State*, 144.
44. Phillips, *Hipbillies*, 119–34.

Chapter Two

1. Morning Due, "A Conference Report: Faggots and Class Struggle" (Wolf Creek, Oregon), 9. Available at Michael J. Lecker's blog "It Was Curiosity," https://itwascuriosity.wordpress.com/wp-content/uploads/2012/12/conference-report-faggots-and-class-struggle.pdf.
2. Morning Due, "A Conference Report," 10.
3. Morning Due, "A Conference Report," 67–68, 71.
4. Morning Due, "A Conference Report," 69–70.
5. Hobson, *Lavender and Red*, 72.
6. Eli Sanders, "Gay Marriage's Jewish Pioneer: Faygele Ben Miriam," *Tablet*, June 6, 2012, www.tabletmag.com/sections/news/articles/gay-marriages-jewish-pioneer.
7. For details on Ben Miriam's Seattle activism, see Atkins, *Gay Seattle*.
8. Patrick Haggerty, "Lavender Country," Paradise of Bachelors, 2023, https://paradiseofbachelors.com/shop/pob-012/. I previously used these lyrics to describe the era's gay liberationist affect; see Ezell, "Between F* Words," 91.
9. Burton-Rose, *Guerrilla, U.S.A.*
10. Burton-Rose, *Guerrilla, U.S.A.*, 33–34.
11. Varon, *Bringing the War Home*, 17–18.
12. Murch, *Living for the City*, 121–22.
13. Hay helped to found the first organized gay movement organization, The Mattachine Society, in 1950, and he was ousted from the Communist Party during the McCarthy era because they considered his homosexuality a liability to their necessarily secretive strategies. See Timmons, *Trouble with Harry Hay*. On rumors of Hay's involvement at the conference, see Hayes, "LaSIS, Dennis Melba'son, and the Early Fey Days—1975–1984," *RFD*, Summer 2010, 18–19.
14. Timmons, *Trouble with Harry Hay*, 254–57; see 257 for quote from Hay's letter to his friend.
15. Morning Due, "A Conference Report," 13.
16. Morning Due, "A Conference Report," 73. The Morning Due account mistakenly names the musician here as "Raspberry." A couple of notes: First, the spiral dance would become central to Starhawk's project to reclaim witchcraft; *The Spiral Dance* was the title of her 1979 book.

However, in his article "Hey Man," from the 1970s, Steven Dansky of the Flaming Faggots critiqued the coupled dancing he saw at GAA Firehouse dances and recommended the more communal circle dance instead. Second, the centrality of the "tipi" in this ritual suggests the "queer settler colonialism" identified by Scott Lauria Morgensen in *Spaces between Us*. Morgensen associates this primarily with West Coast Radical Faerie culture. This makes sense, as it would be Harry Hay who would most conflate Indigenous spirituality with nonbinary gender forms in the figure of the berdache, based on his childhood experience and his readings in anthropology. For an account of Hay's childhood experiences, see Timmons, *Trouble with Harry Hay*.

17. New religious studies scholarship has shown that leftist occultism was by no means new, however. For example, late nineteenth-century French occultists' spiritual theories were often entangled with socialist ones, albeit with a qualified materialist stance. See Strube, "Occultist Identity Formations."

18. Lewis, "'We Are Certain.'"

19. Zowie, "Politics and Faggot Spirituality," *RFD*, Summer 1977, 20. For a helpful caution on the normative, especially white, tendencies of some such spiritual practices, see Malatino, *Side Affects*.

20. Lyle Finley, "This Is YOUR life, LYLE FINLEY," *RFD*, Fall 1975, 43–44. For more on Black radical aesthetic methods of madness, see Bruce, *How to Go Mad*.

21. The period's cultural embrace of antipsychiatry—following on the midcentury work of philosophers and practitioners like Foucault, Deleuze, Guattari, Laing, and Szasz—can be seen, for example, in the 1967 film adaptation of *Marat/Sade* or the 1975 film adaptation of *One Flew Over the Cuckoo's Nest*.

22. Evans, *Witchcraft*, 26.

23. Morning Due, "A Conference Report," 69.

24. For more on this Italian movement, see Virno and Hardt, *Radical Thought in Italy*, and Lotringer and Marazzi, *Autonomia*.

25. Federici would later write her own leftist account of witchcraft, *Caliban and the Witch*. Other key writings from the Wages for Housework movement include Cox and Federici, *Counter-Planning from the Kitchen*, and Dalla Costa and James, *The Power of Women*.

26. The European leftist take on radical mothering is not the only one. For a Black queer reframing, see Gumbs, "'We Can Learn.'"

27. Toupin, *Wages for Housework*. For a detailed analysis of the lessons of this movement, see Weeks, *The Problem with Work*.

28. Plaster, *Kids on the Street*. See chapter 4 for more on Plaster's work. Hanhardt, *Safe Space*, 92.

29. Evans, *Witchcraft*, 170. He also thanked two other writers important to the later development of latter-day gay liberationist political consciousness: New York City gay publisher Larry Mitchell and West Coast psychotherapist Mitch Walker.

30. Hanhardt, *Safe Space*, 104.

31. Evans, *Witchcraft*, 140.

32. Evans, "Arthur Evans (1942–2011)," 2010, at Pagan Press Books website, https://paganpressbooks.com/jpl/EVANS-OB.HTM.

33. Morning Due, "A Conference Report," 3.

34. "RFD Collective Statement," *RFD*, Winter 1976, 4.

35. elliott, "bread & roses revisited (for the sissies)," *RFD*, Winter 1976, 17.

36. Todd, "Getting Out the Vote: An Account of a Week's Automobile Campaign by Women Suffragists." *The American Magazine* 72 (1911): 619.
37. Oppenheim, "Bread and Roses."
38. Hanhardt, *Safe Space*, 93.
39. Hobson, *Lavender and Red*, 74.
40. *RFD*, Winter 1976, 20–21; "Brothers Behind Bars," *RFD*, Winter 1976, 26–31.
41. Burton-Rose, *Guerrilla USA*, 247.
42. Morning Due, "A Conference Report," 3.
43. Evans, *Witchcraft*, 149.

Chapter Three

1. As before, uncited quotes and observations attributed to collectivists are taken from oral history interviews.
2. Zajicek and Lord, *Contemporary Grassroots Women's Movement*, 12.
3. Vider, *The Queerness of Home*, 100–102.
4. Varon, *Bringing the War Home*, 17–18.
5. Michael Oglesby, "A Critique of the Conference," *RFD*, Winter 1976, 18–19.
6. Coralie to Mulberry House, September 24, 1976, Dimid Hayes private collection.
7. Williams, "An Open Letter to the Ozark Food Co-optation Entitled *I Am Tired ...*," undated, Dimid Hayes private collection.
8. Ozark Food Co-op, "Cooptation Blues," November 1976, private collection of Dimid Hayes.
9. For more on the political culture around food co-ops of the 1960s and 1970s, see Cox, *Storefront Revolution*.
10. Williams to Dan, November 16, 1976, private collection of Dimid Hayes.
11. Cunningham, *There's Something Happening Here*, 120.
12. Cunningham, *There's Something Happening Here*, 121–33.
13. Frank, "'Civil Rights of Parents.'"
14. Jones, *Ambivalent Affinities*, 108.
15. Jones, *Ambivalent Affinities*, 118.
16. Mason, *Oklahomo*.
17. Moreton, "Why Is There So Much," 724.
18. Mason, *Oklahomo*, 74.
19. Arkansas Sissies, Letters, *RFD*, Spring 1978, 4.
20. Williams, personal journal, June 23, 1977. Dimid Hayes private collection. Hayes's collection is the source for all citations from Williams personal journal.
21. Williams, personal journal, July 3, 1977.
22. Williams, personal journal, July 14, 1977.
23. "Brothers Behind Bars," *RFD*, Spring 1977, 37.
24. Williams, personal journal, June 1, 1977.
25. Williams, personal journal, June 4, 1977.
26. Williams, personal journal, June 1, 1977.
27. Williams, personal journal, June 6, 1977.
28. Williams, personal journal, June 7, 1977.

29. Williams, personal journal, June 22, 1977.
30. Williams, personal journal, June 24, 1977.
31. Williams, personal journal, July 2, 1977.
32. Williams, personal journal, July 3, 1977.
33. Williams, personal journal, July 3, 1977.
34. Williams, personal journal, July 27, 1977.
35. Williams, personal journal, August 3, 1977.
36. Williams, personal journal, August 16, 1977.
37. Williams, personal journal, August 26, 1977.
38. Williams, personal journal, August 26, 1977.
39. Williams, personal journal, September 3, 1977.
40. For more on Woods's struggle, see "Dessie Woods," The Freedom Archives, 2024, https://search.freedomarchives.org/search.php?view_collection=139.
41. Williams, personal journal, September 17, 1977.
42. Ball, "I'd Rather My Child Be Dead than Homo," *Times-Picayune* (New Orleans), June 19, 1977.
43. Oglesby, personal interview, July 2, 2019.
44. Williams, personal journal, October 1, 1977.
45. Williams, personal journal, October 1, 1977.
46. Williams, personal journal, October 4, 1977.
47. See Melba'son, "Dennis Melba'son Diary," *RFD*, Summer 2010, 21–22, for excerpts that help convey Melba'son's feelings at this time.

Chapter Four

1. Dennis Williams [Dennis Melba'son], personal journal, October 7, 1977.
2. To honor the seriousness of this subjective shift, I will use the name Melba'son for all references to Williams after his relocation to New Orleans.
3. For an overview of psychogeography, see Coverley, *Psychogeography*. For a later psychogeographic view rooted in New Orleans specifically, see Cafard, *Surregional Explorations*.
4. Williams, personal journal, November 9, 1977. Thornton and Oglesby were at that time also considering a move to the Bay Area.
5. Williams, personal journal, October 8, 1977. All of the following quotes appear in Melba'son's October journal. Dates are shared in-text.
6. Williams, personal journal, October 7, 1977. Melba'son mistakenly attributes authorship to Ralph Ellison, but *Black Like Me* had been another formative book for the young Oglesby, so I expect that it had been much on Melba'son's mind in his first days in New Orleans. He may have been reading Ellison's *Invisible Man* simultaneously, too, given that his journal lingered on his own new, classed invisibility.
7. Morning Due, "A Conference Report," 10. The concept of "city chauvinism" adds further evidence for Scott Herring's description of early *RFD*'s "anti-urbanism."
8. Liebling, *The Earl of Louisiana*.
9. Campanella, "Tracing Greek Geography from Bayou Road to the Banks of Bayou St. John," nola.com., May 7, 2014, www.nola.com/entertainment_life/home_garden/article_f1b6cc64-18dc-5139-a7af-2e6e733f8dc0.html.

10. Not only did Oglesby recall finding that the conference's theme of "remembering forgotten dreams" was his own most valuable takeaway, but the fall 1976 issue of *RFD* borrowed that theme as the issue's subtitle.

11. Russo, *The Celluloid Closet*.

12. Hacking, "Making Up People," *London Review of Books*, August 17, 2006, www.lrb.co.uk/v28/n16/ian-hacking/making-up-people.

13. Thanks to contemporary queer witches Ivo Dominguez, T. Thorn Coyle, and Storm Faerywolf for their explanations of this concept. See also Victor H. and Cora Anderson, *Etheric Anatomy*.

14. Arend, *Showdown in Desire*.

15. Ezell, "Between F* Words," 5–18. I here offer a close reading not only of Lyle Finley's graphic poem in the Fall 1975 issue of *RFD*, but also a poem by a "Peter" whose narrator refers to himself by "we are always fucking/me always pregnant/always in labor" in the very first issue of *RFD* (Fall 1974).

16. Looking back, the sissies admit that their understanding of Maoism was piecemeal, and that they had little access to the harsh details of actual Maoist land reform.

17. Ross, *Sissy Insurgencies*, 171–89, 171–72. It has also been argued that in New Orleans in the 1950s and 1960s, when gay Mardi Gras krewes formed, street-based gender nonconformity might have been buttressed by carnival culture. However, early gay krewes, even those mostly composed of white men, often struggled to find safe private venues for themselves. For an overview of gay Mardi Gras history and its costumes, see Smith, *Unveiling the Muse*. Note, too, that, when discussing Ross's analysis, I retain his spelling ("sissy") to keep a distinction between Black historical experience and that of the mostly white gay liberationist collectivists who would use the spelling "sissie".

18. Smith, *Unveiling the Muse*, 170–71. The pre-Stonewall history of such places as Black entertainment districts whose sexual openness long attracted white queers can be found in Kevin Mumford, *Interzones*. Also, Ross's focus on the relationship between the street and the "televisual" is important here because it offers context for GAA zap strategies to widen and politicize gay anger by broadcasting street-level homophobia into homes for all to see.

19. Mumford, *Not Straight, Not White*, 99–124.

20. Plaster, *Kids on the Street*, 71.

21. Plaster, *Kids on the Street*, 181–85.

22. Bell, *Dancing the Gay Lib Blues*, 64. Bell met Rivera as Ray, before she used the name Sylvia with him. I have updated the name and pronouns in Bell's passage.

23. See the documentary film *Pay It No Mind: The Life and Times of Marsha P. Johnson*.

24. In his journal, Melba'son at this time already personally used the spelling "sissie" to reflect this investment in the multiple and collective. For the sake of consistency and clarity, I have used this spelling throughout the book, although it seems that LaSIS followed Melba'son's lead in adopting this spelling, thereby introducing it to the wider collectivist culture.

Chapter Five

1. Cornbelt, letter to the editors, *RFD*, Spring 1978, 5.
2. Kim Brettingen, letter to the editors, *RFD*, Spring 1978, 3.

3. "Buttons," *RFD*, Winter 1978, 21. Here, sissies continue their practice of unconventional spellings as a mode of queering normative concepts. I could find no rationale for this particular spelling of "majik," however.

4. The biographical content and quotes about Speakman are taken from his interview.

5. This observation is taken from Hayes' interview.

6. Original "Sissie Effeminism" bibliography, Dimid Hayes private collection; *RFD*, Summer 1978, 31. There are some small differences between the original bibliography and the one published by the West Coast *RFD* editors. The latter added a 1977 *Advocate* article by California writer Mark Thompson and pointed readers to their own *RFD* issue 13 (Fall 1977) on spirituality. This addition blurred authorship of the list, between the Bay Area *RFD* editors and the newly forming LaSIS, potentially implying that sissie culture, as it was defined and cultivated by LaSIS's information labor, was primarily a West Coast phenomenon. At the same time, the 1976 Wolf Creek conference had to be recognized as a catalyst. I give the spelling "sissie" to LaSIS's radical figure after the creation of this bibliography, even though Melba'son had used it in his journal just before leaving Arkansas.

7. McKinney, "'Finding the Lines to My People,'" 57.

8. "Sisssie Effeminism," n.p.

9. McKinney, "'Finding the Lines,'" 58.

10. This neologism reminds me of the possibility that, as Jack Halberstam has suggested in *In a Queer Time and Place*, the gendered and developmental dimensions of biography must be rethought in order to better account for gender transitions. I would further suggest that radical spiritual and political conversions may deserve similar reframing.

11. McKinney, "'Finding the Lines,'" 64.

12. "Sissie Effeminism," cover sheet.

13. Morning Star, "Jesse's Dream Skirt," *Magnus: A Socialist Journal of Gay Liberation*, Summer 1977, 24–26.

14. Marian Buchanan, "Jesse's Dream Skirt Project," *Marian Buchanan* (blog), June 29, 2015–February 19, 2020, https://marianbuchanan.com/category/jesses-dream-skirt-project/. This is a series of blog posts by illustrator Buchanan, including her research into Mack and the history of the original story.

15. Atlantis Summer 1977 Publishing List, Mary Elizabeth Gehman Papers ~ Photographs ~ Collection NA-142, box 1, Newcomb Archives, Tulane University. This "in and out of school" phrase echoes how the "Brothers Behind Bars" feature in *RFD* sought, with Ed Mead, to unite communities divided by institutional divisions. This kind of cross-barrier organizing was a common liberationist strategy.

16. Student and Youth Organizing, *Youth Liberation Pamphlet*, 75.

17. Student and Youth Organizing, *Youth Liberation Pamphlet*, 70.

18. For more on the specific racial dynamics of the Johns Committee, see Jones, "'Until I Talked with You.'"

19. Sears, *Rebels, Rubyfruit, and Rhinestones*, 64.

20. Long, *Cruising for Conspirators*.

21. Sears, *Rebels, Rubyfruit, and Rhinestones*, 67.

22. Allured, *Remapping Second-Wave Feminism*, 197–214.

23. Arend, *Showdown in Desire*.

24. House of Representatives, *Theory and Practice of Communism*, 7842–7909.

25. Sears, *Rebels, Rubyfruit, and Rhinestones*, 71.

26. For a crucial portrait of gay liberation's genesis and survival in New Orleans, see Perez, *Political Animal*. For more on the Upstairs Lounge fire, see Fieseler, *Tinderbox*; Downs, *Stand by Me*; Delery-Edwards, *Up Stairs Lounge Arson*.

27. Sears, *Rebels, Rubyfruit, and Rhinestones*, 275.

28. Letter from Robinson to David Williams, quoted in Sears, *Rebels, Rubyfruit, and Rhinestones*, 393n.

29. Reich, "Gay Parents Need Childcare," *Impact*, August 1978, 16.

30. At that time LaSIS was also discussing strategies for eldercare, as well as advocacy around issues of disability.

31. Devore and Logsdon, *Crescent City Schools*. This book provides rich analytical context for the strike as well as the wider conditions of New Orleans education.

32. LaSiS, "Solidarity Forever," *RFD*, Fall 1978, 3. The following quotes from the playlet come from this source.

33. James K. Glassman, "New Orleans: I Have Seen the Future, and It's Houston," *The Atlantic*, July 1978, 10ff. It is possible that LaSIS members had read Glassman's summer article, which was critical of New Orleans and the Superdome.

34. LaSIS could not have known at that time just how entrenched this racist injustice was. Tyler was not released from prison until 2016. See "Gary Tyler's Lost Decades," *New York Times*, February 5, 2007.

35. The Supreme Court would rule in favor of Kaiser the following year, in 1979.

36. "Buttons," *RFD*, Winter 1978, 21.

37. Stryker, *Transgender History*; Luther Hillman, "'Wearing a Dress Is a Revolutionary Act,'" in *Dressing for the Culture Wars*, 91–122.

38. "Sissie," *RFD*, Winter 1978, 4, David M. Rubenstein Rare Book & Manuscript Library, Duke University.

39. "Sissy," *RFD*, Fall 1978, 3.

40. "Sissie Terror in the Photo Booth," *RFD*, Winter 1978, 4–5.

41. "Sissie," *RFD* Winter 1978, 4–5. The following quotes from "Sissie" in the following analysis come from these two pages. At this point Aurora still referred to himself as an effeminist in his writing, but the overall title for the collective piece did not use that term.

42. "Sissie," *RFD*, Winter 1978, 4.

43. In 1979, LaSIS's information activism would also include writing and distributing a pamphlet *STOP RAPE*, written from a sissie perspective, and they would also staff rape crisis hotlines.

44. "Sissie," *RFD*, Winter 1978, 4.

45. Alan G. Robinson, "What Is Reporting the Public Record?," *Impact*, August 1978, 2.

46. McKinney, *Information Activism*. As a librarian, I want to point out that LaSIS encouraged the readers of the "Sissie Effeminism" bibliography to pressure public libraries to stock the titles on the list, ordering directly from Atlantis.

47. Renfro, *Stranger Danger*, 18, 19.

48. "Sissie," *RFD*, Winter 1978, 4.

49. Rodriguez, "Trans Generosity," 418.

50. Rodriguez quotes from Muñoz, *Cruising Utopia*, 1, in "Trans Generosity."

Chapter Six

1. Perez and Palmquist, *In Exile*. Oglesby remembers his frustration at LaSIS's use of the phrase "middle-class exiles."

2. This chapter includes biographical information and occasional quotes from newly introduced collectivists. Unless otherwise noted, these come from collectivist interviews.

3. The couple would eventually introduce LaSIS's work to West Coast feminist Sally Gearhart, who expressed admiration for it.

4. "Sissie," *RFD*, Winter 1978, 4.

5. Gross, letter to the editors, *RFD*, Fall 1978, 10.

6. For more on the Glenmary Sisters and FOCIS, see Lewis and Appleby, *Mountain Sisters*.

7. For more on Lewis, see her *Helen Matthews Lewis*.

8. Gross, letter to the editors, *RFD*, Fall 1978, 10.

9. Abbott's observations on this and following pages were given in his interviews.

10. William Cutler, "Statement of Purpose of the Georgia GLF," *Good Gay Times*, clipping, March 8, 1971, Atlanta Lesbian Feminist Alliance Papers, box 15, Gay Liberation Front, folder 36, David M. Rubenstein Rare Book & Manuscript Library, Duke University.

11. Lorraine Fontana, "Gay Convention," *Great Speckled Bird*, November 20, 1972, Atlanta Lesbian Feminist Alliance Papers, box 16, Southeast Gay Coalition, folder 3, David M. Rubenstein Rare Book & Manuscript Library, Duke University. Sears draws on Fontana's journalism to describe the event in *Rebels, Rubyfruit, and Rhinestones*, 108–11.

12. Bill Smith, "Gay Is Gone," article clipping without periodical title, July 23, 1973, Atlanta Lesbian Feminist Alliance Papers, box 15, Gay Liberation Front, folder 36, David M. Rubenstein Rare Book & Manuscript Library, Duke University.

13. Chesnut and Gable, "'Women Ran It,'" 241–84; Mims, *Drastic Dykes*, 64–90. See also Hogan, *The Feminist Bookstore Movement*.

14. "Gay Meetings," *Good Gay Times*, clipping, August 10, 1972, Atlanta Lesbian Feminist Alliance Papers, box 15, Gay Liberation Front, folder 36, David M. Rubenstein Rare Book & Manuscript Library, Duke University. Contrary to Duberman's sense that the Effeminists had little impact, this is further evidence to support Dansky's argument that they inspired small collectives all over the country, and that their influence was persistent, especially for overtly feminist gay men.

15. I draw these details about the origins of early Running Water Farm gatherings from my article "Returning Forest Darlings," which itself draws primarily upon oral history interviews with attendees Abbott, Wilson, Hayes, Englebert, and Pyne. In the text, I name which attendee offered individual observations. The memories of the Atlanta conference are Abbott's.

16. I make an abbreviated form of this argument about early Running Water's continuities with and departures from the Wolf Creek Faggots & Class Struggle conference in Ezell, "Returning Forest Darlings," 79–80.

17. Glover, "Southern Celebrations," *RFD* 17, Fall 1978, centerfold.

18. Niman, *People of the Rainbow*.

19. The quotes and biographical detail in this section about Wilson come from my interview with him.

20. Abbott, *Mortal Love: Selected Poems*, 41.

21. Hayes, "A Letter of Action," Dimid Hayes private collection. Note: On February 8, 2016, Hayes emailed me an annotated copy, dated May 2011, of the original draft.
22. Knopp, "Gentrification."
23. "Women's Section," *Impact*, October 1977, 11.
24. Marilyn Duckworth, "Parsons Talks with Impact," *Impact*, September 1978, 4. Duckworth used this statistic strategically as she made plain to new police superintendent James Parson that he was beholden to New Orleans citizens, including those in neighborhoods with a high concentration of lesbian and gay residents.
25. "Vote Morial Mayor," *Impact*, November 1977, 20.
26. Alan Robinson, "Toups & the Task Force," *Impact*, June 1978, 2.
27. Campanella, *Bourbon Street*.
28. "Hey! Remember Decatur Street?," *Impact*, February 1978, 21.
29. "Realities of Real Estate," *Impact*, April 1978, cover.
30. "From Gertrude Stein," *Impact*, May 1978, 4.
31. *Impact*, July 1978, photo at 31.
32. See especially Harry Wingfield, "Gay Unity," *Impact*, July 1978, 2–4.
33. PTA, "PTA," *Impact*, August 1978, 4. Here, as was common in the gay liberationist rhetoric of the time, "third world" referred to racialized groups oppressed as such within colonialist and imperialist systems. Other quotes and paraphrases in this paragraph about the PTA's political stances also come from this August article.
34. LGBT+ Archives Project of Louisiana, "Timeline of LGBT+ History in New Orleans," https://lgbtarchiveslouisiana.org/timeline-of-lgbt-history-in-new-orleans/.
35. Dimid Hayes, "A Letter of Action." The quotes in the following analysis come from this document.
36. "A Celebration of Gay Men," Running Water Farm mailing list, October 6–8, 1978, Running Water Farm, directories, poetry, event flyers, 1978–84, III, box 49, folder 12, Franklin Abbott papers, Q108, Special Collections and Archives, Georgia State University. It is interesting to note that two other Louisianans did go to the second gathering. One was Michael Reid, a provocative young man who had raised older attendees' eyebrows at the New Orleans gay liberation rally when he announced himself the head of the "United Gay Chicken's Coalition." The other Louisianan was Skip Ward, from just outside Alexandria, who would become a leader of the Louisiana Lesbian and Gay Political Action Caucus (LAGPAC) and spearhead Louisiana-wide activism, including the first State Gay Conference, held in 1981. Aurora also registered as "Haus" on the mailing list, a German variant of "House," which he more commonly used elsewhere. Duane Riddle, a newer Mulberry House member, also attended.
37. Brotherlover, "Sissie Networking," *RFD*, Winter 1978, 20. Brotherlover seems to imagine a pre-internet profile template—but for collectives.
38. Sears, *Rebels, Rubyfruit, and Rhinestones*, 86. The following details of Pyne's life are also taken from Sears.
39. Pyne's background and his Venceremos experience are profiled in Lekus, "Queer Harvests."
40. Both Haze and Mushroom appear in Sears, *Rebels, Rubyfruit, and Rhinestones*, and Mushroom's editorial work with the Southern lesbian publication *Sinister Wisdom* is referenced in Harker, *The Lesbian South*, 144.

240 Notes to Chapter Seven

41. Quoted in Sears, *Rebels, Rubyfruit, and Rhinestones*, 348.
42. Pyne told me that he didn't settle on this name until around 1990, though.
43. Milo Pyne, contact letter, *RFD*, Winter 1976, 44.
44. "RFD Country," *RFD*, Winter Solstice 1974, 3.
45. Herring, *Another Country*, 93–96.
46. *RFD*, Winter 1978, map at 20.
47. Hayes, "A Letter of Action."
48. For a description of Black Mississippi Delta resistance, see Woods, *Development Arrested*.

Chapter Seven

1. See Shively, "Fag Rag."
2. *CBS Reports*, "The Homosexuals," written by Harry Morgan, Mike Wallace, and William Peters, reported by Mike Wallace, aired March 7, 1967, Paley Archive, The Paley Center for Media. The following descriptions and quotes from this episode come from viewing a digitized version on site at the archive.
3. *ABC News Close-Up*, "Homosexuals," directed, written, and produced by Helen Whitney, aired December 18, 1979, Paley Archive, The Paley Center for Media. The following descriptions and quotes from this episode come from viewing a digitized version on site at the archive.
4. In *Sissy Insurgencies*, Marlon Ross gives us a model for how to read sissy performativity across different platforms and audiences at once, allowing us to better understand the necessary multivalence of sissy performance.
5. Ross, *Sissy Insurgencies*, 170, 227–31.
6. Dennis Melba'son to Dav, March 1, 1979, Dimid Hayes private collection. Melba'son's writing became more eccentric at this time, after Milk's assassination, as he developed a shorthand that eliminated most vowels.
7. Clement and the Church of the Beloved Disciple were important precedents in formally linking the Independent Catholic churches and gay liberation. See Plaster, *Kids on the Street*, 74.
8. "Police Reports," *Times-Picayune* (New Orleans), May 11, 1979.
9. "LaSIS Update," *RFD*, Summer 1979, 3.
10. Running Water Farm newsletter from Stepping Stone, Fall 1979. Conference, Radical Faeries, "Gatherings" at Running Water, 1979–81 (box 1, folder 6), Gay Spirit Visions records, W127, Archives for Research on Women and Gender, Special Collections and Archives, Georgia State University, Atlanta.
11. Running Water Farm newsletter from Stepping Stone, Fall 1979.
12. Faygele Ben Miriam, *RFD*, Spring 1979, 4.
13. *RFD*, Summer 1979, 3. It's also interesting that, in retrospect, historian John D'Emilio argued that the 1979 march did not, in fact, result in a truly national movement, citing several similar issues as factors. D'Emilio, "The 1979 March's Place in History," *Gay & Lesbian Review Worldwide*, March–April 2005, 33–34.
14. Sears, *Rebels, Rubyfruit, and Rhinestones*, 306.
15. My account of the 1979 Arizona conference draws primarily from Stuart Timmons, *Trouble with Harry Hay*.

16. Timmons, *Trouble with Harry Hay*, 251n. Timmons argues, though, that both Hay's association with the California essentialists and other intellectuals' emphatic embrace of social constructivism led to polarized interpretive camps unable to see Hay's more nuanced theory.

17. This would become a dominant strain of Radical Faerie culture, critiqued for its queer settler colonial dimensions in, for example, Morgensen, *Spaces between Us*.

18. Walker, *Visionary Love*, 18.

19. Walker, *Visionary Love*, 16, 12.

20. "The Faeries Gather: A True Tale," *RFD*, Winter 1979, 30.

21. A surviving mailing list from the 1980 Radical Faerie gathering reveals pages and pages of crayon writing, doodles, "punny" gathering names, and inside jokes. "Faerie Directory," Conference, Radical Faeries, "Gatherings," at Running Water, 1979–81, II, box 1, folder 6, Gay Spirit Visions records, Q127, Archives for Research on Women and Gender, Special Collections and Archives, Georgia State University, Atlanta.

22. Timmons, *Trouble with Harry Hay*, 250.

23. *RFD*, Winter 1979, 45.

24. *RFD*, Winter 1979, 64.

25. *RFD*, Winter 1979, 35.

26. *RFD*, Winter 1979, 35.

27. *RFD*, Winter 1979, 36.

Chapter Eight

1. *RFD*, Winter 1979, inside front cover.

2. Editorial comment, *RFD*, Summer 1979, 18.

3. Melba'son, book review of Mitch Walker's *Visionary Love*, *RFD*, Fall 1980, 85.

4. Melba'son, book review of Mitch Walker's *Visionary Love*, 82.

5. Melba'son, book review of Mitch Walker's *Visionary Love*, 84.

6. In a Running Water Flier announcing the September 1979 gathering, Ben Miriam reported, "After intense discussion last time, the general feeling was that this is specifically faggot space; children welcome." Conference, Radical Faeries "Gatherings" at Running Water, Gay Spirit Visions records, box 1, folder 6, W127, 1979–81, Archives for Research on Women and Gender, Special Collections and Archives, Georgia State University, Atlanta.

7. Englebert's biographical details and commentary come from his interview.

8. Editorial comment, *RFD*, Summer 1979, 2.

9. June Boyd, "June Boyd: A Black Strong Woman," *RFD*, Summer 1979, 4.

10. Ed Mead, letter in "Brothers Behind Bars," *RFD*, Winter 1979, 20. For more on the exploitative development of Appalachia as a carceral region, see Judah Schept, *Coal, Cages, Crisis*.

11. Editorial comment, *RFD*, Summer 1979, 16.

12. Clear Englebert, letter to the editors, *RFD*, Spring 1980, 3.

13. Editorial comment, *RFD*, Summer 1979, 2.

14. Running Water Farm mailing list, June 15–17, 1979. Conference, Radical Faeries "Gatherings" at Running Water, Gay Spirit Visions records, box 1, folder 6, W127, 1979–81, Archives for Research on Women and Gender, Special Collections and Archives, Georgia State University, Atlanta.

15. David Speakman (House), "Faggots & Friends . . ." *RFD*, Winter 1978, 12.

16. Ezell, "Returning Forest Darlings," 86.

17. Cathy Gross, "That I Am a Dyke. And Not Weird," *RFD*, Spring 1980, 57.

18. Gross would eventually adopt the name Cathy Hope, which she holds today.

19. Englebert shared that Pearl's birth name was Paul Sudds, and that he had changed his name to Pearl after attending his first Running Water gathering. He lived in Atlanta but had also hitchhiked to Birmingham, where Pyne and Englebert picked him up on the way to New Orleans, where they worked on *RFD* with LaSIS. He changed his name to "Purl" and then "Purly," before, according to Clear, he later died of AIDS.

20. Dimid Hayes, "LaSIS, Dennis Melba'son, and the Early Fey Days—1975–1984," *RFD*, Summer 2010, 20.

21. Now housed with Duke's ALFA papers, one draft is filed in a folder labeled "Effeminists," indicating its likely reception by the Atlanta lesbians as an expression of sissie effeminism. Atlanta Lesbian Feminist Alliance Papers, box 16, Southeast Gay Coalition, folder 29, Effeminists, David M. Rubenstein Rare Book & Manuscript Library, Duke University.

22. Milo Pyne, "A Faeryist Not-Man-ifesto," *RFD*, Fall 1980, 57. The following quotes are also from this page.

23. My fuller description of this sanctuary practice can be found in Ezell, "Returning Forest Darlings." I am grateful to editors A. Naomi Paik, Jason Ruiz, and Rebecca M. Schreiber for their vision and guidance for how to reframe sanctuary.

24. Pyne, "Faeryist Not-Man-ifesto," 58.

25. Muñoz, *Cruising Utopia*, 29.

26. "Gay Community Land Trust," *RFD*, Summer 1980, 37–38.

27. Timmons, *Trouble with Harry Hay*, 275.

28. 1981 Short Mountain flyer, James T. Sears Papers, box 136, folder 2, Short Mountain Minutes, 1980–89, David M. Rubenstein Rare Book & Manuscript Library, Duke University.

29. Clear Englebert, "Profiles and Interviews: A Visit with Clear Englebert in S. E. Tennessee," *RFD*, Fall 1981, 50–52.

30. LaSIS, "On the Question of Names," *RFD*, Summer 1981, 14–16.

31. Although I maintain the "sissie" spelling in the unquoted material here, the collective had dropped the collectivist "-ie" by this point, possibly owing to a change in membership.

32. They also seemed to subtly distinguish themselves from Harry Hay's "not-man" subjectivity by not including it among the three figures listed, but also by referring to their definitions as part of a "Sissy Un'man'ifesto" (as different from Pyne's more faerie-invested "Faeryist Not-Man-ifesto").

33. LaSIS, "Faerie Fund," *RFD*, Spring 1981, 15.

34. Dennis Melba'son, "Excerpts from a Journal Written for a Friend in Prison," *RFD*, 1980, 10–15. The account of Melba'son offering the Cernunnos Shawl and his reflection on the Kali Fire ritual can both be found in these published excerpts.

Conclusion

1. LaSIS, "On the Question of Names," *RFD*, Summer 1981, 16.

2. This was not an altogether new practice. For an earlier example from 1960 of gay adult adoption between couples, see Syrett, *An Open Secret*.

3. These details about Melba'son's death were shared in Dimid Hayes, "LaSIS, Dennis Melba'son, and the Early Fey Days—1975–1984," *RFD*, Summer 2010, 18–20.

4. Dimid Hayes, "LaSIS, Dennis Melba'son."

5. In the 1980s, some women—notably Linda Kybek and Louise Coggins—appeared as leaders in Short Mountain meeting notes and minutes, and a women's mailing list was kept for women-only events. Also, Wimmin's Ridge was established as a sanctuary space for women at SMS. Much later, Ida, a neighboring community developed an important transgender community. See Short Mountain women's mailing list, James T. Sears Papers, box 136, folder 13, Short Mountain Women, David M. Rubenstein Rare Book & Manuscript Library, Duke University.

6. For more on this longer history, see Frazier, *The East Is Black*; Kelly and Esch, "Black Like Mao."

7. Muñoz, *Cruising Utopia*, 19–32.

8. Pyne, editorial statement, *RFD*, Winter 1979, inside front cover.

9. Muñoz, *Cruising Utopia*, 4.

10. Morgensen, *Spaces between Us*, 147–48. Such early Short Mountain residents include Jombi and Valencia Wombone.

11. This reality suggests the importance of looking further at exceptional case studies such as the Ozarks women of color rural collective Arco Iris, formed in the late 1970s—touched on in both Zajicek and Lord, *Contemporary Grassroots Women's Movement*, and Thompson, *The Un-Natural State*.

12. Varon, *Bringing the War Home*, 17–18.

Bibliography

Archival Collections

Atlanta, GA
   Archives for Research on Women and Gender, Special Collections & Archives,
      Georgia State University
     Franklin Abbott Papers
     Gay Spirit Visions Records
     Gender & Sexuality Periodicals Collection

Durham, NC
   David M. Rubenstein Rare Book & Manuscript Library, Duke University
     Atlanta Lesbian Feminist Alliance (ALFA) Papers
     James T. Sears Papers

New Orleans, LA
   Louisiana Research Collection, Tulane University
     Gay & Lesbian Newspapers
   Newcomb Archives, Tulane University
     Mary Elizabeth Gehman Papers

New York City, NY
   The Paley Center for Media

Personal Collections

Dimid Hayes, Santa Fe, New Mexico

Newspapers and Magazines

Advocate	*Magnus: A Socialist Journal of Gay Liberation*
American Magazine	*Morning Due: A Journal of Men against Sexism*
Atlantic	*motive*
Esquire	*New Orleans Times-Picayune*
Fag Rag	*New York Times*
Gay and Lesbian Review Worldwide	*RFD*
Impact	*Tablet*
London Review of Books	

Oral Histories

Abbot, Franklin. Interview with the author, December 14, 2015.
Englebert, Clear. Interview with the author, February 28, 2016.

Hayes, Dimid. Interview with the author, August 3–4, 2016.
Hope, Cathy (Gross). Interview with the author, October 18–19, 2016.
Kendrick, Jack. Interview with the author, September 4, 2019.
Laughlin, Trella. Interview with the author, July 3, 2019.
Oglesby, Michael. Interview with the author, July 2, 2019.
Pyne, Milo. Interview with the author, July 1, 2016.
Speakman, David (House/Aurora). Interview with the author, April 1, 2017.
Thornton, Charlie. Interview with the author, July 2, 2019.
Wilson, Mikel. Interview with the author, February 22, 2016.

Dissertations and Theses

Ezell, Jason. "Between F* Words: Rural & Gay Liberationist Refrains in the Southeast, 1970–1981." PhD diss., University of Maryland, 2017.
Gumbs, Alexis Pauline. "'We Can Learn to Mother Ourselves': The Queer Survival of Black Feminism." PhD diss., Duke University, 2010.
McCreery, Patrick. "Miami Vice: Anita Bryant, Gay Rights, and Child Protectionism." PhD diss., New York University, 2010.
Serby, Benjamin J. "Gay Liberation and the Politics of the Self in Postwar America." PhD diss., Columbia University, 2020.
Van Cleve, Stewart Jon. "Beyond the Yellow Brick Road: Queer Localization in the Age of Anita Bryant, 1974–1980." Master's thesis, Portland State University, 2013.

Published Primary and Reference Sources

Abbott, Franklin. *Mortal Love: Selected Poems*. Liberty, TN: RFD Press, 1999.
Anderson, Cora. *Fifty Years in the Feri Tradition*. Portland, OR: Harpy Books, 2010, 1994.
Anderson, Victor H. and Cora Anderson. *Etheric Anatomy: The Three Selves and Astral Travel*. Portland, OR: Harpy Books, 2004.
Bell, Arthur. *Dancing the Gay Lib Blues: A Year in the Homosexual Liberation Movement*. New York: Simon and Schuster, 1971.
Blazer, Judith. "Diana Rivers." *Encyclopedia of Arkansas*. https://encyclopediaofarkansas.net/entries/diana-rivers-6514/.
Dansky, Steven. "Hey Man." In *The Stonewall Reader*, edited by Jason Baumann and the New York Public Library. New York: Penguin, 2019.
Dansky, Steven, John Knoebel, and Kenneth Pitchford. "The Effeminist Manifesto." In *We Are Everywhere: A Historical Sourcebook for Gay and Lesbian Politics*, edited by Mark Blasius and Shane Phelan. New York: Routledge, 1997.
"Dessie Woods." *The Freedom Archives*. http://search.freedomarchives.org/search.php?view_collection=139.
Evans, Arthur. *Witchcraft and the Gay Counterculture*. Boston: Fag Rag Books, 1978.
Flaming Faggots. "The Flaming Faggots." In *Gay Flames*, edited by Konstantin Berlandt and Robert L. Bland. New York: Gay Liberation Front, 1970.
Hinton, William. *Fanshen: A Documentary of Revolution in a Chinese Village*. New edition. New York: Monthly Review Press, 2008.

House of Representatives, Second Session, Ninety-Second Congress. Hearings before the Committee on Internal Security. *The Theory and Practice of Communism in 1972 (Venceremos Brigade)*, part 2. Washington, DC: US Government Printing Office, 1973.

Jay, Karla, and Allen Young, eds. *Out of the Closets: Voices of Gay Liberation.* Twentieth anniversary edition. New York: NYU Press, 1992.

Johnson, Marsha P. Interview with Allen Young. "Rapping with a Street Transvestite Revolutionary." In *The Stonewall Reader*, edited by Jason Baumann and the New York Public Library. New York: Penguin, 2019.

Kasino, Michael, dir. *Pay It No Mind: The Life and Times of Marsha P. Johnson.* New York: Redux Pictures, 2012.

Lauritsen, John. *Religious Roots of the Taboo on Homosexuality: A Materialist View.* New York: COME! UNITY Press, 1974, 2012. https://paganpressbooks.com/jpl/RELROOTS.pdf.

Lauritsen, John, and David Thorstad. *The Early Homosexual Rights Movement (1864–1935).* New York: Times Change Press, 1974.

Martello, Leo. *How to Prevent Psychic Blackmail: The Philosophy of Psychoselfism.* New York: Hero Press, 1966.

Mitchell, Larry, and Ned Asta. *The Faggots & Their Friends between Revolutions.* New York: Calamus Books, 1977.

Newton, Huey. "The Women's Liberation and Gay Liberation Movements." 1970. In *History Is a Weapon.* www.historyisaweapon.com/defcon1/newtonq.html.

Offen, Hal. "Afterword." In *Arthur Evans's The Evans Symposium.* New York: White Crane Books, 2018.

Oppenheim, James. "Bread and Roses." In *The Cry for Justice: An Anthology of the Literature of Social Protest*, edited by Upton Sinclair. Philadelphia: John C. Winston Co., 1915.

Pharr, Suzanne. Interviewed by Kelly Anderson. Voices of Feminism Oral History Project, Smith College, Northampton, MA. June 28–29, 2005. https://compass.fivecolleges.edu/object/smith:1342650.

Radicalesbians. "The Woman-Identified Woman." 1970. In *History Is a Weapon.* www.historyisaweapon.com/defcon1/radicalesbianswoman.html.

Starhawk. *The Spiral Dance: A Rebirth of the Ancient Religion of the Goddess.* Twentieth anniversary edition. San Francisco: HarperOne, 1999.

Student and Youth Organizing. *A Youth Liberation Pamphlet.* 2nd edition. Ann Arbor, MI: Youth Liberation Press, 1977.

Walker, Mitch. *Visionary Love: A Spirit Book of Gay Mythology and Trans-mutational Faerie.* San Francisco: Treeroots Press, 1980.

Wittman, Carl. "Refugees from Amerika: A Gay Manifesto." 1970. In *History Is a Weapon.* www.historyisaweapon.com/defcon1/wittmanmanifesto.html.

Young, Allen. "The Cuban Revolution and Gay Liberation." In *Out of the Closets: Voices of Gay Liberation*, edited by Karla Jay and Allen Young. Twentieth anniversary edition. New York: NYU Press, 1992.

Secondary Sources

Adler, Margot. *Drawing Down the Moon: Witches, Druids, Goddess-Worshippers, and Other Pagans.* New York: Viking Press, 1979.

Ahmed, Sara. *Queer Phenomenology: Orientations, Objects, Others*. Durham, NC: Duke University Press, 2006.

Allured, Janet. *Remapping Second-Wave Feminism: The Long Women's Rights Movement in Louisiana, 1950–1997*. Athens: University of Georgia Press, 2016.

Arend, Orissa. *Showdown in Desire: The Black Panthers Take a Stand in New Orleans*. Fayetteville: University of Arkansas Press, 2010.

Atkins, Gary L. *Gay Seattle: Voices of Exile and Belonging*. Seattle: University of Washington Press, 2003.

Bailey, Marlon M. *Butch Queens Up in Pumps: Gender, Performance, and Ballroom Culture in Detroit*. Ann Arbor: University of Michigan Press, 2013.

Bronner, Stephen Eric. *Moments of Decision: Political History and the Crises of Radicalism*. 2nd edition. New York: Bloomsbury, 2014.

Bruce, La Marr Jurelle. *How to Go Mad Without Losing Your Mind: Madness and Black Radical Creativity*. Durham: Duke University Press, 2021.

Burton-Rose, Daniel. *Guerrilla USA: The George Jackson Brigade and the Anticapitalist Underground of the 1970s*. Oakland: University of California Press, 2010.

Cafard, Max. *Surregional Explorations*. Chicago: Charles H. Kerr, 2012.

Campanella, Richard. *Bourbon Street: A History*. Baton Rouge: LSU Press, 2014.

Capo, Julio, Jr. *Welcome to Fairyland: Queer Miami before 1940*. Chapel Hill: The University of North Carolina Press, 2017.

Charles, Douglas M. *Hoover's War on Gays: Exposing the FBI's "Sex Daviates" Program*. Lawrence: University Press of Kansas, 2015.

Chesnut, Saralyn, and Amanda Gable. "'Women Ran It': Charis Books and More and Atlanta's Lesbian-Feminist Community, 1971–1981." In *Carryin' On in the Lesbian and Gay South*, edited by John Howard. New York: NYU Press, 1997.

Clifton Chas S. *Her Hidden Children: The Rise of Wicca and Contemporary Paganism in America*. Lanham, MD: AltaMira Press, 2006.

Cohen, Cathy J. "Punks, Bulldaggers, and Welfare Queens: The Radical Potential of Queer Politics?" *GLQ: A Journal of Lesbian and Gay Studies* 3, no. 4 (1997).

Coverley, Merlin. *Psychogeography*. 3rd edition. Harpenden: Oldcastle Books, 2018.

Cox, Craig. *Storefront Revolution: Food Co-ops and the Counterculture*. New Brunswick, NJ: Rutgers University Press, 1994.

Cox, Nicole, and Silvia Federici. *Counter-Planning from the Kitchen: Wages for Housework: A Perspective on Capital and the Left*. New York: New York Wages for Housework Committee, 1975.

Cunningham, David. *There's Something Happening Here: The New Left, the Klan, and FBI Counterintelligence*. Berkeley: University of California Press, 2004.

Dalla Costa, Mariarosa, and Selma James. *The Power of Women and the Subversion of the Community*. Bristol: Falling Wall Press, 1975.

Decenes, Carlos Ulises. *Circuits of the Sacred: A Faggotology in the Black Latinx Caribbean*. Durham, NC: Duke University Press, 2023.

Delery-Edwards, Clayton. *The Up Stairs Lounge Arson: Thirty-Two Deaths in a New Orleans Gay Bar, June 24, 1973*. Jefferson, NC: McFarland, 2014.

Devore, Donald E., and Joseph Logsdon. *Crescent City Schools: Public Education in New Orleans, 1841–1991*. Lafayette: University of Southwestern Louisiana, 1991.

Downs, Jim. *Stand by Me: The Forgotten History of Gay Liberation*. New York: Basic Books, 2016.

Duberman, Martin. *Has the Gay Movement Failed?* Berkeley: University of California Press, 2018.

Duberman, Martin. *Stonewall*. New York: Dutton, 1993.

Elbaum, Max. *Revolution in the Air: Sixties Radicals Turn to Lenin, Mao, and Che*. New York: Verso Books, 2002.

Eller, Cynthia. *Living in the Lap of the Goddess: The Feminist Spirituality Movement in America*. New York: Crossroad, 1993.

Enszer, Julie. "'How to Stop Choking to Death': Rethinking Lesbian Separatism as a Vibrant Political Theory and Feminist Practice." *Journal of Lesbian Studies* 20, no. 2 (2016).

Ezell, Jason. "'Returning Forest Darlings': Gay Liberationist Sanctuary in the Southeastern Network, 1973–80." *Radical History Review*, no. 135 (October 2019).

Faderman, Lillian. *The Gay Revolution: The Story of the Struggle*. New York: Simon and Schuster, 2015.

Federici, Silvia. *Caliban and the Witch: Women, the Body, and Primitive Accumulation*. Chico, CA: AK Press, 2004.

Fieseler, Robert W. *Tinderbox: The Untold Story of the Up Stairs Lounge Fire and the Rise of Gay Liberation*. New York: Liveright, 2018.

Frank, Gillian. "'The Civil Rights of Parents': Race and Conservative Politics in Anita Bryant's Campaign against Gay Rights in 1970s Florida." *Journal of the History of Sexuality* 22, no. 1 (2013).

Frazier, Robeson Taj. *The East Is Black: Cold War China in the Black Radical Imagination*. Durham, NC: Duke University Press, 2014.

Gitlin, Todd. *The Sixties: Years of Hope, Days of Rage*. Toronto: Bantam Books, 1987.

Goss, Robert E. "Silencing Queers at the Upstairs Lounge: The Stonewall of New Orleans." *Southern Communication Journal* 74, no. 3 (2009).

Gosse, Van. *Rethinking the New Left: An Interpretative History*. New York: Palgrave Macmillan, 2005.

Gray, Mary L. *Out in the Country: Youth, Media, and Queer Visibility in Rural America*. New York: NYU Press, 2009.

Halberstam, Jack. *In a Queer Time and Place: Transgender Bodies, Subcultural Lives*. New York: NYU Press, 2005.

Hanhardt, Christina. *Safe Space: Gay Neighborhood History and the Politics of Violence*. Durham, NC: Duke University Press, 2013.

Harker, Jaime. *The Lesbian South: Southern Feminists, the Women in Print Movement, and the Queer Literary Canon*. Chapel Hill: The University of North Carolina Press, 2018.

Herring, Scott. *Another Country: Queer Anti-Urbanism*. New York: NYU Press, 2010.

Hobson, Emily. *Lavender and Red: Liberation and Solidarity in the Gay and Lesbian Left*. Oakland: University of California Press, 2016.

Hogan, Kristen. *The Feminist Bookstore Movement: Lesbian Antiracism and Feminist Accountability*. Durham, NC: Duke University Press, 2016.

Howard, John. *Men Like That: A Southern Queer History*. Chicago: University of Chicago Press, 2001.

Hutton, Ronald. *The Triumph of the Moon: A History of Modern Pagan Witchcraft*. Oxford: Oxford University Press, 1999.

Johnson, Colin R. *Just Queer Folks: Gender and Sexuality in Rural America*. Philadelphia: Temple University Press, 2013.

Johnson, E. Patrick. *Sweet Tea: Black Gay Men of the South*. Chapel Hill: The University of North Carolina Press, 2008.

Johnson, Emily Suzanne. *This Is Our Message: Women's Leadership in the New Christian Right*. Oxford: Oxford University Press, 2019.

Jones, Jennifer Dominique. *Ambivalent Affinities: A Political History of Blackness & Homosexuality after World War II*. Chapel Hill: The University of North Carolina Press, 2023.

Jones, Jennifer Dominique. "'Until I Talked with You': Silence, Storytelling, and Black Sexual Intimacies in the Johns Committee Records, 1960–5." *Gender & History* 30, no. 2 (2018).

Kelley, Robin D. G., and Betsy Esch. "Black Like Mao: Red China and Black Revolution." *Souls: A Critical Journal of Black Politics, Culture, and Society* 1, no. 4 (1999).

Kissack, Terence. "Freaking Fag Revolutionaries: New York's Gay Liberation Front, 1969–1971." *Radical History Review* 62 (1995).

Knopp, Lawrence. "Gentrification and Gay Neighborhood Formation in New Orleans: A Case Study." In *Homo Economics: Capitalism, Community, and Lesbian and Gay Life*, edited by Amy Gluckman and Betsy Reed. London: Routledge, 1997.

Latner, Teishan A. *Cuban Revolution in America: Havana and the Making of a United States Left, 1968–1992*. Chapel Hill: The University of North Carolina Press, 2018.

Lecklider, Aaron. *Love's Next Meeting: The Forgotten History of Homosexuality and the Left in American Culture*. Berkeley: University of California Press, 2021.

Lekus, Ian. "Queer Harvests: Homosexuality, the U.S. New Left, and the Venceremos Brigades to Cuba." *Radical History Review* 89 (Spring 2004).

Lewis, Abram J. "'We Are Certain of Our Own Insanity': Antipsychiatry and the Gay Liberation Movement, 1968–1980." *Journal of the History of Sexuality* 25, no. 1 (2016).

Lewis, Helen Matthews. *Helen Matthews Lewis: Living Social Justice in Appalachia*. Lexington: University Press of Kentucky, 2012.

Lewis, Helen M., and Monica Appleby. *Mountain Sisters: From Convent to Community in Appalachia*. Lexington: University of Kentucky Press, 2003.

Liebling, A. J. *The Earl of Louisiana*. New York: Simon and Schuster, 1961.

Long, Alecia. *Cruising for Conspirators: How a New Orleans DA Prosecuted the Kennedy Assassination as a Sex Crime*. Chapel Hill: The University of North Carolina Press, 2021.

Long, Alecia. "'Death Delights to Serve the Living': Reconsidering the Life and Legacy of Clay L. Shaw." *Louisiana History* 57, no. 4 (2016).

Lotringer, Sylvére, and Christian Marazzi, eds. *Autonomia: Post-Political Politics*. Los Angeles: Semiotext(e), 2007.

Luther Hillman, Betty. *Dressing for the Culture Wars: Style and the Politics of Self-Presentation in the 1960s and 1970s*. Lincoln: University of Nebraska Press, 2015.

Malatino, Hil. *Side Affects: On Being Trans and Feeling Bad*. Minneapolis: University of Minnesota Press, 2022.

Marotta, Toby. *The Politics of Homosexuality*. Boston: Houghton-Mifflin, 1981.

Mason, Carol. *Oklahomo: Lessons in Unqueering America*. Albany: SUNY Press, 2015.

McKinney, Cait. "'Finding the Lines to My People': Media History and Queer Bibliographic Encounter." *GLQ: A Journal of Lesbian and Gay Studies* 24, no. 1 (January 2018).
McKinney, Cait. *Information Activism: A Queer History of Lesbian Media Technologies.* Durham, NC: Duke University Press, 2020.
Mims, La Shonda. *Drastic Dykes and Accidental Activists: Queer Women in the Urban South.* Chapel Hill: The University of North Carolina Press, 2022.
Moreton, Bethany. "Why Is There So Much Sex in Christian Conservatism and Why Do So Few Historians Care Anything about It?" *Journal of Southern History* 75, no. 3 (2009).
Morgensen, Scott Lauria. "Arrival at Home: Radical Faerie Configurations of Sexuality and Place." *GLQ: A Journal of Lesbian and Gay Studies* 15, no. 1 (2009).
Morgensen, Scott Lauria. *Spaces between Us: Queer Settler Colonialism and Indigenous Decolonization.* Minneapolis: University of Minnesota Press, 2011.
Mumford, Kevin. *Interzones: Black/White Sex Districts in Chicago and New York in the Early Twentieth Century.* New York: Columbia University Press, 1997.
Mumford, Kevin. *Not Straight, Not White: Black Gay Men from the March on Washington to the AIDS Crisis.* Chapel Hill: The University of North Carolina Press, 2016.
Muñoz, José Esteban. *Cruising Utopia: The Then and There of Queer Futurity.* New York: NYU Press, 2009.
Murch, Donna. *Living for the City: Migration, Education, and the Rise of the Black Panther Party in Oakland, California.* Chapel Hill: The University of North Carolina Press, 2010.
Newton, Esther. *Mother Camp: Female Impersonators in America.* 2nd edition. Chicago: University of Chicago Press, 1979.
Niman, Michael I. *People of the Rainbow: A Nomadic Utopia.* Knoxville: University of Tennessee Press, 2011.
Ongiri, Amy Abugo. "Prisoner of Love: Affiliation, Sexuality, and the Black Panther Party." *Journal of African American History* 94, no. 1 (2009).
Packer, Jeremy. *Mobility without Mayhem: Safety, Cars, and Citizenship.* Durham, NC: Duke University Press, 2008.
Paik, A. Naomi, Jason Ruiz, and Rebecca M. Schreiber. "Sanctuary's Radical Networks." *Radical History Review* no. 135 (October 2019).
Perez, Frank. *Political Animal: The Life and Times of Stewart Butler.* Jackson: University Press of Mississippi, 2022.
Perez, Frank, and Jeffrey Palmquist. *In Exile: The History and Lore Surrounding New Orleans Gay Culture and Its Oldest Gay Bar.* Hurlford, Scotland: LL-Press, 2012.
Perkins, Blake. *Hillbilly Hellraisers: Federal Power and Populist Defiance in the Ozarks.* Urbana: University of Illinois Press, 2017.
Phillips, Jared M. *Hipbillies: Deep Revolution in the Arkansas Ozarks.* Fayetteville: University of Arkansas Press, 2019.
Plaster, Joey. *Kids on the Street: Queer Kinship and Religion in San Francisco's Tenderloin.* Durham, NC: Duke University Press, 2023.
Renfro, Paul M. *Stranger Danger: Family Values, Childhood, and the American Carceral State.* Oxford: Oxford University Press, 2020.
Rodriguez, Nelson M. "Trans Generosity." In *Critical Concepts in Queer Studies and Education: An International Guide for the Twenty-First Century*, edited by Nelson M.

Rodriguez, Wayne Martino, Jennifer C. Ingrey, and Edward Brockenbrough. London: Palgrave Macmillan, 2016.
Ross, Marlon B. *Sissy Insurgencies: A Racial Anatomy of Unfit Manliness.* Durham, NC: Duke University Press, 2022.
Rossinow, Doug. *The Politics of Authenticity: Liberalism, Christianity, and the New Left in America.* New York: Columbia University Press, 1998.
Russo, Vito. *The Celluloid Closet: Homosexuality in the Movies.* New York: Harper and Row, 1987.
Salomonsen, Jone. *Enchanted Feminism: Gender and Divinity among the Reclaiming Witches of San Francisco.* New York: Routledge, 2002.
Schept, Judah. *Coal, Cages, Crisis: The Rise of the Prison Economy in Central Appalachia.* New York: NYU Press, 2022.
Schwartz, Marvin. *In Service to America: A History of VISTA in Arkansas, 1965–1985.* Fayetteville: University of Arkansas Press, 1988.
Sears, James T. *Rebels, Rubyfruit, and Rhinestones: Queering Space in the Stonewall South.* New Brunswick, NJ: Rutgers University Press, 2001.
Shively, Charley. "Fag Rag: The Most Loathsome Publication in the English Language." In *Insider Histories of the Vietnam Era Underground Press,* part 2, edited by Ken Wachsberger. East Lansing: Michigan State University Press, 2012.
Smith, Howard Philips. *Unveiling the Muse: The Lost History of Gay Carnival in New Orleans.* Jackson: University Press of Mississippi, 2017.
Stein, Marc. *City of Sisterly and Brotherly Loves: Lesbian and Gay Philadelphia, 1945–1972.* Philadelphia: Temple University Press, 2013.
Stein, Marc. *Rethinking the Gay and Lesbian Movement.* New York: Routledge, 2012.
Stone, Amy. *Gay Rights at the Ballot Box.* Minneapolis: University of Minnesota Press, 2012.
Strube, Julian. "Occultist Identity Formations between Theosophy and Socialism in fin-de-siècle France." *Numen* 64 (2017).
Stryker, Susan. *Transgender History.* Berkeley, CA: Perseus Books, 2008.
Syrett, Nicholas L. *An Open Secret: The Family Story of Robert and John Gregg Allerton.* Chicago: University of Chicago Press, 2021.
Thompson, Brock. *The Un-Natural State: Arkansas and the Queer South.* Fayetteville: University of Arkansas Press, 2010.
Timmons, Stuart. *The Trouble with Harry Hay: Founder of the Modern Gay Movement.* Boston: Allyson Books, 1990.
Toupin, Louise. *Wages for Housework: History of an International Feminist Movement, 1972–1977.* Edited by Kathe Roth. Vancouver: University of British Columbia Press, 2018.
Varon, Jeremy. *Bringing the War Home: The Weather Underground, the Red Army Faction, and Revolutionary Violence in the Sixties and Seventies.* Berkeley: University of California Press, 2004.
Vider, Stephen. *The Queerness of Home: Gender, Sexuality, and the Politics of Domesticity after World War II.* Chicago: University of Chicago Press, 2021.
Virno, Paolo. *A Grammar of the Multitude: For an Analysis of Contemporary Life.* Los Angeles: Semiotext(e), 2004.
Virno, Paolo, and Michael Hardt, eds. *Radical Thought in Italy: A Potential Politics.* Minneapolis: University of Minnesota Press, 1996.

Weeks, Kathi. *The Problem with Work: Feminism, Marxism, Antiwork Politics, and Postwork Imaginaries*. Durham, NC: Duke University Press, 2011.
Woods, Clyde. *Development Arrested: The Blues and Plantation Power in the Mississippi Delta*. New York: Verso Books, 1998.
Zajicek, Anna M., and Allyn Lord. *The History of the Contemporary Grassroots Women's Movement in Northwest Arkansas, 1970–2000*. Fayetteville: University of Arkansas Press, 2000.

Index

Italic page numbers refer to illustrations.

Abbott, Franklin, 158–59, 213
abortion, 88
Advocate (magazine), 170
alternative childcare, 131–40
American Psychiatric Association (APA), 60
Anderson, Cora, 18
Anderson, Victor, 18
antidiscrimination law, 5
anti-LGBTQ+ book-banning initiatives, 219
antipsychiatry ideology, 59, 61, 62, 109, 110, 181, 232n21
anti-rape politics, 145–46, 150, 187
antiwar movements, 2, 41, 60, 133
Appalachian Regional Commission (ARC), 16–17, 31
Arco Iris community, 231n42, 243n11
Arizona Radical Faerie conference, 25, 178, 187, 189–92, 193, 198
Arkansas Sissies of Mulberry House. *See* Mulberry House collective
"Ascent, Lament, and Admonition" (Abbott), 158–59, 214
Asta, Ned, 198, 199
Atlanta Gay Liberation Front (GLF), 132
Atlanta Lesbian Feminist Alliance (ALFA), 15, 51, 154, 201
Atlanta Little Five Points collective, 15
Atlantis collective, 82, 123, 131, 148, 151, 223, 237n46
Aurora Corona (David Speakman), 123–24, 209–10, 237n41
autonomist communism, 63

"Back in the Closet Again" (Lavender Country), 56, 68
back-to-the-land culture, 16, 38, 40–45, 54, 216. *See also* countercultural movements; faerie farms; hipbilly counterculture; hippie countercultural movement; Short Mountain Sanctuary
Barstow, Paul, 55
Bay Area Gay Liberation (BAGL), 64
Ben Miriam, Faygele (John F. Singer), 55–57, 64, 69, 73, 91, 123, 155, 196
Benson, George, 85
Benson conference, 25, 178, 187, 189–92, 193, 198
Berkham, Alexander, 110
Berzon, Betty, 187
bibliographies, 126–31, 144, 153, 237n46
Black Gay Caucus, 70
Black like Me (Griffin), 106
Black Panther Party, 8–9, 14–16, 58, 132, 169, 199, 211, 217, 218, 229n55. *See also* civil rights movement
Black United Teachers of New Orleans (UTNO), 135–36
Bland, Bob, 168
bombings, 11–12, 56, 69, 216
Books as Seeds (bookstore), 195
Boyd, June, 199, 217
Bread and Roses cooperative, 68
"bread & roses revisited (for the sissies)" (elliott), 66, 71, 72
Briggs Initiative, 125, 130, 138, 173, 177
Broshears, Ray, 19
Brotherlover, Stacy, 123–26, 131, 134, 135, 141, 144, 148, 150, 168, 209; "Sissie Networking," 168, 170, 173, 178, 198, 239n37
Brown, H. Rap, 37–38
Brown, Rita, 69
Bryant, Anita, 23, 83, 177–78, 216
Budapest, Zsuzsanna, 18, 201–2
"Burning Times" (Murphy), 155

Burton-Rose, Daniel, 11, 57
Butterworth Farm, 50
Butz, Earl, 80

Cafe Lafitte, 151
Caldwell, Betty, 151
California Briggs Initiative, 125, 130, 138, 173, 177
Campanella, Richard, 108
capitalism, 20, 51, 80, 146, 198–99
Carlotta Rose (Jack Kendrick), 39–40, 41, 42–43, 111
Casa Maricon Commune, 179–80, 182–83
CBS Reports (television series), 179, 180, 183
Celluloid Closet (film), 111
censorship, 219
Chapel Hill Revolutionary Movement, 168–69
Charlotte Gay Liberation Front (GLF), 132
Charlotte Women's Center, 42
childcare, 3, 54, 66, 67, 97, 131–40, 156
child protectionism, 131–40, 177, 184, 214, 215–16, 219, 229n72. *See also* Save Our Children movement
Christianity. *See* white Christian supremacy
Church of the Beloved Disciple, 182
City of Night (Rechy), 144
civil rights movement, 2, 8, 22, 49, 73, 106, 162. *See also* Black Panther Party
Cleaver, Eldridge, 8
Clement, Robert, 182
Close-Up (television series), 25, 178–80, 183, 184, 209, 215
collective defense strategy, 15, 24, 52, 90–97. *See also* Ozark collectivism; *and names of specific initiatives*
collective houses, 1, 13–17, 21–22, 75. *See also names of specific collectives*
"Collective Statement" (*RFD*), 65–67
communal living, 1, 13–17, 21–22, 75
Communities (magazine), 42
The Confederacy of Dunces (Toole), 107
Cooptation Blues, 79, 80

countercultural movements, 30–41, 211. *See also* back-to-the-land culture; hipbilly counterculture; hippie countercultural movement
Country Women (magazine), 16, 42, 51
Covenant of the Goddess, 18
covens, 18, 21. *See also* feminist witches and witchcraft
Cravens, Russell, 153
Crews, Dwight, 132–33
Cuba, 22, 38–39, 79, 80, 133, 202
Cuban Venceremos Brigade, 2, 15, 22, 45, 133, 169
Cummins Correctional Unit, 91
Cunningham, David, 84

Dalla Costa, Mariarosa, 63
Dansky, Steven, 2
Dellinger, David, 84
Desert Sanctuary, 187, 189, 192
The Diagnostic and Statistical Manual of Mental Disorders (APA), 60
Dinner at Eight (film), 43, 111
discrimination cases, 55, 83. *See also* homophobia
domestic liberation, 76–83
Double F (journal), 128
Douglass, Frederick, 79, 80
Drastic Dykes, 42
dream museum, 182, 183, 215
dreamwork, 150, 159, 182, 192, 213–15. *See also* "remembering forgotten dreams"
Duberman, Martin, 13, 16

ecofeminism, 64, 155, 202–4
Edwards, Sam, 40, 42–43
EEOC (Equal Employment Opportunity Commission) case, 55
effeminists: figure of, 6, 206; on reproductive labor, 54, 97, 109, 115, 214. *See also* street queens
Effeminists (group), 3, 127, 149, 238n14
Elbaum, Max, 14
Eller, Cynthia, 4–5
elliott, jai d., 66, 71, 72

Elwha Land Project, 50
Englebert, Clear, 156, 194–95, 197
Enszer, Julie, 14
essentialism, 188, 193, 241n16
Evans, Arthur, 4–6, 16–17, 19–21, 51, 58, 123, 205
exceptionalism, 107, 193

Faderman, Lillian, 4
faerie farms, 50–51, 73, 124. *See also* Short Mountain Sanctuary
faeries: figure of, 178, 190, 193, 205; as term, 1. *See also* Spiritual Conference for Radical Faeries
Faeries of All Colors Together (FACT), 218
"A Faeryist Not-Man-ifesto" (Pyne), 201–3, 206, 215
faggot: figure of, 6–13, 45–51, 66; genealogy of, 2–6, 211–12; as term, 1, 2. *See also* faggot witchcraft
Faggots and Class Struggle conference, 6, 10, 24, 51–65, 73, 214, 235n10
The Faggots & Their Friends between Revolutions (Mitchell and Asta), 198–99, 201
faggot witchcraft, 17–21, 52–74, 102. *See also* faggot; New Orleans witchery
Fag Rag (magazine), 5, 8, 9, 11, 20, 46, 217
Fag Rag Books, 19
fairy tale tropes, 83, 148, 199–201, 212, 214
Falwell, Jerry, 88
Fanon, Frantz, 152
fanshen, 110, 122, 167, 193, 211, 213
Fanshen (Hinton), 116
Fariña, Mimi, 68
farming. *See* back-to-the-land culture; faerie farms
Fayetteville, AR, 36–37
Federici, Silvia, 63, 232n25
feminist collectives, 40–42. *See also* Southern lesbian feminism
feminist witches and witchcraft, 4–5, 18–20, 64, 213. *See also* New Orleans witchery
Feri, Anderson, 112
Fernandez, Dolores, 133
Fire, Kathy, 197, 199

Fitzgerald, Grant-Michael, 118
Flaherty, Terry, 101–2
Flaming Faggot (Pitchford), 7
Flaming Faggots (group), 2–4, 10, 46, 119, 124, 217
flâneur, 102
FOCIS House, 152
food justice, 24
Frank, Gillian, 84
Fryer, John E., 60

Gabriner, Vicki, 15
Gallmeyer, Ann, 133
Gandhi, Indira, 30
Gandolfo, Charles, 113
Garcia, Jackie, 181
Garrison, Jim, 132
Gaslight (Bergman), 111
Gate Hill Coop, 40
Gay Academic Union, 187, 189
Gay Activists Alliance (GAA), 4–5, 17, 218
Gay American Indians (organization), 70
"Gay Awareness and the First Americans" (Hay), 193
A Gay Bibliography (Gittings), 127, 129
gay ghetto, 117–18, 153–54
Gay Latinos Alliance, 70
"Gay Liberation" (Hay), 58
Gay Liberation Front (GLF): Atlanta, 132; Charlotte, 132; Georgia, 153–54; New Orleans, 132–33, 161; New York, 2–6, 37, 119
gay militancy, 35, 40, 56–58, 78
Gay Spirit Visions, 210–11
Gay Sunshine (journal), 39
Gearhart, Sally, 238n3
genderfuck, 141, 187, 214
George Jackson Brigade, 11–12, 20, 57, 68–69, 196
Georgia Gay Liberation Front (GLF), 153–54
German Red Army Faction (RAF), 69
Gertrude Stein Democratic Club, 133–34, 161, 162, 163, 166
Gitlin, Todd, 14
Gittings, Barbara, 60

Glenmary Sisters, 152
GLF (Gay Liberation Front): Atlanta, 132; Charlotte, 132; Georgia, 153–54; New Orleans, 132–33, 161; New York, 2–6, 37, 119
God Is the Author of Segregation (KKK), 85
Goldman, Emma, 106, 128
A Good Book Store (bookstore), 195
Gorman, Bob, 32, 34, 230n14
Gosse, Van, 14
Great Speckled Bird (newspaper), 33, 154, 195
Greensboro massacre and protest, 202
GRID (gay-related immune deficiency), 209

Hacking, Ian, 111
Haggerty, Patrick, 56
Hanhardt, Christina, 19, 64, 68
Harker, Jaime, 49
Hart, Lois, 2
Hay, Harry, 58, 178, 187, 190, 191–92, 193, 241n16
Hayes, Dimid (Dean), 43–44, 52, 123, 124–25, 160, 164–65, 198, 209
Haze, Gabby, 156, 169
Hellenism, 107–8
Hemphill, Essex, 217
Herring, Scott, 16, 170
Higgins, Thom, 178
Hillman, Luther, 212
Hillsborough, Robert, 85, 216
hipbilly counterculture, 32–35, 40, 41. *See also* back-to-the-land culture; countercultural movements
hippie countercultural movement, 30–32, 35, 38, 156–57. *See also* back-to-the-land culture; countercultural movements
HIV/AIDS, 209, 242n19
Hobson, Emily, 15, 19, 54, 69
homophobia: Bryant and New Right's campaigns of, 23–24, 83–90, 130, 219; modern initiatives of, 219. *See also* discrimination cases
homosexuality as mental disorder, 60, 61
Homosexuals (docuseries), 25, 178–80, 183, 184, 209, 215

"The Homosexuals" (episode of *CBS Reports*), 179, 182, 184
Hope, Cathy (Gross), 151–53, 195, 199–201, 242n18
housing, 1, 13–17, 21–22, 75. *See also* names of specific collectives
Howard, John, 22
Huckleberry Farm, 42, 44
Hughes, Langston, 213
hunger, 51, 80, 81
Hutton, Ronald, 18

I Am Tired (Williams), 78
I Ching, 195
Impact (newspaper), 126, 134, 161–62, 167
India, 30–31
Indigenous Americans, 193
industrial workerism, 63, 67
Industrial Workers of the World (IWW), 67
infiltration, 20, 84, 132–33, 190
informants, 53, 133, 169, 184
International Wages for Housework movement, 63, 67
Interview with the Vampire (Rice), 113
Itkin, Michael-Francis, 19

Jackson, George, 11
Jackson, Patricia, 41, 48
"Jesse's Dream Skirt" (Morning Star), 130, 131, 149, 182, 214, 215
Joan of Arc, 19
Johnson, E. Patrick, 22
Johnson, Lyndon B., 31
Johnson, Marsha P., 10, 14, 119
Jones, Jennifer Dominique, 85, 88

Kali Fire ritual, 1
Kameny, Frank, 60
Kelly (gay prisoner), 91–94
Kendrick, Jack, 39–40, 41, 42–43, 111
Kennedy, John F., 31
Kilhefner, Don, 187
King, Martin Luther, Jr., 213
King Tut exhibit, 101, 103, 107, 108, 115–16
Kirby, Nicki, 151

Knoebel, John, 2
Knopp, Lawrence, 161
Koch, Leo and Mary, 30, 31
Koch Farm, 31–33, 35, 51, 91
Ku Klux Klan, 37, 84–85, 89

Lambe, Ron, 181, 185
land movements, 203–4
L&RU (Lavender & Red Union), 53, 61–63, 73
land trusts, 203–4
LaSIS collective: alternative childcare and teacher solidarity in, 131–40, 148–49; establishment of, 21–22, 24–25, 122–25; on faerie figure, 205, 209; Gay Pride events by, 211; police targeting of, 184–85; Pyne and, 194; queer solidarity of, 161–67; Short Mountain and, 195–97, 199, 201, 205–6; Sissie Effeminism bibliography, 126–31, 144; sissie performativity by, 179–83; sissie strategy of, 150–53; unqueer street pedagogy of, 140–49. *See also* New Orleans, LA; sissie collectivism
Laughlin, Trella, 41, 42, 48, 50–51, 75
Laveau, Marie, 113
Lavender & Red Union (L&RU), 53, 61–63, 73
Lavender Country (album), 55
Lavender Country (band), 56, 68, 218; "Back in the Closet Again," 56, 68
Lavender Panthers, 68
Lekus, Ian, 22, 172
Lesbian Connections (magazine), 41, 42, 51
lesbian South, 22–23, 29, 40–42, 48, 199–201
The Lesbian South (Harker), 22–23
"A Letter of Action" (Hayes), 168, 173, 178
Lewis, Abram J., 60
Lewis, Helen Matthews, 152, 197
Lexington Six collective, 15
librarians and library services, 223–25
Liebling, A. J., 107
Lindsay, John, 5, 17
living dead, 20–21
Lord, Allyn, 41, 42, 49, 231n42, 243n11

Louisiana Sissies in Struggle. *See* LaSIS collective
Loving v. Virginia, 85

Magdalen Farm, 51, 156
magic, 20–21. *See also* faggot witchcraft; feminist witches and witchcraft; majik
Magnus (journal), 52, 130
majik, 122, 140, 147, 150, 236n3
Maoism, 61, 116, 117, 140, 211, 235n16
Mardi Gras, 106, 183, 235n17
Marotta, Toby, 2, 4
Martello, Leo, 5, 17–18, 64, 227n19
Mason, Carol, 214
Mattachine Society, 190, 231n13
Matthews, Tede, 57, 65
McKinney, Cait, 127
Mead, Ed, 11, 57, 91, 196
Meinhof, Ulrike, 69
Melba'son, Dennis (Dennis Williams), 1, 24, 29–35, 39–40, 44, 101–21, 142–47, 193–94, 209, 211, 213
Metropolitan Museum of Art, 5
Miami-Dade County, FL, 83–84
Mifsud, Stella, 181
militant activism, 2–3, 11–12, 229n55. *See also* gay militancy
military state, 20
Milk, Harvey, 186; assassination of, 23, 25, 173, 178, 180
Mims, La Shonda, 23, 42
Mitchell, Larry, 198
modern paganism, 18, 64, 201–2
moon ritual, 59–65, 71–73
Moreton, Bethany, 219
Morgan, Bobby, 35, 49
Morgan, Robin, 199
Morial, Ernest Nathan "Dutch," 162
Morning Due (journal), 53, 59, 65–66, 69–71
Morning Due collective, 11–12, 56
Mother Earth News (magazine), 42
Ms. (magazine), 42
mud-bath ritual, 191–92
Mulberry Farm, 43, 73, 116, 122, 124, 150, 163

Mulberry House collective, 6, 24; collective defense strategies of, 90–97; domestic liberation and splitting of, 76–83; establishment of, 29, 39–45; faggot figure of, 45–51; introductory letter, 47; sissy figure of, 12, 125
Mumford, Kevin, 11, 118
Murphy, Charlie, 155

National Association of Black & White Men Together, 217
National March on Washington for Lesbian and Gay Rights, 25, 177–78, 186–87, 240n13
New Communist Lavender & Red Union, 10, 14–15
New Communities, Inc., 203–4
"The New Homosexuality" (Burke), 37
New Orleans, LA, 38, 102–9, 215, 239n24. *See also* LaSIS collective
New Orleans Gay Liberation Front (GLF), 132–33, 161
New Orleans witchery, 109–21. *See also* faggot witchcraft; feminist witches and witchcraft
New Right, 83–90, 134–40, 177, 187, 211, 214, 215–16, 219
Newton, Huey, 8, 14, 37
New York Daily News (newspaper), 84
New York Gay Liberation Front (NY-GLF), 2–6, 37, 119
Noble, John, 182, 192, 215
"no woke" educational legislative bills, 219, 224
"Nuclear Realities" (Fire), 197
nudity, 184
NY-GLF, 2–6, 37, 119

Oglesby, Michael, 210; on Faggots and Class Struggle conference, 76–78, 235n10; and Mulberry House, 36–39, 44
Oppenheim, James, 67, 68
Oregon Faggots and Class Struggle conference, 6, 10, 24, 51–65, 73, 214, 235n10
Oregon Women on the Land (OWL), 203–4

Out of the Closets (Young), 38–39, 169, 172, 216
Ozark collectivism, 52–74. *See also* Southeast Network
Ozark Food Co-op, 51, 75, 78–83
Ozark lesbian socialist feminism, 29, 40–42, 48
Ozark Regional Commission (ORC), 16–17, 31, 32
Ozark separatism, 29–45
Ozark Women on the Land (OWL), 50–51

paganism. *See* feminist witches and witchcraft; modern paganism
Panic in the Streets (film), 108
Pay It No Mind (film), 119
peasant (figure), 8, 110, 116, 211
Pendleton, Phillip, 187
Perry, Troy, 38
Pharr, Suzanne, 42, 132
Philippines, 79
Phillips, Jared M., 32, 41
Pied Piper (trope), 84, 212, 214
Pink Triangle Alliance (PTA), 134, 163, 211
Pitchford, Kenneth, 2–3, 7, 227n10
Plaster, Joey, 64
police raids, 2, 5, 53, 184. *See also* surveillance
Prejean, Helen, 209
prisoner correspondence, 91–92, 195, 196
prison system, 33, 80
privilege, 76–79
Project Return, 181–82
Protean Radish (newspaper), 168–69
psychogeographies, 102–9, 213
Putnam House, 33
Pyne, Milo, 168–72, 193, 194, 201–3, 212–13

queerbaiting. *See* homophobia

racism: Duberman on, 13–14; by KKK, 84–85, 89; and Short Mountain collective, 199, 204, 206–7; against Tyler, 137–38, 177, 236n34. *See also* violence
Radicalesbians (group), 46

Radical Faeries (group), 1, 16, 25, 193–207, 231n16, 241n17, 241n21
Radical Faeries conference, 25, 178, 187, 189–92, 193, 198
Radical Study Group, 2, 4
Rainbow Gatherings, 156, 190
Rais, Gilles de, 19
Randy, 96–97
Razordykes, 41
Reagan, Ronald, 187, 214
Reclaiming Collective, 18, 112
Red Queen, 4–6, 16–17, 19–21, 51, 58, 123, 205
Reich, Bob, 80–81, 93, 123
Reid, Michael, 239n36
"remembering forgotten dreams," 109, 126–27, 149, 155. *See also* dreamwork
reproductive labor, 66, 71, 77–78
Revolutionary People's Constitutional Convention, 8, 14
RFD (magazine and print network), 47, 143; about, 2, 6, 16, 29; Black queer poets in, 217–18; "Collective Statement," 65–67; faerie figure in, 193, 201; influence of, 50; legacy of, 210; sissy figure in, 141–45, 167–68; Thornton on, 39; Troxler on hipbillies, 35–36; women's work in, 195, 199–200
Riddle, Duane, 80
rituals, 59–65, 231n16
Rivera, Sylvia, 4, 10, 14, 118–19, 227n16
Rivers, Diana, 40–41, 93, 94, 210
Roan Mountain, 157–60
Robb, Thomas Arthur, 88
Robinson, Alan, 133–34
Roe v. Wade, 88, 219
Ross, Marlon, 24–25, 144, 180, 240n4
Running Water Farm, 22, 25, 155, 156–59, 164–66, 178, 185, 189, 190, 193, 210
Rushton, Bill, 133–34

Safe House (Beale et al.), 128
Saint, Assotto, 217
San Francisco Gay Freedom Day, 69
sanity, 61, 110–11
Sassafras community, 40, 41, 42, 44, 93

Save Our Children movement, 23–24, 76, 83–90, 130, 177, 215–16, 219, 229n72
Saxe, Susan, 15
Schneider, Charlene, 161
Schwartz, Marvin, 32, 34
Scott, Barbara, 132
Sears, James T., 22, 131–32
separatist movements, 14, 19
sex radicals, 19
Shakur, Assata, 80
Shaw, Clay, 133
Shively, Charlie, 178
Short Mountain, Inc., 204
Short Mountain Reinhabitation Project, 200–201
Short Mountain Sanctuary, 21–22, 25, 169, 178, 192, 193–207, 210, 243n5. *See also* sissie collectivism
Simos, Miriam, 18
Singer, John, 55–57, 64, 69, 73, 91, 123, 155, 196
sissie: figure of, 6, 12–13, 66–67, 211–16; psychogeography of, 102–9; in *RFD*, 141–45, 167–68; as term, 1, 66, 235n24, 236n6
sissie collectivism, 21–22, 25; national, 177–92; in South, 150–73, 197–200. *See also* LaSIS collective; Short Mountain Sanctuary
sissie effeminism, 134, 144
"Sissie Effeminism" bibliography, 126–31, 144, 153, 237n46
sissie majik, 122, 140, 147, 150, 236n3
"Sissie Networking" (Brotherlover), 168, 170, 173, 178, 198, 239n37
Sissie Networking (map), 170–73, 202
Sissie Terror in the Photo Booth (photographs), 143
"Sissy" (photo), 142
sissy liminality, 119
Snake Pit raid, 5
Solidarity Forever campaign, 137–40
solidarity processes, 4, 8–10, 61, 199–207
soul alignment, 112
Southeastern Conference for Lesbians and Gay Men, 189

Southeast Network, 1, 22, 185–86, 199–207
Southern lesbian feminism, 22–23, 29, 40–42, 48, 199–201
Speakman, David, 11, 123–24
Spiderworts (group), 202
The Spiral Dance (Starhawk), 18–19, 231n16
Spiritual Conference for Radical Faeries, 25, 178, 187, 189–92, 193, 198
STAR (Street Transvestite Action Revolutionaries) House, 14, 119
Starhawk, 18–19, 112, 231n16
state violence, 20
Stein, Gertrude, 134, 228n23. *See also* Gertrude Stein Democratic Club
Stepping Stone corporation, 185–86
STIFs (straight-identified faggots), 66–67, 125
Stone Hill House, 93
Stonewall Riots, 8, 30, 40, 56, 119, 123, 172, 187
"Stonewall South," 22, 131–32
Stop WOKE Act (2022), 224
A Streetcar Named Desire (Williams), 113–14
street heresy, 110
street pedagogy, 25, 140–49, 215
street queens, 10, 14, 38, 118–19, 146, 212. *See also* effeminists; *and names of specific queens*
Sudds, Pearl, 200, 242n19
suicide, 30, 110, 150
surveillance, 20, 53, 184–85. *See also* police raids; violence
Susan B. Anthony Coven #1, 18
Sybil (film), 112
Symbionese Liberation Army, 57

teacher solidarity, 131–40, 148–49
Tennessee Valley Authority (TVA), 197, 203, 213
"That I Am a Dyke" (Gross), 199–200
Thompson, Brock, 42
Thornton, Charlie, 36–39, 44, 210
The Three Faces of Eve (film), 111
Todd, Helen, 67
Torch (newspaper), 87, 88
Toups, Ann, 162

Tronti, Mario, 62
trucking collective, 75
TVA (Tennessee Valley Authority), 197, 203, 213
Tyler, Gary, 137–38, 177, 236n34

unqueer (term), 145, 207. *See also* street pedagogy
UpStairs Lounge, 38

Varon, Jeremy, 14, 57, 76, 219
Venceremos Brigadiers, 2, 15, 22, 45, 133, 169
Vider, Stephen, 13, 21, 75
violence: bombings, 11–12, 56, 69, 216; and Lavender Panthers, 68; police raids, 2, 5, 53, 184; by racist organizations, 84–85. *See also* racism; surveillance
Visionary Love (Walker), 193, 203
VISTA (Volunteers in Service to America) program, 31–35, 44
voodoo, 113. *See also* New Orleans witchery

Walker, Mitch, 187, 193–94
Wallace, Mike, 179
Ward, Skip, 239n36
War on Poverty, 31, 35
Weathermen, 15
Weeks, Kathi, 46
white Christian supremacy, 23–24, 25, 75–97, 150, 197–98, 214, 219
White Citizens' Councils, 37, 84
Williams, Dennis. *See* Melba'son, Dennis (Dennis Williams)
Williams, Roger, 92–95
Wilson, Mikel, 155, 156–58, 170
Witchcraft and the Gay Counterculture (Evans), 5, 17, 19, 64, 73, 128, 205
witches and witchcraft. *See* faggot witchcraft; feminist witches and witchcraft; New Orleans witchery
witch hunts, 19–20
Wittman, Carl, 49, 58, 217
Wolf Creek, 52, 58, 63–64, 65, 70–71. *See also* Magdalen Farm

"The Woman-Identified Woman" (Radicalesbians), 46
Women's Centers, 41–42
women's suffrage movement, 67
Woods, Dessie, 96, 177
workerism, 63, 67

Yellowhammer community, 41, 42, 44, 50
Young, Allen, 38–39, 169

Zajicek, Anna M., 41, 42, 49, 231n42, 243n11
zaps, 5, 17, 18, 19, 57, 139, 178, 214, 227n18, 235n18

www.ingramcontent.com/pod-product-compliance
Lightning Source LLC
Chambersburg PA
CBHW021852230426
43671CB00006B/360